D1374356

Princess Peacock

World Folklore Advisory Board

Princess Peacock

Tales from the
Other Peoples of China

Retold by Haiwang Yuan

Foreword by Zhang Chunde

World Folklore Series

A Member of the Greenwood Publishing Group

Westport, Connecticut • London

Library of Congress Cataloging-in-Publication Data

Yuan, Haiwang.
   Princess Peacock : tales from the other peoples of China / retold by Haiwang Yuan ;
   foreword by Zhang Chunde.
      p. cm. — (World folklore series)
   Includes bibliographical references and index.
   ISBN 978-1-59158-416-2 (alk. paper)
   1. Tales—China. 2. Minorities—China—Folklore. 3. Minorities—China—Social
life and customs. I. Title.
   GR335.Y73   2008
   398.20951—dc22   2008011521

British Library Cataloguing in Publication Data is available.

Library of Congress Catalog Card Number: 2008011521
ISBN: 978-1-59158-416-2

First published in 2008

Libraries Unlimited, 88 Post Road West, Westport, CT 06881
A Member of the Greenwood Publishing Group, Inc.
www.lu.com

Printed in the United States of America

The paper used in this book complies with the
Permanent Paper Standard issued by the National
Information Standards Organization (Z39.48–1984).

10 9 8 7 6 5 4 3 2 1

The publisher has done its best to make sure the instructions and/or recipes in this book are correct.
However, users should apply judgment and experience when preparing recipes, especially parents
and teachers working with young people. The publisher accepts no responsibility for the outcome of
any recipe included in this volume.

To my wife and son

CONTENTS

Part 1: Chinese Ethnicities and Their Culture: An Overview

Part 2: Food, Games, and Crafts

Part 3: The Tales

FOREWORD

Zhang Chunde

China is a country with a long history, rich culture, and multiple nationalities. People of various cultural backgrounds have formed a nation of fifty-six ethnic groups after more than 5,000 years of constant migration, integration, disintegration, and interaction. Working and living together while fighting against many types of adversity, they have created an inexhaustible wealth of folk literature. The folk literature of China's ethnic minorities is a gem in the treasure house of Chinese literature as a whole. Without it, Chinese literature would not be complete, and neither would it be as colorful and abundant as it now is.

For historical reasons, many Chinese ethnic minorities do not have written languages, but they have left a tremendous legacy of their collective memories through oral tradition. Interestingly, the lack of a written language has kept the ethnic minorities' folktales from being edited, modified, and fashioned, as many of the tales from the Han Chinese have been in the process of being disseminated from mouth to letters.

The Han and the ethnic minorities have borrowed from each other in the creation of their folk literatures. An example is the Pangu mythology. Although a textbook legend among the Hans, it had long been an oral tradition of ethnic Yao. This apparently illustrates a hereditary relationship. On the other hand, the themes "Romance of Three Kingdoms" and "Weaving Girl and Cowherd," well-known by the Han Chinese, have found their way into folktales retold by some of the ethnic minorities.

Each ethnic minority in China boasts a tremendous collection of oral literature. Recently the thirty-volume *Complete Collection of Chinese Folktales* was published, sponsored by the Ministry of Culture of the PRC, the State Ethnic Affairs Commission, and Chinese Folk Literature and Art Society, and edited by the National Art Science Planning and Piloting Work Group. Each volume averages 1.5 million words. Even this is only the tip of the iceberg; there are far more folktales that need collecting. Therefore, it is extremely difficult to convey to English-language readers the complexity and richness of the ethnic minority folk literature in a 300-page book like this. Fortunately, Professor Haiwang Yuan from Western Kentucky University has done an admirable job. He has, as it were, plucked a flower from each of the ethnic minority group's gardens of folk literature and meticulously formed a beautiful parterre, hoping that it will arouse readers' interest in the gardens that each of the flowers represents. I have the conviction that his expectations will be met.

To help English-language readers understand unfamiliar tales from the Chinese ethnic minorities, Yuan has provided a brief introduction to the many aspects of the ethnic minorities in general and to the cultural background of each of the stories in particular. The appendix of motifs and tale sources will be of great help to scholars of folk literature around the world. This effort has contributed greatly to the research in Chinese ethnic minority folk literature and added to endeavors to salvage the human record and world cultural heritage.

Although it embraces globalization and is building a market economy, China has begun to realize the significance of preserving non-material cultural relics. But under the onslaught of dominant cultures from home and foreign lands, traditions of ethnic minorities are facing great challenges. Their preservation has become an urgent matter. This book is a noteworthy attempt to focus attention on the folk literature of Chinese ethnic minorities.

Princess Peacock: Tales from the Other Peoples of China will suit readers of different ages, tastes, and educational backgrounds, and I strongly recommend it to those who are interested in learning about China and its ethnic minorities. This book and its companion, *The Magic Lotus Lantern and Other Tales from the Han Chinese* (2006), constitute a window from which readers can have a better glimpse of the Chinese psyche. I hope that readers will like them both. As a veteran scholar of the Yi ethnicity, it is a pleasure and honor to write this foreword to the book.

Zhang Chunde

professor of ethnic languages, Yunnan Nationalities University, Kunming, China;
member of the Nationalities Studies Advisory Council, Yunnan Province, China;
director of the Center for the Study of Nationalities in Western China,
Yunnan Nationalities University, Kunming, China

ACKNOWLEDGMENTS

A number of people have helped make this book a reality. First I must thank the Faculty Summer Scholarship Committee of Western Kentucky University (WKU) for funding my fieldwork in China for the second time. I am indebted to my editors at Libraries Unlimited, Barbara Ittner in particular, for quality control, as well as to Emma Bailey, production manager, Sharon DeJohn, copyeditor, Mike Florman, layout designer, and Gaile Ivaska, cover designer. I am deeply grateful to freelance writer Dory Hudspeth, my student assistant Kaylee Holoway, and my son Hao Yuan, for graciously proofreading my manuscript. I greatly appreciate the generosity of writer and artist Dai Yuru and her editor, Yang Jie, for allowing me to use the exquisite illustrations from her book *Yunnan Nationalities' Headdresses and Costumes*. My thanks also go to WKU student Sarah Martin for her illustrations. I thank Larry Caillouet, professor at WKU; Yang Changbin, director of the Kaili College Library of Guizhou; Wang Gang, a librarian from the Yunnan Agriculture University; and Liang Yong, a photographer from the Honghe Hani Autonomous Prefecture of Yunnan, along with his wife She Huixian, for permitting me to use the beautiful photos they have taken. I'm thankful to Ma Hui, librarian at Honghe University, for connecting me with Liang Yong and sending me his photos. I especially thank Zhao Shilin, director of the Yunnan Nationalities University Library, who has lent me all the help he could, including granting me access to his university's museum exhibits and introducing me to the celebrated Yi ethnologist Professor Zhang Chunde, who kindly agreed to write the foreword for this book. Minjie Chen, a doctoral student at University of Illinois Urbana-Champaign, granted me an interview. My niece Ling Ding, then in China, helped me locate information unavailable in the United States. I am indebted to my wife Shizhen for caring and helping me while I was writing. I also must express my gratitude to the administration of WKU Libraries, Dr. Michael Binder and Dr. Brian Coutts in particular, who have given me the time and resources to write. Finally, I thank my colleagues for showing their moral support. Charles Smith and Bryan Carson actually helped me locate the map and provided related copyright information.

INTRODUCTION

China has fifty-six officially recognized nationalities, with Han accounting for over 91 percent of the country's total population of 1.3 billion. The rest of the nationalities are called *shaoshu minzu,* or ethnic minorities. Like Han, each of the fifty-five ethnic minorities has a rich tradition of folklore, most of which has been passed down through the ages by word of mouth. Many of the ethnic minorities didn't have written languages until the mid-twentieth century.

Unlike Han folktales, the tales from Chinese ethnic minorities have largely maintained their original flavor, having seldom been adapted or edited by scholars. Confucius taught that one should "stay at a respectful distance from ghosts and gods" and focus on personal moral uplift. This tradition of indifference to otherworldliness has to some extent stifled the fanciful imagination of the Han Chinese. Their minority compatriots have greatly enriched the treasure house of Chinese literature.

The number of stories from ethnic minorities is staggering. A single project to record the oral tradition of one ethnic group, the Dongxiang, yielded 1,500 to 1,600 tales. Another research project conducted recently produced a forty-six-million-word anthology of Chinese folktales, primarily from ethnic minorities. The voluminous collections of ethnic folktales provide an author with inexhaustible resources. At the same time, they present a tremendous challenge: It's impossible to give a full picture of China's ethnic minorities by telling and retelling all their stories—which may number in the millions—in a 300-page book.

Nonetheless, this volume is an effort to give American readers a fair view of China as a multi-ethnic nation of diverse cultures. Intended as a companion to *The Magic Lotus Lantern and Other Tales from the Han Chinese* (2006), this book samples one tale from each of the fifty-five Chinese ethnic minorities, in hopes of rousing the reader's interest in learning more about China's ethnic folkways. The expectation is that each tale will provide a glimpse of the wealthy cultures of a particular ethnic group. Several criteria have been followed to create a representative sampling.

First was to include tales already well-known among the ethnic minorities. (Whether or not they are familiar to the Han Chinese was not a consideration.) Although the jokes of Nesridin Afendi are very popular among Uygurs, they are not included here because their authorship is also claimed by peoples of West and Central Asia. In addition, Afendi is already a celebrity in the English-speaking world.

Another requirement was that the tales cover a wide range of types, such as "animal tales," "moral tales," "magic tales," "tales of love and romance," "tales of creation and ethnic origin," "tales of how things came to be," "tales of deities, immortals, and legendary figures," and "legends about places." However, it was no simple job to categorize the tales, because some fall into several groups. For example, "Three Brothers" tells a moral story as well as describing ethnic origins. Therefore, the placement of the tales in categories is somewhat arbitrary. Readers, especially teachers and librarians, may reclassify the tales as they see fit when using them in their classrooms.

A third step was to exclude tales whose content may not be suitable for young readers, because this book is in part targeted to that age group. The excluded tales are predominantly those about human origin with graphic descriptions. Tales of dubious brother–sister relationships have been modified for a younger audience; in these cases, the motif appendix includes the original content so that the tales can still be useful for researchers.

A fourth step was to select the tales with historical perspectives. Throughout China's history various peoples have come together, separated, and come together again. The tales reflect this history. On the one hand, tales like "Sax—Mother of the Dongs" and "Liu Sanjie—A Fearless Folk Song Singer" expose the Han's oppression of ethnic minorities. On the other hand, "Forty Girls," "Three Brothers," "Seven Brothers," and "Princess Wencheng" reveal times of ethnic harmony and peaceful coexistence, demonstrating either a common ancestry or a unity fused by royal matrimony.

The last step, but not the least, was the use of various sources. Although most of the tales in the book are based on the works of others who recorded them in writing, some were collected by the author during his field trip to China in summer 2007.

Brief introductory remarks precede each of the stories, identifying their ethnic affiliations and providing the background knowledge needed to better comprehend and appreciate them.

To gain a holistic understanding of China's cultures, readers may want to use this book with *The Magic Lotus Lantern and Other Tales from the Han Chinese*, particularly when doing a comparative study or research on the diffusion or spread of cultures. The book is intended for a broad readership. Ethnologists and folklorists will find it useful for their research in Chinese ethnic minorities. College and school students studying Chinese as a second language may adopt it as supplemental cultural resource. Teachers and librarians can employ it to facilitate their cultural programs and studies. Parents, especially those who adopt children from China, may read the stories to their children. Businesspeople who seek a better understanding of China can learn more about its different peoples' customs and etiquettes. Tourists of China may find the book a complement to their travel guides, as many of the country's scenic spots are habitats of ethnic minorities; in fact, anyone who is interested in learning more about China will benefit from the book, because it shows more than the one face of China they have seen through the mass media.

Regarding the names of the Chinese ethnic groups, this book follows the *Names of Nationalities of China in Romanization with Codes (GB/3304—1991)*, issued by the Standardization Administration of China on April 1, 1992. For example, the standardized form Uygur is used instead of its variant Uighur, and Buyei instead of Bouyei. An exception applies to Zang and Chosen, the former being replaced by Tibet and the latter by Korean when they appear in non-Chinese publications like this book. As for the ethnic names of persons and places appearing in the stories, Romanization of their original script is applied where it is available, as in the case of "Songtsan Gambo" and the lake "Bukûri." Otherwise, Chinese Pinyin is employed, such as "Ashima," and "Jiuqian Mountains."

There is a Chinese saying, "An abbot's job is to lead one into the door of a monastery; it's up to him to read enough of the Buddhist Scripture to become a monk." This is the philosophy of this book. The intention of this collection is to give American readers a glimpse of the immensity of Chinese minority ethnic cultures and thereby of China's culture in general. Their interest kindled, it is hoped readers will embark of their own accord on a journey to explore a civilization that is ancient, mystic, profound, and, most important, incredibly diversified.

MAP OF CHINA

Chinese Linguistic Groups

SINO-TIBETAN
- ☐ Mandarin
  - 1. Northern
  - 2. Eastern
  - 3. Southwestern
- Southern
  - 1. Wu
  - 2. Gan
  - 3. Xiang
  - 4. Min
  - 5. Hakka
  - 6. Yue
- Tibetan
  - 1. Amdo
  - 2. Khams
  - 3. Dbusgtsang
- Kam-Tai
- Miao-Yao

INDO-EUROPEAN
- Tajik

AUSTRO-ASIATIC
- Mon-Khmer

ALTAI
- Turkic
  - 1. Kazakh
  - 2. Uygur
  - 3. Kirghiz
- Mongolian
- Manchu-Tungus
- Korean

—— Province-level boundary

Boundary representation is
not necessarily authoritative.

0   500 Kilometers
0   500 Miles

PART 1

Chinese Ethnicities and Their Culture: An Overview

OVERVIEW OF CHINESE ETHNICITY

Brief Historical Background

According to a Chinese ethnologist, the early Chinese fell into roughly three groups, living in three distinct regions. Farmers inhabited the vast plains of Central China and later became the bulk of Huaxia, predecessors of the ethnic Han; nomadic herdsmen roamed the northern grasslands; and people who hunted and engaged in primitive farming lived on the southwestern plateaus. The interactions of these three groups have contributed to the evolution of China into the multi-ethnic nation it is today (Zou, 2004).

Classification of Ethnicities

Throughout China's long history, no government bothered to define its ethnic peoples. Then, in the 1950s, China began "allowing groups to apply for national minority status" (Heber, 1989; Lee, 1997). Although more than 400 groups applied, only 55 received official recognition. Thus, some of the minority ethnic groups recognized today consist of several branches with different names and varying customs. For example, Mosuo is now part of the Naxi group. Sani and Ani belong to the Yi ethnicity. And the dozen distinct aboriginal groups in Taiwan fall under the name Gaoshan (High Mountains).

For decades, members of many ethnic minorities hid their affiliations to avoid persecution. Since China relaxed its social control in the early 1980s, some twelve million have restored their ethnic status. But the 1990 census showed that there were still 749,341 Chinese belonging to none of the fifty-six officially recognized groups. This number includes the 2,000 to 8,000 Jews believed to reside in China today (Gladney, 2004, 9). There is evidence that Kaifeng, capital of the Northern Song dynasty (A.D. 960–1126), once had a large community of Jewish immigrants. But due to isolation and lack of religious leaders, they gradually disappeared. Beginning in the 1930s, modern Jewish communities re-emerged in China. It is estimated that a total of 40,000 once lived in Harbin, Shanghai, and Tianjin.

When New China, or the People's Republic, was established in 1949, the majority of those Jews left the country for other parts of the world.

The number of legal aliens in China has reached 250,000. This further complicates the issue of China's ethnic identification. The immigrants come from 136 countries, including Japan, Korea, the European Union, and the United States ("China—Paradise of Foreign Immigrants," 2006).

Policies Toward Ethnic Minorities

During the Han dynasty (202 B.C.–A.D. 220), the Huaxia- or Han-dominated governments pursued various policies toward ethnic minorities. The Tang (A.D. 618–907) and the Song (A.D. 960–1279) courts adopted the *jimi* (controlling and winning over) strategy (Zou, 2004), which basically promoted integration. The Manchu rulers of the Qing dynasty (1644–1911) advocated harmony between Manchu and Han, but harmony often proved elusive. In the mid-1950s the concept of ethnic autonomy found its way into the Chinese Constitution. This allows ethnic minorities to remain distinct and to have their own leaders. Mark Bender, an East Asian studies professor from The Ohio State University, observes, "Since the end of the Cultural Revolution in the late 1970s, there has been general improvement in the implementation of minority policies, though ethnic tensions simmer in some regions in the west" (Bender, 2006).

Currently there are five autonomous regions at the provincial level. These are Inner Mongolia, Guangxi, Tibet, Ningxia, and Xinjiang. There are also 30 autonomous prefectures and 120 autonomous counties, where ethnic minority communities concentrate.

Subtle changes have occurred in the relations among ethnic peoples over time. Rizvan Mamet and his colleagues recently conducted research on interethnic marriage. The conventional belief is that Muslims in Xinjiang are more traditional than the Han Chinese and therefore are less likely to marry people of other ethnic groups. The research reveals, however, that that perception is inaccurate: "Uyghur females in Xinjiang are 68 percent more likely to marry out than the Han females" (Mamet et al., 2005). The Dai people have no problem with marrying outside of their ethnicity, either. Offspring of the Hans and the Dais now even form a separate branch of the Dai group, the Han-Dai.

Social behavior can unconsciously reinforce the harmonious relationship between neighboring ethnic peoples. This is true of the Han and She peoples in Zhejiang. Some Han Chinese customarily place their newborns in a She family for temporary adoption, believing this may enhance the babies' chance to survive. This practice, despite its lack of scientific grounding, has helped foster a closer tie between the two ethnic peoples.*

Folktales may shed some light on the harmony enjoyed by ethnic peoples in China. "Seven Brothers," retold in this book, explains that seven ethnic groups shared the same ancestry. The beautiful tale of an Aini sister and a Dai sister-in-law (not included in this book) also illustrates ethnic accord. This tale explains the asymmetrical nature of the clothing of these two groups. A Dai woman wears a vest and a long skirt, whereas an Aini girl dresses in a long-sleeved top and a short skirt. According to the tale, the Dai sister-in-law bought a piece of cloth to make a blouse for each woman. But she accidentally cut one half larger than the other. She made the Aini sister a long-sleeved top and herself a sleeveless vest. When the Aini sister learned of her Dai sister-in-law's selflessness, she made a short skirt for herself and gave the long skirt to her.

Chinese history demonstrates how different peoples came together, separated, and came together again. Although there were suppressions and revolts in the past, and there are still some sporadic separatist rumblings that may be considered when studying Chinese ethnic minorities, for the most part peoples of the various ethnic groups in China have been living fairly peacefully together for a very long time.

Additional Reading

Lynn, Aliya Ma. *Muslims in China*. Indianapolis: University of Indianapolis Press, 2007. 118pp. ISBN-10: 0880938528; ISBN-13: 978-0880938525.

Safran, William. *Nationalism and Ethnoregional Identities in China*. New York: Routledge, 1998. 208pp. ISBN-10: 0714644765; ISBN-13: 978-0714644769.

---

*Minjie Chen, telephone interview conducted on April 2, 2007 in Tianjin, China.

PEOPLES

Population

In 2005 there were 123,330,000 minority ethnics living in China, accounting for 9.44 percent of China's total population (Zhonghua renmin gonghe guo guojia tongji ju, 2006). The 2000 census showed that eighteen ethnic minority groups had more than a million people each, fifteen had over 100,000 each, another fifteen each had fewer than 100,000, and seven each had a population below 10,000. The Zhuang, with 16,178,811, are the largest ethnic minority in China. The Lhoba, with only 3,000 people, are the smallest (China, 2002).

In 1982, the Chinese government began to enforce planned birth among ethnic minorities. Today, each family of an ethnic minority with less than ten million people is allowed to have up to three children. Planned birth doesn't apply to Tibetans in agricultural and pastoral areas. Neither is it enforced upon ethnic groups having fewer than 10,000 people each (Di jiu jie quanguo renmin daibiao dahui changwu weiyuan hui di ershi wu ci huiyi, 2001).

As a result of the disparity in family planning policies, ethnic minority populations are growing faster than that of the Han Chinese. In the decade between the fourth census in 1990 and the fifth in 2000, the Han Chinese increased 11.22 percent, while the ethnic population rose 16.7 percent (China, 2002).

Geographic Distribution

Distribution of Chinese ethnic populations has the characteristics of what scholars call *xiao jizhong, da fensan* (a high level of concentration in specific regions and wide scattering throughout the country). Though accounting for less than 10 percent of China's total population, ethnic minorities are found in a large part of the country. The ethnic Hui are scattered nearly all over the country. A single ethnic group, such as the Miao, can be found in nine provinces, extending from Guizhou to Hainan. The people of Tujia can also be found in four different parts of the country. In 2000 sixteen of the thirty-one Chinese provinces and administrative regions had significant ethnic communities. On the other hand, sixteen ethnic groups exist in Yunnan Province only.

Minority ethnic and Han Chinese also "penetrate" each other's "territories." Forty percent of the She people live in the Han-dominated provinces Jiangxi and Zhejiang, in East China. At the same time, the Han population has surpassed that of the Mongols in Inner Mongolia and is expected to surpass the Uygurs in Xinjiang soon (Zhongguo minwei, 2006).

Political events and economic development have played a role in the changes among ethnic minority populations and their geographical redistribution. To "garrison the frontier" that bordered the Soviet Union, the Chinese government sent millions of Han Chinese to the sparsely populated Xinjiang region. Zhao Shilin, an ethnologist at Yunnan Nationalities University, reports that there were 101,900 Jingpo people in 1953. But a decade later, the number had dropped sharply, to 57,800. It took another twenty years to climb back to 93,000. Professor Zhao explains that China's political turmoil in the 1950s and 1960s made it difficult for the Jingpos to hang on to their traditions, so they had to flee to neighboring Burma (Zhao, 2002).

In the past three decades, China's economy has grown tremendously. Its wealth, however, is far from being equally distributed among its people. Regions along the east coast are much more fortunate than the rest of the country. This imbalance, combined with easier migration, has resulted in large numbers of Chinese, ethnic minorities included, leaving their impoverished homelands. According to one study, 10 to 18 percent of the population, mostly of ethnic minorities, in Guizhou, Chongqing, Hainan, and Hebei, had moved out between 1900 and 2000. At the same time, ethnic minority population gained significantly in the more developed Shanghai, Guangdong, Beijing, Zhejiang, and Tianjin (Jiang, 2006).

Due to preferential family planning policies, however, the population of ethnic minorities has increased in their home regions, canceling out the losses to emigration. The ethnic populations have increased in most of China's provinces and regions. There were 340,580 more Tibetans in 2000 than in 1990 (Jiang, 2006). The seeming deficit in some of the regions is attributed to the influx of Han Chinese.

Continued migration is redrawing the demographic map of China's ethnic minorities. In 1990, only Beijing had members of all China's ethnic groups living in it; a decade later, ten more regions have followed suit (Zhou, 2003).

Additional Reading

China. *2000 nian di wu ci quan guo ren kou pu cha zhu yao shu ju* (*Major Figures on 2000 Population Census of China*). Beijing Shi: Zhongguo tong ji chu ban she, 2001. 64pp. ISBN: 7503735554.

Iredale, Robyn R., Naran Bilik, and Fei Guo. *China's Minorities on The Move: Selected Case Studies*. Armonk, N.Y.: M.E. Sharpe, 2003. 183pp. ISBN-10: 0765610248; ISBN-13: 978-0765610249.

LANGUAGES

The Huis and Manchus speak Mandarin (*Putonghua*) and write Chinese characters (*hanzi*) because they have largely been assimilated with the Han Chinese. The rest of the fifty-five ethnic minorities share more than 120 languages, some written but most spoken. There are more languages than ethnicities because people officially categorized in one ethnic group may still have cultural differences. This is true of the Dai people, who speak four varying dialects and write with three different scripts. Likewise, the Mongols, though speaking one tongue, have two writing systems.

Generally speaking, the 120 ethnic tongues belong to the Altaic, Indo-European, Sino-Tibetan, South Asian, and South Island families. Hieroglyphic, syllabic, or alphabetic languages, they are linguistically Tibetan, Uygur, Arabic, Korean, Thai, Latin, and Slavic.

In China, all languages are legally equal, although *Putonghua* (Mandarin) is designated as the national language. The Bill of Autonomous Regions of Ethnic Peoples (2001), asserts that leaders of different ethnic backgrounds working in ethnic regions are encouraged to learn each other's languages. Leaders of ethnic Han are required to learn the language of the ethnic people among whom they work. Bonuses are given to those who can speak more than two ethnic languages.

In the early 1950s seven teams of linguists visited thirty-three ethnic minorities in sixteen regions to help them develop written languages. They helped the Zhuang, Yi, Buyei, Miao, Dai, Dong, Hani, Lisu, Li, Va, Tu, and Naxi people create alphabetic writing systems on a voluntary basis. They also assisted the Jingpo, Lahu, Uygur, and Kazak people in improving their existing Romanized scripts. In 1996 the government standardized the syllabic system for the Yi people. At the same time, China established national standards to encode Mongolian, Tibetan, Yi, Uygur, Kazak, and Kirgiz scripts for computer input. The first two have been adopted by the International Organization for Standardization (ISO).

The beauty of the ancient *Dongbawen* (scripts of Eastern Ba) has caught the attention of ethno-linguists as well as tourists from home and abroad. Using pictures to represent ideas, it is allegedly older than *Jiaguwen* (oracle-bone scripts) of the Shang dynasty (sixteenth to eleventh centuries B.C.), which is the precursor of contemporary Chinese characters.

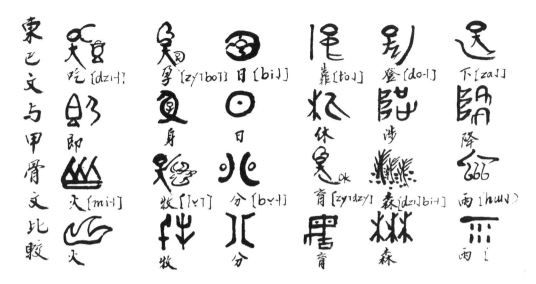

Comparison of the heliographic *Dongba* script (first and third rows) with the Han Chinese bronze script (second and fourth rows)

Another interesting language is *nüshu* (women's scripts). Professor Gong Zhebing from Wuhan University first discovered it in Jiangyong County in Hunan Province in 1982. Despite its pictographic appearance, *nüshu* is, in fact, a spelling language. As its name implies, it's a language exclusively used by women, of the ethnic Yao and Zhuang peoples. Its origin is disputable. Some linguists trace it to the middle of the seventeenth century. Others find similarities in *Jiaguwen*. The reason for its creation may be elusive, but it is commonly considered a backlash against male dominance, which denied women the right to learn.

Today, ethnic languages face serious challenges. A recent study shows that more than half of the 120 ethnic languages are spoken only by groups of ethnic peoples numbering fewer than a thousand each. More than twenty are on the brink of extinction, because they are spoken or written by populations of fewer than a thousand. Only a dozen Hezhen elders still know how to speak their mother tongue, and fewer than a hundred Manchus understand theirs. Mu Shihua, a researcher of Naxi nationality at the China Academia of Social Science, complains that in a Naxi family of three generations, only the grandparents know how to speak the beautiful Naxi language. Their grandchildren think it will affect their intellectual development and refuse to learn it. The researcher concludes that, like other ethnic youths, the young Naxis, who care very much about making money, consider the study of their mother tongue to be a waste of time. Other scholars put the blame on local authorities, saying that they emphasize economic development more than ethnic cultural preservation.

On the other hand, the largest electronics producer in China, Haier, has just announced their first television sets with Mongolian menus available. Haier is also planning to produce television sets with Uygur, Tibetan, and Korean languages as an option in their control menus ("Shou tai shaoshu minzu yuwen dianshi jijiang toufang shichang," 2006). Technology will help preserve these languages, at least to some extent.

Additional Reading

Ramsey, S. Robert. *The Languages of China.* Princeton, N.J.: Princeton University Press, 1989. 355pp. ISBN-10: 069101468X; ISBN-13: 978-0691014685.

HOMES

Current waves of economic development in China are quickly washing away traditional buildings in cities and even some rural areas. A pun on this frenzy is circulating among foreign residents in Beijing: China is "chai-ne" ("being demolished"). Everywhere one turns, there are swiveling cranes towering over massive construction sites. A good illustration of traditional China being demolished is the dwindling numbers of *siheyuan* (compounds of houses surrounding a courtyard), time-honored dwellings of Beijing residents. They are being replaced by Western-style high rises. Local governments zealous for higher GDP (Gross Domestic Product) numbers are bent on real property development, often sacrificing traditional architecture.

Fortunately, many Chinese have come to realize the importance of their cultural heritage. The China Nationalities Museum in Beijing and the Ethnic Cultural Park in Kunming are making efforts to preserve traditional ethnic homes. They highlight life-sized replicas of traditional ethnic homes built by ethnic craftsmen with materials shipped from original ethnic habitats.

Geographic conditions and availability of construction materials generally determine the architectural styles of ethnic homes:

- Wood-structured *diaojiaolou* (houses on high poles) and *mulengfang* (houses of square timber)
- Stone-structured *shibanfang* (slab houses) and *diaolou* (castle houses)
- Bamboo-structured *ganlan* (pole-railing houses) and *zhulou* (bamboo houses)
- Thatched-wood structured *qianjiaolou* (thousand-foot houses) and *chuanlou* (boat-shaped houses)
- Immature-soil structured cave-houses and houses of the Turpan style

Diaojiaolou are often built against mountains and along rivers. They are popular among the Dong, Miao, Sui, and Tu peoples. Although wood poles prop up the façade above the water, the rear part of the structure sits against the mountainside, serving as residential quarters.

Zhulou are the home of the Dai and Lhoba. Constructed mostly of *zhu* (bamboo), the richest natural resource for home building in South China, *zhulou* houses are thatched with straw and supported by wooden columns. More columns indicate greater family riches. The

---

Homes   **11**

columns are square to deter snakes from climbing up them. A thick column in the center of the house is believed to hold the family's good fortune. Hosts encourage their guests to put their arms around it before their departure to share their good luck with them.

A *zhulou* house of the Dai people has two stories; that of the Lhoba has three. The first story holds domestic animals, the second is the dwelling area, and the top is for storage. The Dai dwelling floor is dominated by a large living room. This is flanked by a cooking area and a partitioned bedroom. All family members sleep on the same long bed, separated only by their mosquito nets of different colors: Black nets are for older people, white ones for the children and grandchildren, and red ones for the newlyweds. As devout Buddhist followers, the Dai cannot imagine how people sleep separately in different rooms; in doing so, they believe, their souls would be separated. *Zhulou* has gone through many changes. Today it is no longer built solely of bamboo and wood. Bricks and concrete are being used more and more in place of natural materials. In Xishuangbanna, an enclave of the Dai people in Yunnan, *zhulou* houses made of bamboo, of half bamboo and half bricks, and of bricks and concrete stand side by side, revealing the evolution of the structure through different stages.

Houses of the Hani people look like mushrooms, which is why they are called *muogufang* (mushroom houses). With earth walls as the foundation and bamboo and wood poles supporting a thatched roof, a mushroom house has three stories, which function the same as those in bamboo houses do. Floored with planks, the second story is partitioned into three rooms and has two staircases on opposite sides. The one on the left is for men, and the one on the right for women. A man who accidentally set his foot on the wrong staircase would become a laughingstock in his community.

Courtesy of Hou Yong and She Huixian, Honghe Hani Prefecture, Yunnan

Hani mushroom house in Yunnan

Nomadic Mongols live in domed, portable tents, known to Westerners as yurts (or sometimes ger). Mongols call them *benbugegeri* (domed houses) or *Mongolegeri* (Mongolian houses). The Han Chinese call them *menggubao*, meaning "homes of the Mongols." A yurt consists of *hana* (wood palings) and *wuni* (wood beams). They prop up a felt cover fastened with leather ropes. A yurt has more space on the inside than it appears to have from the outside. A hearth sits in the center facing the entrance. Surrounding the hearth against the walls of the yurt are cupboards and trunks, painted with beautiful Mongolian motifs. In front of the furniture are thick carpets. The carpeted area serves as a living room during the day and a bedroom at night. A yurt doesn't need inside support, but noble families have four elaborately decorated columns at the heart of the yurt. Like the Dai people, the Mongols encourage their guests to rub the columns so they can share their good luck.

According to Wang Ping, director of the China Nationalities Museum, religious beliefs are also a factor in shaping the styles of ethnic homes. A Tibetan house must have a room or recess designated for worship.

Additional Reading

Knapp, Ronald G. *China's Old Dwellings*. Honolulu: University of Hawaii Press, 2000. 362pp. ISBN-10: 0824820754; ISBN-13: 978-0824820756.

Knapp, Ronald G. *Chinese Landscapes: The Village as Place*. Honolulu: University of Hawaii Press, 1992. 328pp. ISBN-10: 0824814134; ISBN-13: 978-0824814137.

CLOTHING

Traditional clothing has cultural value. It defines ethnic minority groups and even identifies different communities within the same group. Forty-seven branches of the Yi dress in as many as 120 different styles of costume. This diversity across and within ethnic groups adds to the colorful mosaic of Chinese culture.

Each piece of garment or jewelry tells a story of the ethnic group to which its wearer belongs. Naxi women's sheepskin shawls, decorated with a pattern of seven stars, have at least a couple of folktales behind them. One tells of a young woman's fight against a monster of drought. The monster unleashed eight more suns into the sky, trying to destroy the earth and its residents. The young woman fought the monster until her death. Heavenly God bid a snow dragon swallow seven of the nine suns and turn the eighth into a moon. He then made the dragon throw up the suns and shaped them into stars. So the young woman would always be remembered, he embedded the stars in the back of her cape.

A woman of a Yi branch may wear a hat shaped like a rooster's comb. The story says that the bird and the centipede had been good friends. They were alienated only after the centipede refused to return a horn it had borrowed from the rooster. When their village was infested with centipedes, the Yi took advantage of their enmity and raised many roosters to stamp out the pests. Their combs have since become symbols of good fortune.

Some traditional ethnic clothing may not be as mythical, but it reveals the origin of an ethnic minority's name. Xibe, for example, means "hooked leather belt." The ethnic Xibe are so called because hooked leather belts are an integral part of their traditional costumes. The Bais call themselves "white people" (*Baini*); they use a lot of white color in their costumes ("Exhibition on Costumes," 2002). Black dominates the apparel of the Naxis. They associate the color black with infinite darkness, which they interpret as invisible ("Guya chunpu de Naxi zu fushi," 2006). Part of their name, "*na,*" means black in the Naxi language.

Ethnic costumes are significant in other ways as well. A Tibetan man in his thick robe bares his right arm, a custom that has religious as well as practical significance. Some believe they do so to model Sakyamuni, founder of Buddhism. Others reason that it is convenient to have an arm free for labor.

**Hat that originated from a tale about a rooster. Courtesy of Dai Yuru and Yunnan
Fine Arts Publishing House**

Costume patterns and decorative motifs vary among ethnic groups. The most distinct feature on a particular piece of garment knitted with white and red yarns is a square pattern on the front of a vest. The pattern is said to be a seal, symbol of authority of the God of Yao, and regarded as a talisman by those who wear it.

Ethnic minority women acquire their skills of embroidery and wax printing when they are very young. They make costumes not only for themselves, but also for their children and grandchildren. Mothers usually pass on to their daughters prized costumes and ornaments in hopes that they can carry on the time-honored tradition.

Current Changes

In regions out of reach of commercialism, ethnic traditions remain largely intact. Elsewhere, however, the younger generation has begun to abandon ethnic clothing. Easier transportation and migration expose young people to modern fashions like T-shirts and jeans. They wear their ethnic costumes only during festivals or on important occasions like weddings.

On the other hand, changes can be a two-way street: Ethnic costumes have had a great impact on fashion design in China as well as in the outside world. An example is the *Qipao*. Once a long and loose robe worn by Manchu women, it has become a national fad, with some modifications. Laces embroidered with ethnic Chinese motifs have also found their way onto dresses sold worldwide.

Today, greater attention is given to ethnic costumes not only for preservation, but also for profit. "A full set of original costumes and ornaments can be sold for a million *yuan* (US$128,500). The average price tag for a tailor-made traditional Tibetan costume ranges between 40,000 and 50,000 *yuan* (US$4,830-6,038)" (Yu, 2004). These items are expensive because fewer ethnic women know how to make them.

The profit-making craze poses a grave danger to traditional ethnic costumes. Some foreign collectors have jumped upon the opportunity to acquire them in large quantities, worrying the Chinese. It has been reported that the Japanese National Ethnology Museum alone has collected several thousand sets of Chinese ethnic costumes, some of which can no longer be found in China ("Zhongguo shaoshu minzu fuzhuang liushi yanzhong," 1999).

Realizing the value and the uniqueness of their costumes, many ethnic communities have built themselves into tourist attractions, bringing in cash and investment to improve their economies. The idea of preserving Chinese ethnic cultures—ethnic clothing and ornaments included—while making a profit is apparently behind the building of two large ethnology museums/parks in Beijing and Kunming, where tour guides from various ethnic backgrounds showcase their traditional dress to visitors from home and abroad.

Replica of a Lhasa street corner in the Beijing Ethnic Museum

Additional Reading

Wang, Fu-shih, ed. *Ethnic Costumes and Clothing Decorations from China.* Hong Kong: Hai Feng Publishing, 1986. 336pp. ISBN-10: 0887348068; ISBN-13: 978-0887348068.

Zang Yingchun. *Chinese Minority Costumes.* Translated by Yu Hong, Beijing: Wu zhou chuan bo chu ban she, 2004. 218pp. ISBN-10: 7508503791; ISBN-13: 978-7508503790.

RELIGIONS

Chinese ethnic minorities subscribe to a variety of religions, including Buddhism, Lamaism, Daoism, Shamanism, Christianity, Catholicism, Orthodox, Islam, and various forms of native folk beliefs. Although some ethnic groups have a single religion, others have multiple ones. Chinese Russians subscribe to Orthodox Christianity only. Most Tibetans believe in Lamaism or Tibetan Buddhism, a combination of Buddhism and native non-Buddhist beliefs. Ten ethnic groups are followers of Islam: Bonan, Dongxiang, Hui, Kazak, Kirgiz, Salar, Tajik, Tatar, Uygur, and Uzbek. And many from the Daur, Ewenki, Hezhen, Manchu, Oroqen, Tu, and Xibe groups are devoted to shamanism, an ancient practice in which a shaman (one that knows) acts as an intermediary between the natural and the spiritual worlds.

Nearly half of the fifty-five ethnic minority groups adhere to the religious traditions of their ancestors, which see a spirit behind everything in nature—a tradition known to us as animism. The Jino people worship the sun. A Jino woman can be easily identified by the symbol of a shining sun sewed on the back of her blouse. The Jino people also worship their ancestors, as do the Han and some other ethnic minorities. The Naxi people not only believe in Lamaism and Daoism, but also hang on to their native creed, known as *Dongbajiao* (the religion of Eastern Ba). Polytheistic and naturalistic in nature, it borrows from Lamaism.

In the nineteenth century, Christianity, including Catholicism, came to China. Christian beliefs gained ground not only among Han Chinese but also among ethnic minority peoples. France alone established seven parishes with a thousand cathedrals in Inner Mongolia ("Shaoshu minzu zongjiao xinyang," 2006). Christians can be found among a dozen ethnic groups.

The Great Cultural Revolution (1966–1976) affected the religious lives of all Chinese. Many ethnic groups were forced to give up their traditional religious practices. However, "In the post-Mao era, China's society and religion are both becoming increasingly pluralistic. State policies toward religion are also evolving" (Lai, 2006). Since the 1980s, $4,500,000 has been spent on renovating the famed Potala Palace in Tibet. Recent statistics from China's Bureau of Religious Affairs show that in 2006, the country had more than 1,500 Taoist temples, 16,000 Christian churches, and 17,600 Buddhist temples, in addition to 1,700 public places for believers of Lamaism. Chinese Muslims, who pray outside their homes, now see the number of mosques multiplying quickly, and Mecca welcomes more and more Chinese Muslim pilgrims each year.

Protestant church in a Miao village in the vicinity of Kunming, Yunnan

Additional Reading

Gazangji. *Tibetan Religions. Series of Basic Information of Tibet of China.* [Beijing]: China Inter-
continental Press, 2003. 162pp. ISBN-10: 7508502329; ISBN-13: 9787508502328.

Israeli, Raphael. *Islam in China: Religion, Ethnicity, Culture, and Politics.* Lanham, Md.: Lexington
Books, 2002. 350pp. ISBN-10: 0739124196; ISBN-13: 978-0739124192.

CUSTOMS

Like all civilizations, the fifty-five Chinese ethnic minority groups have their unique customs, rituals, and taboos. A detailed discussion would require a full-length book. Following is a sampling of customs and taboos of a few ethnicities.

Tibetans and Mongolians give their guests *kha-btags* (ritual scarves). Made with materials of varying qualities, the scarves also differ in color and length. The longer a scarf is, the more significant it becomes. Silk *kha-btags* are the most valuable and are predominantly white in color, because Tibetans believe white symbolizes purity, honesty, and kindheartedness. Colored *kha-btags* are usually dedicated to Buddhist deities.

Kha-btag giving can be very ceremonious. How a *kha-btag* is presented depends on the seniority of the recipient. When giving a *kha-btag* to an elder or a superior, one must bring the upper body a little forward while holding the *kha-btag* with both hands above the head. When giving it to peers, one need only hang it over the hands or wrists of the recipient, who holds them out. If the recipient is a junior or subordinate, one places the *kha-btag* around his or her neck.

A *kha-btag* conveys different feelings when used in different situations. It can be a gesture of New Year greetings, a sign of welcome to visitors, a symbol of good wishes to newlyweds, or a message of mourning to the dead and of solace to the living.

Like other Chinese ethnic minorities, Mongols are very hospitable. The first thing they do when they have visitors is offer them *naicha* (milk tea) or other beverages. Drinking *naicha* is very ceremonial. Holding the cup with the left hand, one dips into the cup with the index finger of the right hand three times and snaps away the moisture on the finger. The first time, one flicks it forward above the head to consecrate heaven. Next one tosses it onto the floor to sanctify the earth. Finally, one applies it to one's forehead to bless one's ancestor. Only then may one start drinking from the cup. Anyone who doesn't feel like drinking it may politely put the cup away.

The Uygurs are a hospitable people, too, unless someone disregards their customs and social taboos. They believe a person's gaze possesses an evil power that can bring ill fortune to them. That is why they hate it when people stare at them or the things they possess. Visitors and tourists must be careful when shopping; paying too much attention for too long to a piece of merchandise without buying it may invite resentment from a Uygur shopkeeper.

Other ethnic peoples have their taboos as well. As a rule of thumb, it is advisable to stay away from religious ceremonies and funeral services of an ethnic community. These occasions are considered sacred or private. Some ethnic people also hate to see their hearths violated. A visitor should never touch the tripod above the fire, nor should he or she step on the fire itself. Doing so would bring bad luck to the household.

Eating dogs, repulsive as it is to many Westerners, is customary in some areas of Asia. However, many Chinese ethnic groups consider dog-eating taboo, including the Miao, Manchu, Mongol, Yao, Tibet, Yi, and the ten Muslim ethnic groups. Muslims in China, as elsewhere in the world, also prohibit the consumption of pork and alcohol.

Each ethnic group has its own particular marriage traditions. The wedding of an ethnic Bai couple takes three days to complete. "Four," which means "safe and sound" to the Bais, is a favorite number used to arrange dinner tables. Each has food served in a set of four containers and vessels.

A Yao wedding involves an unusual practice. While the bridegroom dances and sings with relatives and friends around a bonfire outside, he leaves his bride alone in the bridal chamber. The Mosuos, a branch of the Naxi ethnic group, still practice *zouhun* (walking marriage). This means that the men visit their spouses during the night and return to their parents' homes when day breaks. "Fatherless" children are raised by their mothers' family members. The Hanis have turned the tradition of *qianghun* (bride kidnapping) to the bride's benefit. The bride's parents "refuse" to marry their daughter so as to "force" the bridegroom to kidnap her. By doing so, they hope the bridegroom will value their daughter more and treat her better after marrying her. A bride of the Zhuang, Yi, Tibet, and Gaoshan ethnic groups is expected to "cry" instead of rejoicing on setting out for her bridegroom's home. By "crying" she demonstrates her unwillingness to leave her parents, who have invested so much in her upbringing. This practice is known as *kuhun* (crying marriage).

A Dai man is married into his wife's family. Before living with his wife, he has to perform hard labor for three years. If he fails the test, he will be booted out, and the bond is automatically dissolved. If he succeeds, however, his fate will change completely. He will become the housekeeper, leaving the outdoor labor to his wife for the rest of their lives.

Most Chinese today either bury or cremate their dead. Some of the Tibetans, Yugurs, and Monbas still expose the bodies to birds of prey, a custom known as *tianzang* (celestial burial). However, burials in water (*shuizang*), on trees (*shuzang*), or on cliffs (*yazang*), once practiced by some ethnic minority groups, have now become obsolete.

Mourning behaviors also vary from ethnicity to ethnicity. In the Dai tradition, after one passes away, his or her family members will put up a *fan* (long narrow banner) in their community's Buddhist temple. The *fan* is believed to be a ladder leading the soul of the dead to heaven. Once there, it needs no attention from the living. That means it requires no annual visitation, unlike the Han and most other ethnic Chinese.

For all their different traditions, one common trait of Chinese ethnic groups is their respect for the elderly. The Jingpos hold a *jinglaohui* (party of respecting the old) each year at which the young vie with one another to invite the elderly to dine. The Hanis have a *jinglaojie* (festival of respecting the old). Young Hanis plant trees as a wish that the elders' lives be as evergreen. Ethnic minorities like the Dong, Korean, and Bai observe similar rites.

Mongolian girl presents *kha-btag* and *naicha* to the author to welcome him to her yurt

Additional Reading

Chun, Ge. *Ershi yi shiji Zhongguo shaoshu minzu fengqing lu (Customs of the Ethnic Groups in China)*. Beijing Shi: Zhongguo huabao chubanshe, 2004. 236pp. ISBN: 7800246930.

Yeh, Ta-ping, et al. *The Bride's Boat: Marriage Customs of China's Fifty-Five Ethnic Minorities.* Beijing: New World Press, 1993. 204pp. ISBN/ISSN: 7800051803.

FESTIVALS

While enjoying official holidays with the rest of the country, China's ethnic minorities also have their own festivals to celebrate. The governments of the various ethnic regions decide whether to offer paid leaves for ethnic holidays and festivals.

As a result of cultural interaction, twenty-nine of the fifty-five officially recognized minority ethnic groups celebrate the Chinese New Year, though each in its own way. Other minority ethnic groups enjoy their unique traditions of festivity exclusively, such as the Koreans' *shutoujie* (Hair-combing Festival), the Dongs' *guniangjie* (Festival of Girls), and the Jingpos' *munao zongge* (Singing and Dancing Festival).

Because of media exposure and tourism, some of the unique ethnic holidays and festivals have become nationally known, including the Tibetan's *Shoton*, the Yi's Torch Festival, Mongol's *Nadam*, and the Dai's Water-splashing Festival, to name a few. Today, tourists needn't miss some of these festivals if they come at the wrong time of the year: The Water-splashing Festival of the Dais is reenacted daily to entertain visitors to the Dai community near Jinghong, capital of Xishuangbanna in Yunnan. They also needn't worry if they are in the wrong place; the Yi's Torch Festival can be experienced in the Ethnic Park in Kunming.

A Chinese ethnic minority may have a number of branches that live apart from one another. Each follows a different tradition and has its own celebrations. On the other hand, because of their common cultural background, several ethnic minorities observe the same holidays. The ten Muslim ethnic groups share Corban, Rozi Heyt, and *Shengjijie* (the Festival of Commemorating Muhammad).

In addition, ethnic groups of distinct cultural backgrounds may also celebrate similar festivals, though details of the celebrations differ from one ethnicity to another. For example, torch festivals are popular with not only the ethnic Yi, but also the Bai, Hani, Lahu, Naxi, and Pumi. The custom of water splashing is shared among the Achang, Blang, De'ang, and Va, as well as the Dai. *Sanyuesan* (the Third Day of the Third Moon Festival) is celebrated concurrently by the Bai, Li, Buyei and Miao peoples.

Many festivals originated from the daily lives of ethnic people. They celebrate their labor, the animals that help them with their labor, and the crops that result from their labor. The Dai, Dong, Hani, Pumi, and She celebrate *xinmijie* (the New Rice Festival) or *changxinjie* (the New Grain-tasting Festival) at the first harvest of rice, a time close to the autumnal equinox. The *changxinjie* of the ethnic She features ancestor worship, dancing, and *pange* (a singing contest between men and women that can last several days). Traditional food includes *ciba* (cakes made of glutinous rice), a recipe for which is available in this book. Ethnic minorities like the Blang and Qiang treat their farm cattle with such respect that they celebrate them in the *xiniujiaojie* (the Festival of Washing Cattle's Hooves) and *niuwanghui* (the Fair of Cattle King). Others who share the same tradition include the Li, Mulao, and She.

Some festival activities reveal lifestyles of the past and the present. Horse racing is a favorite of many ethnic minorities, including the Sui, who do it at *duanjie* (the Year End Festival). The Tu do it at *leitaihui* (the Singing Contest). The Mongols do it in *Nadam* (Recreation Gathering). And the Pumi do it on *danianjie* (Grand New Year Day). Perhaps most exciting is *diaoyang*, which is part of the Muslim's Corban celebration. This race involves catching a lamb as a trophy.

Like the holidays of the Han Chinese,* many holidays and festivals of ethnic minorities are associated with tales or legends. The Water-splashing Festival is an example. One story tells of a monstrous father and his seven daughters. The monster treated the Dai people so badly that his daughters decided to get rid of him. They managed to learn that he could only be killed by his own hair. While he was fast asleep, they plucked a tress of his hair, made it into a bow, and placed it against his neck. It cut his head off immediately. Before they had time to rejoice, the girls were alarmed to find the head reeling on the floor, spewing fire and scorching everything in its path. To prevent the fire from spreading to the Dai community, one of the girls picked up the burning head, and it immediately cooled off. But it smeared her beautiful dress, so her sisters splashed water on her to wash off the soot and ashes. Hence began the tradition of water splashing in April, the beginning of the Dai's New Year.

Another version of the story involves a Dai prince who slaughtered a ravaging fire dragon of nine heads. When his people found him badly burned, they saved his life by pouring a great amount of water on him to clean his wounds and soothe his pain.

Twenty of China's ethnic minorities have their own calendars. Some also have zodiac animals, like the Han Chinese. The ethnic Yi begin the zodiac with their totem, the tiger, instead of the rat. The Tibetan New Year starts from the first day of the first Tibetan month, which is neither the Chinese nor the Western New Year's Day.

Ethnic festivals number in the hundreds. Tibetans alone enjoy more than 150. The multitude of ethnic holidays and festivals adds to the diversity and richness of Chinese culture.

Statue of Dai prince slaughtering the nine-headed fire dragon

Additional Reading

Breuilly, Elizabeth, et al. *Festivals of the World: the Illustrated Guide to Celebrations, Customs, Events, and Holidays.* New York: Checkmark Books, 2002.

Stepanchuk, Carol, and Charles Choy Wong. *Mooncakes and Hungry Ghosts: Festivals of China.* San Francisco: China Books & Periodicals, 1991. 145pp. ISBN-10: 0835124819; ISBN-13: 9780835124812.

---

*Examples are tales about the origins of the Chinese New Year, the Dragon Boat Festival, and the Moon Festival, retold in *The Magic Lotus Lantern and Other Tales from the Han Chinese* (Libraries Unlimited, 2006).

PERFORMING ARTS, CINEMA, AND TELEVISION

Natural singers, members of Chinese ethnic minorities have a rich tradition of performing arts. More than 20,000 musical pieces, 7,000 dramas, 2,000 play scripts, and 200 musical instruments have been collected in the past few decades in Yunnan Province alone ("Wenhua yishu," 2006).

Music

Duige are songs in antiphonal style sung by men and women either one-to-one or group-to-group. They are specific to many of the Chinese ethnic minorities. Notable are the Bai, Dong, Hani, Li, Miao, Mulao, She, Yi, and Zhuang. They sing *duige* to have fun, to combat fatigue during labor, or to help youngsters find potential spouses. To add to the excitement of festival celebrations, contests of *duige* are also held. One such event can be found in the story "Liu Sanjie—A Fearless Folk Song Singer," retold in this book.

Baisha xiyue, the pride of the Naxi people, dates back to the Yuan dynasty (1280–1368). It had been lost in oblivion until its rediscovery in the early 1950s. A classical orchestral music, it has twenty-four *qupai* (tunes) played with ancient ethnic musical instruments.

Dage (The Great Song) of the ethnic Dong is an unaccompanied traditional folk chorus. It has become world famous for its contrapuntal melody, which is amazingly attuned with the theory and technique of Western music.

In addition to the chanting used by Lamas to help recite Buddhist scriptures, animated secular forms of music are also prevalent in Tibet. Much of Uygur, Uzbek, and Tajik music is based on the Twelve Muqam scales. The Hanis are known for their musical form *haba,* the Tujias for *longchuandiao,* the Salars for *salarqu,* the Yaos for *anchunge*, and the Huis for *huar'er*. Famous professional ethnic singers include Hu Songhua of the Manchu, Song Zuying of the Miao, Qubi'awu of the Yi, Kelimu of the Uygur, Tengger'er of the Mongols, and Caidan Zhuoma of Tibet.

There are roughly four families of ethnic musical instruments:

- *jizou* (percussion)
- *chuizou* (wind)
- *lazou* (bow-string)
- *tanzou* (pluck-string)

The Korean *changgu* (long drum), the Tibetan *shengu* (spiritual drum), and the Uygur and Uzbek *sabayi* (a combination of clubs and iron rings) are examples of percussion instruments. The Gin's *danxian* (unicord) and Yi's *sanxian* (tricord) are examples of the numerous pluck-string instruments. The twenty or so bow-string instruments include the famous Mongolian *matouqin* (horse-headed fiddle). A tale of its origin is retold in this book (see p. 227). *Hulusi* (a bottle gourd with pipes of different lengths), one of many ethnic wind instruments, is a favorite of the Dai, Achang, Va, De'ang, and Blang alike. It is gaining popularity among the Han Chinese as well.

Dance

Members of Chinese ethnic minorities are also talented dancers. The twenty-six larger ethnic minority groups in Yunnan alone have 1,095 kinds of dances, with a total of 6,718 choreographic movements (Ma, 2004). Even one of the smallest ethnic minority groups, the Oroqen, boasts a long list of dances, one of which (*yihenaren*) is a ritual dance for the occasion of passing on genealogical records. Tibetans are noted for their *guozhuang* dance. Young men and women move rhythmically from right to left in a big circle, dancing while singing. Many other ethnic groups, like the Uygur, Korean, and Mongolian, are also known as gifted dancers.

Different dances are performed on different occasions. The Jingpo people dance *munao zongge* and *dingge* to celebrate or rejoice, and *gebenge* and *jinzhaizai* to mourn or worship. One branch of the Yi, identified by their beautiful embroidered waistbands, sometimes dance around a bonfire—an event at which a young man and woman court each other. The Naxi people dance their *halili* and *dongba* to celebrate their ethnic festivals.

Many ethnic dancers have achieved national and even international recognition. Dao Meilan of the Dai is famed for her "Princess Peacock Dance"; Ayi Tula of the Uygur is known for her "Picking Grapes Dance"; Cui Meishan of the Korean, is noted for her "Long Drum Dance"; Muode Gema of the Mongols is famous for her "Cup and Bowl Dance"; and Yang Liping of the Bai is celebrated for her "Lark's Soul," "Two Trees," and "Drizzle."

Lisu couple playing *kouxian* (mouth cord) and *sanxian* (three-cord fiddle).
Courtesy of Dai Yuru and Yunnan Fine Arts Publishing House

Drama

Theatrical arts among ethnic minorities are as diversified and colorful as other performing arts. *Zangju* (Tibetan drama) is known in Tibet as *lhamo*, which means "fairies." It is said that the drama was first started by seven *lhamoes*. Unlike conventional dramas known to the average Chinese, different parts of *Zangju* are distinguished by their masks instead of their costumes. Human voices are employed in place of a band to accompany the performance. A show consists of three parts, beginning with a dance to pay tribute to Buddhist gods and closing with a ritual of good wishes. The bulk of the show in between consists of dancing, singing, and lyric reciting in plain and rhymed languages. A full-length *Zangju* can last from one to five days.

Dongxi (Dong Opera) evolved from the Yi's tradition of storytelling and ballad singing. It drew heavily from Han operas. *Baiju* (Bai Opera) uses both the Bai dialect and Mandarin. There are as many as thirty variant tune types to represent the parts of different ages, genders, and emotions. Only a high-pitched *suona* (Chinese horn) and some instruments of percussion are used during long interludes between singing. The topics of *Baiju* are both indigenous stories and the classics of the Han Chinese (Yang, 2000). "A Cloud of Love from a Princess" is a celebrated *Baiju*. It is retold in this book (see p. 154).

Hui and Manchu artists, such as Cheng Yanqiu and Ma Lianliang, have made immeasurable contribution to the national theatrical art called *Jingju* (Beijing Opera). The brilliance of their stardom has masked their ethnic identities; most their fans don't even know their ethnic backgrounds.

Cinema

Movies relating to ethnic minorities fall into two categories: those about ethnic topics and those made by ethnic producers. *Yaoshan yanshi* (*Romance of the Yao Mountains*), released in 1933, was the first movie China had ever produced about its ethnic minorities.

These films cover many topics and genres, but love is a particularly popular theme. Outstanding are *Lusheng liange* (*Love Song to the Tune of* Lusheng), about the Lahu people; *Wu duo jinhua* (*Five Golden Flowers*); about the Bai; and *Bingshan shang de lai ke* (*Guests from the Icy Mountains*), about the Uygur and Tajik. Most of them starred actors and actresses from the ethnic groups.

Ethnic artists have worked hard to succeed in the Han-dominated movie industry. *Tulufan qingge* (*Love Songs of Turpan*) is one of the most recent examples of a film directed by members of an ethnic group; its directors, Jinlini and Xie'er Zhati, are both Uygurs.

Television

Although television now reaches more than 90 percent of China, even in the Tibet and Xinjiang Autonomous Regions, TV programs made by ethnic people are still rare (Xu, 2005). To encourage the production of more and better programs featuring ethnic peoples, the Chinese government set up the biannual *Junma* (Fine Horse) Award in 1986. By 2002, a total of 459 programs made by TV stations in regions where ethnic minorities live had received this award. *Xinjiang guniang* (*A Girl from Xinjiang*) is one of the few TV plays directed by and starring exclusively Uygurs; its director is Zouliya Sima Aiyinuowa.

Additional Reading

Li, Wei, and Xingrong Zhang. *From China's S.W. Borders Minority Dances, Songs, and Instrumental Music of Yunnan: a Video Survey*. Van Nuys, Calif.: Aspara Media for Intercultural Education, 2001. ISBN 1880519232.

Rees, Helen. *Echoes of History: Naxi Music in Modern China*. New York: Oxford University Press, 2000. 278pp. ISBN-10: 0195129504; ISBN-13: 978-0195129502.

FINE ARTS

Chinese ethnic minorities began creating artworks in prehistoric times. They first painted on rock faces. Cliff paintings can be found on the Tianshan Mountains in Xinjiang, the Heishan Mountains in Gansu, and the Yinshan Mountains in Inner Mongolia. They are also part of the scenery along the Zuojiang and Heilongjiang Rivers.

Among the artistic relics of the early ethnic minorities in Yunnan, the *Nanzhao zhongxing huajuan* (*A Painting Scroll of the Zhongxing Period of the Nanzhao Reign*) and the *Zhang Shengwen huajuan* (*A Painting Scroll by Zhang Shengwen*) are the most distinguished. They were created by Bai and Yi artists around the tenth century.

A century later, Hu Huan emerged as a great painter of horses and hunting scenes. He was from Qidan, a descendant of the ancient Xianpi ethnicity. His *Zhuoxietu* (*A Scene of Repose during a Hunting Trip*) documents a moment when a great number of Qidan hunters were about to enjoy their long-awaited break after a hunting trip. Hu's contemporary, Yelüpei, a Qidan prince who later adopted the Han Chinese name Li Zanhua, was equally adept at depicting horses and horsemen.

The Naxi's *Shenlutu* (*Painting of the Sacred Path*) is one of the many genres of *Dongba* paintings. On a cloth canvas 15 meters (49.21 feet) long, it features several hundred images of beings from heaven, earth, and the underworld. As its name suggests, the painting was designed to lead one's soul out of hellish suffering to heaven. Naxi artists of the older generation imitate the time-honored *Dongba* paintings, while young artists today are more innovative.

One can't discuss Tibet and art without talking about *thangkas* or *tankas*. These are painted scrolls or embroidered banners used primarily for religious purposes. Borrowing traditional techniques from the Han Chinese, Hindus, and Nepalese, *thangkas* are painted with precision and rich colors. Extracted from natural pigments, the red, yellow, blue, and white colors symbolize authority, virtue, solemnity, and purity, respectively. *Thangkas* come in different sizes and are embroidered, woven, appliquéd, painted, or beaded. Themes of the *thangkas* include religion, biography, history, folkways, and even medicine ("Xizang yishu," 2006).

Tibetans are also adept at creating murals, which can be found in every monastery. They illustrate Buddha and his followers. Some murals record historical events, such as the marriage of Songtsan Gambo and Princess Wencheng, a tale retold in this book (see p. 168).

Another fascinating art form, sand painting, is done by Tibetans of the Tantric Buddhist sect. Buddhists of this faction believe in a harmony of opposites. While meditating, they use sands of brilliant colors to create symmetrical diagrams of Mandala, which is a plan of the spiritual world of fulfillment. When the painting is finished, the Buddhist artists scrape the sand and cast it into flowing water. They do so to demonstrate that nothing is permanent.

Some ethnic groups are especially skilled carvers. The Buyei people are known for the carved wooden masks used in their opera, known as *nuoxi*. Their wood carving talent can also be found in their architecture and furniture. In addition, they carve ink slabs with folklore motifs. Their Longxi brand enjoys a national reputation.

The Oroqens carve birch bark. Their *adawale*, a tub-like container for stowing away one's jewelry and new clothes, is famous. It is so treasured by the Oroqens that a bride takes it along with her as part of her dowry.

Calligraphy is the specialty of the Manchus. Weng Fanggang (1733–1818), Liu Yong (1719–1804), Yong Rong (1752–1823), and Tie Bao (1752–1824) are known as the Four Great Master Calligraphers in Chinese history. Aisin Gioro Pujie and Qi Gong are among celebrated contemporary calligraphers.

During the Yuan dynasty (1271–1368), many Mongolian painters rose to fame. After learning the craft from the Han Chinese, they perfected the techniques. Some of the notable artists were Li Huosun, Yu Chuhan, and Boyan Shouren. Chaoke Batu and Esu Ritai are two of the most accomplished Mongolian oil painters today.

In September 2005, an art show called Minzu tuanjie song (Ode to Ethnic Unity) was held in Beijing. It featured eighty-two visual artists from all ethnicities of China. Among the artists were Li Youxiang from the Derung, Zhao Xian from the Xibe, Zhaxi Yingqian from the Monba, Maji Ritai from the Tu, Lan Faqin from the She, and Nie Zhongbang from the Tujia. Efforts such as this to preserve and promote ethnic traditions of artistic creation will surely offset the challenges from both foreign and Han Chinese cultural infiltration.

Additional Reading

Kreijger, Hugo. *Tibetan Painting: The Jucker Collection*. London: Serindia, 2001. 190pp. ISBN-10: 1570628653; ISBN-13: 978-1570628658.

Rose, Eileen M., and Abby Rose Dalto. *Create Your Own Sand Mandala for Meditation, Healing and Prayer*. Alresford, England: Godsfield, 2003. 96pp. ISBN-10: 1841812056; ISBN-13: 978-1841812052.

LITERATURE

The literature of ethnic minorities is an inseparable part of Chinese literature as a whole. Many members of ethnic minorities share Märchen, epics, and ballads. Some claim literary forms peculiar to themselves. The Nu and She people are especially known for their *xushige* (epic songs). The Xibe are talented in *nianshuo* (reading and telling), while the Tu are gifted tellers of fables. The Uygurs, Uzbecs, and Tartars are known for humorous tales.

Ethnic literature's long history traces back to the Han Chinese classic *Shijing* (*The Book of Songs*), which was compiled between the eleventh and the sixth centuries B.C. Even today, a recital of *Shijing* lyrics is part of a wedding in the Tujia community in Hunan Province.

The epic, rare in Han Chinese literature, is a literary tradition of almost all ethnic minorities. The theme of love pervades this literary form, such as in the Dai tale "Princess Peacock," retold in this book (see p. 158). Some epic tales are historic. Most notable are *Gesa'erwang zhuan* (*Legend of King Gesaer*) of the Tibetans, *Jiangge'er* (*The World Conqueror*) of the Mongols, and *Manasi* (*Hero Manasi*) of the Kirgiz. These are all works of great length. *Gesa'erwang zhuan*, for example, has over a million lines of verses in 120 episodes.

Chinese efforts to document and preserve ethnic epics started in the 1930s. The first to be published was the Yi epic *Axi de xianji* (*Ancestors of the Axi People*), in 1945. Since the 1950s, dozens of genesis epics from the ethnic minorities of Southwest China have been published. They include the Naxi's *Chuangshiji* (*The Genesis*) and the Yao's *Miluotuo*. Both are retold in this book (see pp. 185 and 195).

Although oral tradition dominates ethnic literature, writings in ethnic languages have never been in short supply. Bai writers began to pen their poems and lyrics as early as the third century B.C. Tajik's educated elite started to write two centuries later. Intellectuals of Tibet and the Zhuang became creative in the seventh century. Shortly thereafter, the Dai and Tujia did the same. The twenty-six major ethnic minorities in Yunnan have authored more than 100,000 volumes of literary classics in twenty-three different scripts. Of the 50,000 volumes of ancient literature discovered in Dunhuang, an ancient city on the Silk

Road, more than 10 percent were written in various ethnic languages. Among the collection, a Tibetan text titled *Tsambo zhuanlüe* (*A Brief Biography of Tsambo*) is of great literary value.

Turki works of significance appeared in the tenth century. *Aiqing changshi* (*An Epic of Love*), by Nizhali, a Uygur poet of the mid-1800s, has had a far-reaching impact on literary creation in West and Central Asia. The most distinguished Mongolian work, *Menggu mishi* (*Mongolia's Secret History*), appeared in the 1440s.

Although ethnic languages have been used primarily to write about ethnic topics, ethnic minorities have also borrowed from Chinese stories. The Chinese classics *Sanguo yanyi* (*Romance of Three Kingdoms*) and *Xixiangji* (*Record of the West Chamber*) were retold in the Daur language long ago. *Dongyong yu Liu guniang* (*Dongyong and Sister Liu*) is a Gin version of the ethnic Han Chinese "Cowherd and Weaving Girl," a story retold in *The Magic Lotus Lantern and Other Tales from the Han Chinese* (Yuan, 2006).

Some ethnic authors wrote about the Chinese in Chinese. Topping the list is the renowned Manchu author Pu Songling (1640–1715), who compiled and retold hundreds of tales about supernatural beings in his *Liaozhai zhiyi* (*Strange Stories from a Make-do Studio*). Others include Lao She (1899–1966) and Duanmu Hongliang (1912–1996), both Manchus. Lao She was famous for his novel *Si shi tong tang* (*Four Generations under One Roof*), and Duanmu Hongliang for his *Ke'erqin caoyuan* (*The Khorchin Grasslands*). Shen Congwen (1902–1988), of the Miao, was known for his full-length novel as well as his short stories.

Today, while collecting and compiling volume after volume of ethnic classics, ethnic writers are writing conscientiously about the ethnic themes they know best in both native dialects and Chinese. A group of Nu writers has produced over a hundred full-length and short novels. Outstanding are *Yabiluo xueshan* (*The Yabiluo Snow Mountain*) in the Lisu vernacular and *Nujiang taosheng* (*The Roar of the Nu River*) in Chinese (Gao, 2005). Ethnic subject matter has become an inexhaustible source that writers of all ethnic backgrounds in China are trying to tap.

Literary classic written in the Yi script

Additional Reading

Bender, Mark. *Seventh Sister and the Serpent: Narrative Poem of the Yi People.* Beijing: New World Press, 1982. 65pp. ASIN: B000F8TRR4.

Dan, Jin, et al. *Butterfly Mother: Miao (Hmong) Creation Epics from Guizhou, China.* Indianapolis, IN: Hackett Publishing Company, 2006. 214pp. ISBN-10: 0872208494; ISBN-13: 978-0872208490.

STORYTELLING

Members of Chinese ethnic minorities tell stories to reinforce and perpetuate their unique cultures. Indeed, lacking writing systems, oral tradition serves as the collective memory of many ethnic minorities. Faced with modernization and commercialization, holding on to a tradition becomes all the more difficult. Consequently, many ethnic forms of storytelling are at risk of extinction today.

Unlike the Han Chinese, ethnic minorities treat storytelling less as a profession than as a communal activity. Storytelling is performed more often at festival gatherings than on a stage. A typical scenario involves a knowledgeable elder with a good memory and sense of humor telling stories to youngsters gathered around him or her. Most of the ethnic minorities tell their stories in their own languages. Some, like the Manchu, Bai, and Mongolians, are bilingual or multilingual.

In most cases, storytelling takes the form of talking and singing, sometimes to the accompaniment of certain musical instruments. It is similar to the Han Chinese *shuochang*, a generic term for storytelling under the category of *quyi*, which Mark Bender calls "performing narrative arts" (Bender, 2003). There are more than eighty types of ethnic *shuochang,* one-fifth of the 400 *quyi* forms still extant in China.

Many of the best-known performers of *xiangsheng* (comic monologues and dialogues) are from the Hui and Manchu nationalities. Some of the most renowned have been Bai Quanfu, Chang Baosen, Guo Qiru, Hou Baolin, Ma Sanli, Su Wenmao, Wang Fengshan, and Zhao Zhenduo. In the mid-1990s, a young Tibetan *xiangsheng* performer by the name of Luosang thrilled and soon saddened the nation. He was capable of mimicking the sounds of a band with his mouth. In 1995, his life was cut short by a motorcycle accident at the age of twenty-seven.

Some ethnic minorities create their versions of *xiangsheng* by drawing on ideas and even stories from the Han Chinese. The Tibetan *dangling* is one of these. Some simply perform Han Chinese *xiangsheng* in their ethnic vernaculars, as the Uygur storyteller Abuliz Tuopingti does. Others invent something similar to *xiangsheng*, such as *mantan* (comic monologue), *caitan* (comic dialogue), and *sanlaoren* ("three old men") of the Koreans. Another example, the Mongolian *xiaokeyare*, consists of talking, ventriloquism, and singing.

Ethnic minorities' storytelling often involves a lot of singing, as in the case of the Tibetan *zhongxie*. They do, however, have the conventional form of storytelling known to the Han Chinese as *pingshu* (storytelling with commentary). The Mongol *wulige'er*, Xibe *nianshuo*, and Uygur *wayizileke* are some of the ethnic *pingshu*.

Tanchang, or singing a story to the accompaniment of a plucking instrument, is found in the Uygur *dasitan*, the Tibetan *maqu*, the Bai *dabenqu*, the Zhuang *molun*, and the Mongol *haolaibao*.

The 800-year-old *dabenqu* of the ethnic Bai is based on their folk songs. It is performed by a duo. One performer sings and the other plays a trichord. There are two styles of *dabenge*, the northern and the southern; the former is mild and agreeable and the latter simple and unadorned. *Molun* is popular among the ethnic Zhuang. It was originally performed by a single person, who sang in the Zhuang vernacular while playing a smaller tricord. Beginning in the early 1950s, it has taken in more performers and accompanying instruments, like the *maguhu* (horse-bone fiddle) and *huluhu* (calabash fiddle).

Haolaibao, which means "singing after singing" in Mongolian, falls into the following subsets:

- *danghai haolaibao*, performed by varied numbers of people on broad topics
- *wulegeri haolaibao*, performed with questions and answers
- *dairilacha haolaibao*, sung in an antiphonal style with a satirical tone
- *hu'erren haolaibao*, performed solo with a fiddle

Some ethnic *shuochang* don't require any musical instrument at all, as is the case with the Oroqen *yimakan*. Because the Oroqen don't have a writing system, they have kept *yimakan* alive through their oral tradition. A solo performer sings and narrates alternately in the voices of a child, a man, a woman, or an elder, as required by the plot of the story (Xu, 2005).

Other ethnic storytellers use unconventional musical instruments. A good example is the 500-year-old *linggu* (storytelling with bells and drums) of the Yao people. Performers beat their long drums with bells tied to their wrists or fingers while they sing and narrate in the Yao vernacular.

Members of ethnic minorities are never short of stories to tell. A survey conducted in the early 1990s revealed that the Hui alone possessed over 1,200 tales. Most of the stories that the ethnic minorities tell are about their cultural heroes, their love affairs, or people and things with which they identify. Tibetans sing and talk about King Gesa'er; Mongolians about Jiangge'er, Gada Meilin, and Princess Yandan; Kirgizes about Manas; Manchus about Nisang Saman; Ewenkis about A'ertai Congbao'erfu; Daurs about Shaolang and Daifu; Kazaks about A'erpamisi; Uygurs about Ailipu and Sainaimu; Bais about King Bai; Suis about *Dragon's Daughter and a Fisherman*; and Dongs about King Wumian.

Today, the tradition of storytelling among ethnic peoples faces more challenges than that of the Han Chinese. In addition to the competition of high-tech mass media, most of the ethnic storytellers use their own tongues, which are understood by limited audiences. The greatest danger lies in the fact that it takes dedicated and talented people to preserve their long stories. Fewer young people seem to be interested. Instead, they are drawn to the more exotic and exciting pop culture.

Mongolian young man telling the author a story about the horse-headed fiddle he is holding in his hand

Additional Reading

Chao, Gejin. *Qian nian jue chang ying xiong ge: Weilate Menggu shi shi chuan tong tian ye san ji (The Heroic Songs of The Past: Fieldnotes on the Oirat Mongolian Epic Tradition)*. Nanning Shi: Guangxi ren min chu ban she, 2004. 135pp. ISBN: 7219047185.

Spagnoli, Cathy. *Asian Tales and Tellers*. Little Rock, Ark.: August House Publishers, 1998. 224pp. ISBN-10: 0874835267; ISBN-13: 978-0874835267.

PART 2

Food, Games, and Crafts

*I*n *The Magic Lotus Lantern and Other Tales from the Han Chinese*, a companion to this book, food, children's games, and crafts of the Han Chinese were introduced. This section focuses on the same areas, but related to the fifty-five Chinese ethnic groups. Large or small, each has a unique culture. Materials and ingredients used by Chinese ethnic minorities may be difficult to come by in your community due to cultural, climatic, and geographical differences. In cases where the ingredients are somewhat unusual, alternatives are suggested. In addition, the recipes, as well as the instructions for the games and crafts, provide only general guidelines. Use your imagination and improvise with available materials and ingredients as you see fit. While doing crafts and cooking with children, make sure you take safety precautions. Small children should always be supervised by parents, teachers, or librarians.

FOOD

Ethnic dishes add to the rich and colorful Chinese cuisines. Methods of cooking for these dishes fall into three basic categories. The Derung, Jino, Lahu, and Nu cook their food primarily by exposing it directly to fire. The Blang, De'ang, Jingpo, Lisu, Miao, Pumi, Va, and Yao prepare food mostly by boiling. Because of their frequent interaction with the Han Chinese throughout history, groups such as the Achang, Bai, Buyei, Dai, Hani, Hui, Mongol, Naxi, Sui, Tibetan, Yi, and Zhuang have learned Han culinary skills and have adapted them to their traditional techniques.

The surrounding environment and availability of food resources affect the diets of China's ethnic minorities. Groups who pasture on the grasslands of Inner Mongolia, Xinjiang, and the Qinghai-Tibet Plateau derive their food and beverages from the livestock they herd: cattle, sheep, horses, and even camels. The Kazaks' *shouzhuarou* (boiled lamb eaten with bare hands) is a delicacy now also popular among neighboring ethnic peoples as well as with Han tourists. Over a dozen ethnic minorities, mostly engaging in animal husbandry in the above-mentioned regions, drink *naicha* (tea mixed with milk of pasturing animals) and *suyoucha* (tea mixed with ghee, which is semifluid, clarified butter).

Like the Han Chinese, ethnic minorities in North China generally eat wheat for carbohydrates; those living in the south are more dependent on various types of rice. *Nang* (a type of baked wheat bread) is a favorite of the Uygurs, and *migan* (a kind of rice noodle) is a choice food of the Dais. The Tibetans, Lhobas, and Tus live on the most elevated plateau in the world, and they use *qingke* (highland barley) to make their staple food, *tsamba* (bread made of *qingke* flour and *suyoucha* tea), because crops like wheat, corn, and rice won't grow at very high altitudes. The Yi people, who inhabit the dry and cold mountains, turn to the sturdy buckwheat for food. The Bai, Blang, Dai, Hani, Jino, Naxi, and Yi in Yunnan, a subtropical province where flowers and insects are abundant, have a tradition of eating both. There are more than 200 kinds of edible flowers on their menus, including the chrysanthemum, plum, jasmine, lotus, lily, peony, *yulan* magnolia, and evening primrose. As the Chinese in general have become increasingly conscious of healthy eating, some of the flower cuisines are finding their way into restaurants throughout China. The high-protein-content worms and insects they eat include grasshoppers, crickets, cicadas, bamboo worms, ant eggs, and pupae of wasps and bees (Yang, 2001).

Dish of wasp pupae and bamboo worms

Bamboo, which is abundant in South China, provides not only edible shoots but also materials for kitchen utensils and tableware. *Zhutongfan* (rice cooked in a bamboo tube) is a delicacy of the Dai and Li people. To make *zhutongfan*, soaked rice is put into a bamboo segment at one end, then it is sealed. The bamboo segment is baked on a slow fire until its surface is charred. Then the bamboo segment is cut open, and the cooked rice is served.

In addition to natural resources, religious beliefs also determine ethnic peoples' cuisines. Although they are believers of Lamaism, a branch of Buddhism that forbids the killing of living beings, Tibetans do eat the meat of yaks, cows, and sheep. However, they seldom eat fowls, eggs, and pork. They especially object to eating very small creatures, including fish, believing that this leads to mass killing, a sin loathed by Buddhists. China's Muslim ethnic groups follow the Islamic canon and eat only the meat of ruminant, double-toed herbivores like cows and sheep. The meat of hogs as well as animals that have experienced a natural death is forbidden.

Many ethnic minorities attach spiritual significance to their kitchens, usually located at the center of their living rooms. The Mosuos, a branch of the Naxi, keep their kitchen fires going all the time. If the fire goes out by accident, they have to get their new fire blessed by a religious elder.

Hearth in the middle of a Mosuo family's living room.

As is true in the Han Chinese tradition, particular ethnic foods are associated with cultural events and holidays. For example, the Hani people celebrate their New Year with *nuomi baba* (glutinous rice cakes). The Sui people regard the head of a cooked chicken as the symbol of dignity and serve it only to an elder or the most distinguished guest.

Today, increased travel and the booming Chinese economy have brought many obscure ethnic dishes into average Chinese restaurants. On the other hand, changes are also taking place within ethnic minorities themselves. The Oroqen and Xibe, who once hunted for their meat, now live by animal husbandry and farming. And today most Uygurs use chopsticks to enjoy their traditional *shouzhuafan* (food eaten with bare hands).

At the same time, commercialization has also prompted Chinese entrepreneurs to capitalize on ethnic legacies. The sumptuous *manhan quanxi* (Manchu-Han Complete Banquet) has become all the rage among China's new rich. It was once the Qing (1644–1911) court's banquet, with an average of thirty-six dishes in each of its six courses, lasting as long as two days. Another six-course ethnic royal banquet gaining popularity is the Mongolian *zhama* of the Yuan dynasty (1206–1368). Unlike *manhan quanxi*, *zhama* provides not only good food, but also entertainment such as singing, dancing, and gaming.

China's ethnic minorities often cook with spices and ingredients that are readily available to them, even growing wild. These include catmint, cardamom, *xiangjiang* (a coriander-tasting ginger), *xiangmaocao* (a kind of lemongrass), pseudo-ginseng, Vietnamese coriander, resurrection lily powder, fresh prickly ash (Sichuan pepper) leaves, as well as fresh bamboo, lichen, Chinese quince, wild celery, and Chinese caterpillar fungus. Many of these ingredients are rarely available in Asian groceries in North America, so the recipes chosen for this book do not include these ingredients. They by no means do justice to the diversity and depth of ethnic cuisines.

Recipes

Nang (Uygur Pancake)

Nang, a pastry popular among the Uygur and Uzbek as well as some Central Asian nationalities, is known to the Chinese as the "Uygur bread" or "Uygur pancake." A typical traditional *nang* is shaped like the crust of a pizza and made of wheat flour, water, salt, and yeast. Baked in a special clay oven pit, a *nang* cake is topped with sesame seeds and chopped onion. Various types of *nang* are made today; some even have fillings.

A typical *nang*

Nang (Uygur Pancake)

Ingredients:

1 cup lukewarm water

½ packet yeast

2 oz softened butter

3 cups whole wheat or white flour

1 tsp sugar

pinch salt

4 tbsp raisins

1 egg, beaten

2 tbsp sesame seeds

Directions:

1. Combine the yeast and water in a mixing bowl. Set aside until the mixture becomes foamy.

2. Add the butter to the yeast and then add the flour, sugar, salt, and raisins. Combine into a soft dough.

3. Sprinkle flour on a cutting board or other dry surface and knead the dough for 10 minutes, until smooth.

4. Put the dough into the bowl, cover it loosely with plastic wrap, and let it rise at room temperature for 2 or 3 hours.

5. Turn the dough out of the bowl onto the board and knead for 5 minutes.

6. Return the dough to the bowl and let it rise for 30 minutes.

7. Turn the dough out onto the board and knead it briefly, then roll it out into a circle about ½ inch thick. The center should be thinner than the edges. Preheat the oven to 400°F (204°C).

8. Place the dough on a greased cookie sheet and bake for 15 minutes. Brush the bread with the beaten egg and sprinkle the sesame seeds over it, then bake for another 5 minutes, until lightly browned. Serves 2.

Ban niuroumo (Mixed Ground Beef)

This is a Dai dish. The Dai people, who like many other ethnic minorities in South China have cultivated a taste for bitter, sour, and spicy-hot flavors, are known for barbecuing and dressing cold vegetables and meats in delectable sauces. Spices like lemongrass and long coriander distinguish Dai food from that of the Han Chinese.

The soybean and glutinous rice flours required in the following recipe are usually available in Asian groceries, as well as health food stores.

Ban niuroumo (Mixed Ground Beef)

Ingredients:

> 1½ tbsp cooking oil
> 2 lb ground beef
> 7 tbsp soybean flour
> 3 tbsp glutinous rice flour
> *Seasonings:*
>> 2 tbsp garlic, 2 tsp cilantro, and 2 tsp long coriander, diced together
>> 2 tsp green onion, chopped
>> dash salt
>> 2 tsp chili powder
>> 1¾ tbsp lemongrass
>> pinch ground white pepper
>> pinch powdered chicken bouillon

Directions:

1. Heat cooking oil in frying pan or wok and stir-fry beef until cooked. Set aside beef in a bowl to cool.
2. Sauté soybean and glutinous rice flours in frying pan or wok on low heat until they release an aromatic smell.
3. Add beef and seasonings to pan and combine all. Serves 3–4.

Kao niurou (Barbecue Beef Steak)

This is a dish of the Lahu people, who historically obtained food by hunting, as is evident in the name of their ethnicity: The first syllable means "tiger," and the second means "roasted meat." Today, however, tigers are scarce (if there are any), and they are protected. Thus, the Lahu have turned to domestic animals and other game for their meat.

Kao niurou (Barbecue Beef Steak)

Ingredients:

> 2 lbs beef steak, trimmed and rinsed
>
> 7 tbsp garlic, crushed
>
> 1 tbsp chili powder
>
> pinch lemongrass
>
> dash salt
>
> pinch Sichuan peppercorn powder (available at Asian groceries)
>
> pinch Vietnamese coriander (optional if unavailable)

Directions:

1. Cut steak into rectangular chunks, approximately 1 inch thick, 2 inches wide, and 4 or 5 inches long. Pound the steak to tenderize it

2. Combine the rest of the ingredients, cover the steak with them on both sides, and let sit for 30 minutes.

3. Grill the steak strips on a slow or medium charcoal fire for 10–15 minutes, turning the meat twice, until lightly browned. (The Lahus use chestnut wood, which may or may not be available in Asian groceries.) Serves 2–4.

Sai mi yangrou (Lamb Sweeter Than Honey)

This is a traditional Tibetan dish. Tibetans treat lamb as a tonic to cope with cold weather. A hunter's wife customarily prepares this dish to anticipate the return of her "honey" from his wintry hunting trip (Guan, 2001). Hence, the term "honey" is a symbol of affection rather than a reference to an ingredient.

Sai mi yangrou (Lamb Sweeter Than Honey)

Ingredients:

1 lb lamb

1 egg yolk

1 oz soy sauce

1 tbsp cornstarch, dissolved in water

2½ tsp water

7 tbsp sugar

few drops of vinegar

2 tsp ginger extract (combine 1 part minced ginger and 2 parts water, soak, then strain)

2 cups cooking oil

1 oz ghee (if not available, substitute clarified butter)

Directions:

1. Cut lamb into slices approximately ⅛ inch thick, ⅔ inch wide, and 1 inch long.
2. Combine egg yolk, a third of the soy sauce, half of the dissolved cornstarch, and 1 tsp of the water. Marinate the lamb in this mixture for 30 minutes.
3. Combine the sugar, vinegar, ginger extract, and the rest of the soy sauce, cornstarch, and water to make a sauce. Set aside.
4. Heat the cooking oil in frying pan or wok on high heat until it reaches 320°F or 160°C (meat dropped into the oil should sink to the bottom, then surface) and deep-fry the lamb slices until grayish. Drain the lamb and pour off the oil from the frying pan or wok.
5. Add 2 tsp cooking oil to the frying pan or wok and heat on high. Add the meat and sauce and stir until slightly thickened.
6. Sprinkle ghee (or clarified butter) on top and serve. Serves 2.

Huokao zhurou (**Roast Pork**)

This is a favorite dish of the ethnic Yi. They also like *tuotuorou* (boiled pork chunks), *qiaobaba* (buckwheat cakes), *suancaitang* (sour veggie soup), and deep-fried grasshoppers. Living mostly in mountainous and semi-mountainous areas, in the past the Yi often ate game. Today, however, domestic animals have become their major source of meat.

Huokao zhurou (**Roast Pork**)

Ingredients:

> 8–10 pieces or 2 lbs pork loin or chops
> 1 egg, beaten lightly
> 1 tsp sesame oil
> *Seasonings and flavorings:*
>> 2 tsp ginger, minced
>> 2 tsp green onion, chopped
>> dash of salt
>> pinch five-spice powder (available in Asian groceries)
>> pinch powdered chicken bouillon
>> pinch ground white pepper

Directions:

1. Pound meat to tenderize it.
2. Combine egg, sesame oil, and spices and flavorings. Marinate meat in it for 1 hour.
3. Barbecue meat on grill for 10 minutes or until browned on both sides. Serves 5–8.

Xizhouyu (Fish of Xizhou)

Many ethnic groups enjoy fishing and eating fish. The Bai people, who live in Xizhou near Lake Erhai, are particularly fond of the aquatic food it provides. This includes not only fish but also snails. The following Bai dish calls for grass carp, which is native to Asia. Where it is unavailable, other white-fleshed fish (such as halibut or cod) can be used instead.

Xizhouyu (Fish of Xizhou)

Ingredients:

2 lbs fillets of any flaky, white-fleshed fish, cut into 2- to 3-inch pieces

2 tsp salt

pinch each aniseed powder and fennel seed powder

1¾ cup soy sauce

5 tbsp cooking oil (the Bai use lard)

2 tsp garlic

1¾ oz each ham and soaked Chinese mushrooms, sliced

1 tbsp green onion

1 tbsp ginger root, sliced

3½ oz chicken broth

pinch each powdered chicken bouillon and ground white pepper

1 oz chili oil

Directions:

1. Combine salt, aniseed powder, fennel seed powder, and soy sauce. Marinate fish fillets in mixture for 30 minutes.

2. Heat cooking oil in frying pan or wok. Add garlic and sauté until lightly browned.

3. Add ham, mushroom, green onion, and ginger. Combine thoroughly.

4. Add chicken broth and marinated fish fillets. Bring to a boil.

5. Turn heat down to low and simmer for 20 minutes.

6. Stir in powdered chicken bouillon, ground white pepper, and chili oil. Serves 3–5.

Qingdun niurou (Beef Stew with Light Seasoning)

This is a *qingzhen* dish of the Hui. *Qingzhen*, which literally means "clean and true," is the customary Chinese name for a Muslim. A mosque, for instance, is called a *qingzhensi* (Muslim temple). Beef stew has now become a popular *qingzhen* dish among ethnic groups in China.

Qingdun niurou (Beef Stew with Light Seasoning)

Ingredients:

2 lb beef stew meat, rinsed and patted dry

4 cups water

Spices:

2 tsp ginger root, crushed

1½ tbsp green onion

1 cardamom pod

2 aniseeds

10 Sichuan peppercorns (available at Asian markets)

Flavorings:

2 tsp salt

pinch each powdered chicken bouillon and ground white pepper

Directions:

1. Put steak and water in a saucepan. Bring to a boil and simmer until meat turns gray and water becomes foamy.

2. Drain steak. Submerge in fresh pot of water. Bring to boil again and skim off the foam.

3. Add spices. Turn heat to low and simmer for 5–6 hours or until beef is tender (easily pierced with a chopstick).

4. Add flavorings and simmer for a few more minutes. Remove cardamom, aniseed, Sichuan peppercorns, green onion, and ginger before serving). Serves 4–5.

Suanmugua chaoji (Fried Chicken with Suanmugua)

Mugua, or *suanmugua*, is the fruit of the Chinese quince tree native to Yunnan. Growing beneath the treetops, its large pear-looking fruit is often used as a vegetable in ethnic food. The following dish is a favorite of the Miao people living in Yunnan. Where *mugua* is hard to come by, other fruit (such as pears or apples) can be used instead.

Suanmugua chaoji (Fried Chicken with Suanmugua)

Ingredients:

1 chicken, boned, rinsed, and patted dry

1 egg white, beaten lightly

2 tbsp cornstarch, dissolved in water

4 cups (the Miaos use lard)

3 chili peppers, chopped

2 tsp green onion, c chopped

½ tbsp ginger root, sliced

1 Chinese quince, sliced (if not available, used 2 apples, peeled and sliced)

dash salt

pinch each sugar, ground white pepper, and powdered chicken bouillon

⅓ tsp sesame oil

Directions:

1. Cut chicken into 1-inch cubes
2. Combine egg white with 1½ tbsp cornstarch and marinate chicken in it for 15–20 minutes.
3. Heat cooking oil in frying pan or wok on high heat until it reaches 320°F or 160°C (meat dropped into the oil sinks to the bottom and surfaces). Deep-fry the chicken until cooked. Drain the chicken and pour away the oil.
4. Add 1 tbsp cooking oil to the frying pan or wok and fry chili pepper until lightly browned.
5. Add green onion and ginger and stir fry for a few seconds.
6. Add chicken, fruit, salt, sugar, pepper, and bouillon. Stir for 5 minutes.
7. Add the rest of the cornstarch to thicken and sprinkle sesame oil on chicken. Serves 3–4.

Mugua, fruit of a Chinese quince tree

Huangmen jizirou (Stewed Muntjac Meat)

Ji, or *jizi*, the Chinese muntjac, is known to Westerners as the barking deer. Indigenous to Southeast Asia, it used to be a meat source of the Lisu people in South China. Today, however, the Lisus hunt only to supplement their staple food of corn, which they grow. They get their protein from pork, lamb, and chicken. A dish of chicken cooked with oil extracted from the seeds of female sumac trees (male sumacs yield the materials for paint) is very popular among the Lisu people.

Hunters in North America may find the following traditional Lisu muntjac dish interesting, for they can use venison as a substitute.

Huangmen jizirou (Stewed Muntjac Meat)

Ingredients:

1½ lbs muntjac meat (substitute venison, lamb, or even chicken)

4 tbsp vegetable oil

1–2 chili peppers

pinch Sichuan peppercorns (available at Asian groceries)

½ tbsp sliced ginger root

½ tbsp chopped green onion

2 cup chicken broth (the Lisu use pork broth)

2 tsp salt

pinch cardamom (available at Asian groceries)

½ tbsp sugar

Directions:

1. Cut meat into small chunks, rinse, drain, and pat dry.
2. Heat vegetable oil in frying pan or wok. Fry chili peppers and Sichuan peppercorns until they are lightly browned.
3. Add ginger and green onion. Stir fry for a few seconds.
4. Add meat and stir-fry for 10 minutes, then add broth, salt, cardamom, and sugar.
5. Simmer on low heat, covered, for 3–5 hours or until thoroughly cooked. Serves 3–4.

Bajiao ciba (Rice Cake in Banana Leave)

Ciba (glutinous rice cake) is a traditional food of many ethnic minorities, including the Buyei, Dong, Gaoshan, Gelao, Gin, Hani, Maonan, Miao, Mulao, She, Tu, Tujia, Yao, and Zhuang. To make traditional *ciba*, glutinous rice is soaked, steamed, and ground to a paste in a large mortar. The paste is then divided into multiple pieces and served. Today, *ciba* can have various flavors and coatings, to make it tastier. It is often used as gifts and in festival celebrations.

The following recipe is for a different type of rice cake popular among the Zhuang people. It doesn't have to be ground in a mortar, but does require *bajiao* (banana leaves), which are available at most Asian groceries, especially where Thai foods are sold.

Bajiao ciba (Rice Cake in Banana Leave)

Ingredients:

5 fresh *bajiao* (banana leaves), well soaked and cut into 6-inch-square pieces (substitute reed or bamboo leaves, more readily available at Asian groceries).

2 lbs glutinous rice, soaked overnight or for 12 hours

muslin cloth (cheesecloth)

4 tbsp sugar

2 tbsp honey (for stickiness)

4 tbsp roasted peanuts, crushed

1 tbsp roasted sesame seeds, crushed

1 can red bean paste (available at Asian groceries)

1 tbsp salad oil

Directions:

1. Rinse banana leaves or substitutes. Soak in hot water to soften.
2. Grind soaked rice in blender into a paste.
3. Press and strain rice paste through muslin cloth.
4. Blend strained rice with sugar, honey, peanuts, and sesame seeds. Combine mixture into dough and divide into 10 portions.
5. Stuff each portion with 1 tbsp red bean paste.
6. Coat banana leaves or substitutes with salad oil (to prevent cooked rice from sticking to them) and wrap dough portions with them to make 10 cakes, which can be triangular or oblong.
7. Steam in a double boiler on high heat for 25–30 minutes. Serves 5–10.

GAMES

China's ethnic minorities enjoy their leisure time with songs, dances, sports, and games. Sports and games often relate to their lives. The *zhuo huoya* (catching a live duck) game of the Gin people, who live on the south coast, is a test of their swimming skill, required of them as fishermen. A duck is let loose in the sea, and after it drifts a certain distance from shore, a group of youngsters jump into the water and try to catch it. Men of the Va and Jino ethnic groups practice pitching pebbles to relive the fun of hunting. Women of the Nu play a game of *cuoma* (slubbing hemp to create threads), which is, in fact, the initial step in creating their dresses. Lahu women compete with one another in threading needles.

Many ethnic sports and games are adapted to specific environmental conditions. The Bai, who live near Lake Erhai, enjoy dragon boat racing. The Lisu, who inhabit both sides of the Nujiang Valley, have turned ropeway gliding into a sport. The Hani, who populate areas covered with thick forests, like racing up to the treetops.

Ethnic minorities use whatever materials are available for gaming. The Jino, for example, climb, pull, push, turn, and twist bamboo poles for entertainment because they live where bamboo is plentiful. Working in the rice fields, the Hani enjoy "fighting" with mud. Some ethnic minorities like games involving balls made of straw, bamboo, thread, wool, chicken feathers, or even a pig's gallbladder (Zhao, 2003, 267).

Ethnic minorities play games for various purposes: to entertain, commemorate, mourn, worship, court, or reinforce their life skills. The Uygur and Tajik share the *diaoyang* (sheep snatching) game with some of their Central Asian Muslim brethren as part of their festivals and wedding ceremonies. This game involves a contest between two teams of horsemen. Each team tries to get hold of a lamb and drop it in a large circle drawn on the ground of the opposite team's side. The game is both exciting and demanding. Spectators, men and women, old and young, cheer the contestants with singing and dancing. Another game that involves competing over an animal is less challenging. *Biaoshu*, an aboriginal rodent in the mountainous area where the Lahu live, is used in this game. Before a young man and a young woman can become engaged, each of their families chooses a team of men to hunt *biaoshu* with bows and arrows. The team that captures the most rodents within a set time wins the contest. The would-be bridegroom works the hardest, of course, trying to prove himself (Zhao, 2003, 85).

Mongolian wrestling

Games that may have originally been activities meant for something serious have now become pure entertainment, as in the case of the Korean seesaw. In this exciting game two women raise each other up and down alternately. According to the Koreans, women were confined to their homes in the old days. To satisfy their curiosity about the outside world, they used the seesaw to get a glimpse of what was beyond their courtyard walls.

Some activities combine performing art and sports, such as *datiao*. In this group dance participants form a large circle while stamping their feet rhythmically. Dubbed a Chinese "disco," *datiao* is popular among the Lisu, Hani, Naxi, Pumi, and Yi.

Some games are unique to one ethnic group, such as *damoqiu*, a favorite of the Pumi. In this game, a wooden pole is firmly planted in the ground, leaving three to six feet above ground level. A long pole with a concave area in the middle is placed horizontally on its pointed top. A player straddles each end of the pole. The players then run, push, and hop, holding on to the pole, being hurled up and down and turned around and around with it. It's like a carousel ride but more fun and thrilling.

Other games are common to many ethnic minorities. The Achang, Bai, Blang, Dai, De'ang, Hani, Lahu, and Naxi all have a long tradition of martial arts, though each has a slightly different flavor. More than twenty of China's ethnic minorities race horses. Other common games include swinging, wrestling, dragon boat racing, peg-top playing, and muscle flexing in tugs of war with ropes, bamboo poles, or bare hands.

Some ethnic games have evolved over time. On the one hand, modernity eats away at the tradition, as the soccer ball takes the place of the Naxi's traditional ball of straw or a pig's gallbladder. On the other hand, new ethnic games are constantly emerging. The Tu traditionally walked on stilts when roads were muddy. Now they play a new type of soccer game in which players run on the poles.

Games

Children of China's ethnic minorities have their own games. *Muzhuqi* (chess of sows) is a favorite of the Nu children; *Niujiaoqi* (chess of a bull's horn) is peculiar to ethnic Va; the Hani game of *muji shoudan* (a hen protecting her eggs) cannot be found elsewhere; and Tibetan kids entertain themselves with *zhao niudu* (looking for a calf), instructions for which are given below. Only the Manchu children know how to play *man cheng pao* ("running around in a city").

Boys and girls of the Va and Nu play the same "Eagle and Chicks," which children of many other cultures also play. Instructions for this game are in *The Magic Lotus Lantern and Other Tales from the Han Chinese* (Yuan, 2006). The Hani children play a similar game, in which a "leopard" is used in place of the eagle, and piglets replace the chickens. A step-by-step description of this game is given below. The Tu and Tibetan children's game of *lang chi yang* (a wolf preying on lambs) is yet another variant. The hide-and-seek game prevalent among various cultures in the world has its cousins in the Va's *duo maomao* (hiding from a cat) and the Gin's *an ji gu* (blindly guessing a chicken's name).

Some children's games are gender-specific. Among the Jino, boys prefer slingshots, long jumps, bow shooting, bamboo tube throwing, long distance running, and clay dough molding; girls choose to toy with weaving shuttles and, copying their mothers and grandmothers, play rice pounding, baby-sitting, and clothes making (Zhao, 2003, 220).

Following are instructions for a few games that children of some of China's ethnic minorities play.

An ji gu (A Blind Chicken's Guess)

This is a game played by Gin children. To begin, approximately a dozen children form a circle. A leader passes an object to one child in the circle. (The Gin children use a seashell, but you may choose anything you wish.) The child who gets the object passes it to a child next to him or her. The object is then passed on and on in one direction until someone drops it.

The child who accidentally drops the object becomes the "blind chicken." Playmates blindfold him or her with a towel or handkerchief. Blindfolded, with both hands held out, the child tries to catch a playmate in the circle. The children move around, trying not to be touched. If the child gets hold of someone, he or she has to guess the captive's name by feeling him or her from head to toe. If the guess is wrong, the captive is released back into the circle. The game continues until the child identifies a person correctly, who then takes the role of the "blind chicken" and starts another round of the game.

Zhao niudu (Looking for a Calf)

This is a Tibetan children's game played by six to eight children. One of the children, usually the youngest, acts as the calf and another child, often the oldest, is designated as the seeker to look for it. The "calf" stands in the middle of a circle formed by the other players. The seeker, who is outside the circle, starts the game by asking aloud, "Hey, have you seen a stray calf?"

"What does your calf look like?" ask the children.

"My calf's body is gold and its limbs silver," explains the seeker.

"We don't have such a beautiful calf, but we do have one with mud stains all over its body," the children in the circle shout to their questioner.

To get the "calf," the seeker has to enter through the arches formed by the children's arms. In front of an arch, the seeker asks,

"What's the gate made of?"

"It's made of gold and needs a golden key to unlock it," the children answer.

In front of another arch, the seeker asks again, "What's the gate made of?" The players say that it is made of silver. The names of the materials then change, from agate to coralline, jade, etc., as the questions-and-answers continue. When the seeker comes to the last of the arches, the children forming it let their arms down and cluster together, trying to shut the "gate." Pretending to be frustrated, the seeker roars, "If I turn myself into an old cow, do you think you can block my way any more?" and charges at the tightened circle in an attempt to break in. The other players run around to protect the "calf" in the circle. The seeker wins if he or she captures the "calf." If not, the seeker has to admit defeat. The game either ends or restarts with different children playing the roles of the "calf" and the seeker.

Baozi zhua zhu (A Leopard Catching a Boar)

This game is popular among the Hani children. There is no limit to the number of players. One child is chosen as a leopard, and the rest act as boars. A place against a tree or a wall is designated as the leopard's den.

To begin, the "leopard" sits in the "den." The "boars" line up hand in hand in front of it. They keep asking, "What time is it?" The answer goes hour by hour, starting from seven o'clock in the morning. When the "leopard" answers, "seven o'clock in the evening," it springs up to get at the "boars." The "boars" try to dodge the attack. The "boar" that gets caught will be confined in the leopard's den. The "boars" attempt to rescue the captive without being caught. The "leopard," on the other hand, tries to seize more boars without losing its victim(s).

When all the boars are captured, the last "boar" taken prisoner assumes the role of the leopard. Then the game starts again, with the previous "leopard" joining the "boars."

Dian shizi (Tossing Cobblestones)

This is a popular girl's game of the Va ethnic group. The game requires two or three children, who play by turns. It takes two to three rounds to get a winner. The game uses fifty round smooth stones the size of lima beans. (In fact, dried lima beans are a good substitute for the stones.) To begin, one of the players tosses all the stones or beans up in the air and catches them quickly on the back of her hand. She then tosses up the ones she has caught and tries to catch them in her palm. The next stage of the game begins. The same player has to pick up the stones or beans that fell to the floor, using her thumb and forefinger only. First she tosses up a stone or a bean . Then she quickly picks up another one from the floor before catching the one that is falling from above.

A player fails the round of the game if either she catches the stone or bean she tosses up but fails to pick one up from the floor at once, or she picks up a stone or bean from the floor but misses the one she has tossed up. After the rounds are complete, the child who has made the fewest mistakes and harvested the most stones or beans wins the game.

Naxi children at play

Part 2: Food, Games, and Crafts

CRAFTS

Many members of Chinese ethnic minorities are gifted craftspeople. Their crafts fall roughly into eight categories: *zhijin* (brocading), *cixiu* (embroidering), *yinran* (printing and dyeing), *jianzhi* (paper cutting), *diaosu* (carving), *bianzhi* (braiding), *qiqi* (lacquering), and *jinshu gongyi* (metal crafting).

The brocades (*zhijin*) made by the Tujia, Li, and Zhuang are particularly popular. The Tujia brocade, known as *xilankapu* (knitted floral bedding), involves over 200 patterns of plants, flowers, and wild and domestic animals. Silk is often used for making *zhijin,* but the Miao people favor cotton, the Lis prefer kapok, and the Tibetans use wool to weave a specific kind of brocade that they call *pulu*. The Han Chinese believe that Huang Daopo was their mother of textiles and that she learned the technique from the Li.

Nearly half of the ethnic groups are skillful in embroidery, and each has unique characteristics. Their costumes are often the venues to display their talent at embroidery. There are numerous styles of embroidery: *suxiu* (plain), *caixiu* (colored), *tuxiu* (with raised patterns), *bianxiu* (with braids), *chanxiu* (by tying), *suoxiu* (with lockstitch), *zhouxiu* (on crinkled surface), *tiaohua* (with cross-stitch), *tiexiu* (with patches of cloth), and *lianxiu* (with embedded ornaments of silver, copper, jade, agate, glass, shells, and fish bones) ("*Shaoshu minzu cixiu*" 2006).

Relative geographic isolation has made ethnic minorities self-sufficient in many ways. Some still print and dye the fabrics they use to make their own dresses. Two of the best known techniques are *zharan* (tie-dye) and *laran* (wax-dye or batik). *Zharan* has existed in China for more than 2,000 years. The Bai people are famous for tie-dyeing fibers eleven times with designs of butterflies, pagodas, and flowers. The Miao are known for their traditional *laran* (batik), a technique in which beeswax is applied to hemp, silk, cotton, and wool to create artistic patterns. The fabrics are dyed with pigment from an aboriginal indigo plant at low temperature so that the wax will not be melted in the process. After its completion, the wax is removed, revealing beautiful cracking patterns.

How this technique originated is unknown. A legend, however, holds that a Miao girl wished to add colors to her drab clothes, but did not know how. In a dream, a fairy led her into a garden with bees bustling among various blossoms. When she woke up, she found her dress covered with beeswax. She threw it in a dye of indigo, hoping to mask the smear. She then rinsed it in hot water. What happened next was a sensation: Beautiful white flowers appeared on her dark blue dress. She taught the craft to her friends, and it soon spread to the neighboring ethnic communities. The Miao women in Guizhou today still wear things they have wax-dyed themselves: scarves, girdles, tunics, underdresses, and puttees, which are strips of cloth wound spirally around their legs from ankle to knee.

Laran, **batik or wax printing, in an ethnic Bai community in Yunnan, China**

Paper-cutting is an art mastered not only by the Han Chinese but also by the ethnic minorities, including the Dai, Daur, Hezhen, Manchu, Mongol, Miao, Tibetan, Tu, Uygur, Xibe, and Yugur. Styles of paper-cutting differ. The Dai paper-cuts often contain images of Buddhism, in which they firmly believe. Paper-cutting of the Xibe and Uygur features only flowers, following the Islamic tradition of worshiping no graven images. Mongolian paper-cuts are reminiscent of their nomadic ancestors. Unlike the Han Chinese, who cut paper to decorate their houses, ethnic peoples do so mostly to embellish their clothing. They use paper-cuts as templates to embroider ornamental laces and other fabrics.

Some members of ethnic minorities are brilliant woodcarvers. Their beams, eaves, bedsteads, shrines, tables, window grids, and chairs are festooned with carved decorations of plants and flowers as well as real-world and imaginary mammals and fowl. A ring carved out of an animal bone and worn on the thumb of an Oroqen man's right hand serves as his talisman.

Some members of ethnic minorities braid using rattan, straw, wicker, bamboo, and the Chinese fan palm. The wickerwork of the Mongols, straw hats of the Bais, and bamboo articles of the Dais, De'angs, Lhobas, Maonans, Suis, and Miaos are famous. The Miaos in

Guizhou alone can make a large variety of bamboo ware, including hats, mats, canteens, stools, baskets, sieves, dustpans, and bird cages. The Koreans are especially good at crocheting. The Mongols, Tibetans, Kazaks, and Uygurs are the best carpet producers. Carpets made by the Kazaks and Uygurs, known as the "Xinjiang carpets," are not only durable but have exquisite designs. The largest Xinjiang carpet by far is found in a lounge of the Great Hall of People in Beijing. Weighing 2.5 tons, it covers a floor area of 460 square meters (550 square yards)!

The Bai began to make lacquer ware as early as the tenth century. Semifinished products of wood, bamboo, leather, or horn are coated with a glossy, transparent, resinous material called lacquer. The Pumi and Yi are also great lacquer craftsmen. The lacquered drinking vessels and dinner sets of Liangshan, the largest Yi community in Sichuan, are acknowledged for their beauty and utility.

The Buyei, Miao, Mongol, Sui, and Tibetan craft utensils of gold, silver, copper, tin, or alloys. Silver ornaments are an important part of the Miao women's costumes. A complete set includes a coronet, a necklace, a pendant, bracelets, hair pins, earrings, and neck rings. The largest neck ring weighs as much as two kilograms (4.5 pounds). Coronets and pendants are decorated with complex patterns of butterflies, phoenixes, or dragons. Both the Tibetan and the Uygur are renowned for their knives of superior quality and elegance. Even their sheaths are beautiful, made of silver and brass as well as materials like leather, apricot wood, and cupronickel, which is an alloy of copper and nickel.

There are many more varieties of ethnic craftwork in addition to these. Ethnic pottery, dolls, costumes, and calligraphy of the mystic *Dongba* script are just a few examples. Following are instructions for four handicrafts of China's ethnic minorities.

Wax-Dyed T-Shirt

Having learned about *laran* (wax-dyeing), you can now try your hand at it. To make professional *laran* crafts may require years of training, but don't let that discourage you. Follow the instructions, and you'll be surprised at how much you can accomplish. Always exercise caution when working with hot wax and dyes. Children should be supervised by an adult.

Materials needed:

1 packet of powder or ½ bottle of liquid denim blue fabric dye that doesn't require a high temperature

8–16 oz fluid or solid paraffin (mold or dipping) or beeswax with a melting point lower than 150°F (65°C)

1 100% cotton T-shirt

bucket or large pot to make a dye bath

brush pen (although professionals use brass pens)

1 pair rubber gloves

sheet to protect work area (garbage bag or newspaper is fine)

Instructions:

1. Sketch a picture on the T-shirt with a pencil. (You may sketch on drawing paper before copying it to the T-shirt to create your own pattern.)

2. Heat the wax on a stove. Dip the brush pen in melted wax and trace the pattern on the T-shirt. (Hold the T-shirt up against light to see if the waxed area is transparent. If not, apply wax again.)

3. Soak the waxed T-shirt thoroughly in water at room temperature.

4. Hand-dry the T-shirt slightly by gently squeezing it (make sure not to break and flake off the wax).

5. Dip the T-shirt in he denim blue dye for 15 minutes or until the dye is set, in accordance with product instructions. Rinse 2–3 times and hand-dry slightly (make sure not to break and flake off the wax).

6. Heat 2–3 gallons of water in the bucket or pot until it reaches well above 150°F (65°C). Dip the T-shirt in the hot water until the wax melts, revealing the image you drew on the T-shirt.

7. Rinse, drip dry, and enjoy.

Frame of *Dongba* Script

The *Dongba* script of the Naxi people is one of the oldest writing systems in the world that use pictures to indicate meanings, older than the Han Chinese characters known as *hanzi*. Modern *hanzi*, the simplified version in particular, has largely lost its pictographic beauty. *Dongba* script, on the contrary, still retains its original flavor. You can use the beautiful *Dongba* script to create an ethnic craft yourself.

Materials needed:

1 3½-by-3½-inch easel back or 6-by-4-inch acrylic frame

metallic colored pencils (preferred colors: white, gold, yellow, blue, lawn green, and deep pink) to write on black paper

1 sheet black heavyweight construction paper that fits the frame

Instructions:

1. Cut the construction paper to the size of the frame.
2. Choose an ideograph from the figure (on page 64) and copy it on the construction paper using the metallic pencils (use different colors to write different parts of the script; add color to the background).
3. Place the paper in frame and the craft is completed (see the photograph on page 64).

Dongba ideographic characters. 1. means "happy family." It's a family of three in a house surrounded by grass, water, a sun, and a moon. 2. means "dream come true." Beneath a sleeping man is a closed eye that signifies dreamland. Above him is an open eye looking at a flower that indicates reality. 3. means "wish you happiness." A person points at the water that feeds a flower, as if to tell the plant where its happiness originates.

Easel back frame with *Dongba* script

Lucky Pendant

Pendants are important ornaments used to embellish dwellings and costumes. They have aesthetic as well as cultural significance. A silver crescent pendant shows a Tibetan woman's chastity. A fish-shaped pendant signifies an abundant food supply to the Naxi. Other ethnic peoples also use their totem animals in their pendants. Now that you have learned a few *Dongba* scripts, you can make a simple pendant also.

Materials needed:

1- to 2-foot piece of hemp cord or string

1-inch Chinese copper bell (if not available, substitute a liberty bell)

3-inch wooden cutout heart (available in craft stores)

4-inch wooden cutout house (available in craft stores)

10 glass beads of various colors (preferably crimson, dark olive green, maroon, sea green, black, coral, and midnight blue); keep away from small children.

markers or pens that can write on wood (preferably black, white, crimson, lawn green, yellow, and coral)

Instructions:

1. Drill 2 holes for hanging and stringing, one on the top part of each cutout and the other on its bottom part, ½-inch from each edge. (Ask an adult to help with a power drill.)

2. Add a casual color background to each wooden cutout or leave as is.

3. Copy the *Dongba* ideogram "love" (from the drawing below) on the wooden heart cutout and "happy family" (from the drawing on p. 64) on the wooden house cutout with markers or pens. (Use different colors for each part of an ideogram.)

4. Make two strings of beads with the hemp cord and five beads each. Leave 2 inches of cord on each end for stringing.

5. Thread a section of hemp cord into the top of the wooden heart to make a 2- to 3-inch loop for hanging.

6. Connect one end of a bead string to the bottom of the wooden heart and the other end to the top of the wooden house.

7. Connect one end of the other bead string to the bottom of the wooden house and the other end of the bead string to the bell. When the pendant is complete, hang it wherever you like.

Dongba ideograph "love," showing a woman offering a
needle and thread to a man, an indication of care

Yi Doll

China's ethnic minorities are known for their diverse costumes
and ornaments. Each ethnic group and subgroup (branch) can be
identified by its characteristic costume. In the following activity,
you are going to make a doll wearing one of the many costumes of
the Yi people. *Note:* Always exercise caution when working with
hot glue and scissors. Children require adult supervision.

Materials needed:

half-finished doll, 7 inches tall (available in craft stores),
preferably with black hair

3½-by-11-inch (9-by-28-cm) piece of white fabric

3½-by-11-inch (9-by-28-cm) piece of yellow fabric

4-by-11-inch (10-by-28-cm) piece of black fabric

4-by-4-inch (4-by-4-cm) square of black fabric

7-inch piece of black chenille

7-inch piece of white chenille

7-inch piece of red chenille

7-inch piece of gold chenille

Tools needed:

1 pair scissors

hot glue gun and glue

12-inch ruler

Instructions:

To make the headpiece:

1. Plait the black, white, and red chenille. Cut to 6 inches (15 cm) long.

2. Glue the plait to one side of the black fabric square 1 inch from the edge. Leave 1 inch of plait on either side. The side with the plait serves as the front of the headpiece (Step 1 in the drawing).

To make the skirt:

1. Glue together the white, yellow, and black fabrics to make an 11-by-11-inch (28-by-28-cm) striped square, with the black stripe being the bottom of skirt (Step 2 in the drawing).

2. Glue the gold chenille where the yellow and black fabric come together.

3. Cut the square into a circle with an 11-inch (28-cm) diameter (Step 3 in the drawing).

4. Fold the fabric circle in half, then in half again, into a cone shape (Step 4 in the drawing).

5. Trim ⅔ inch (2 cm) off the tip of the cone (Step 5 in the drawing).

To make the doll:

1. Pull the skirt onto the doll above the waistline, covering the arms. Spot glue the skirt to the body. Make sure that the skirt is evenly pleated (Step 6 in the drawing.).

2. Glue the headpiece onto the doll's head, with 2 inches falling down the back. Glue the headpiece to both sides of the head so the front arches (Step 7 in the drawing).

3. The doll is complete. You may want to add various ornaments.

Steps in making a Yi doll

Part 2: Food, Games, and Crafts

PART 3

The Tales

Animal Tales

    Historically, the official records of the Han Chinese dismissed animal stories as unorthodox. They often appeared in political contexts; a minister would use them to make his case to a monarch, fearing that more pointed advice would invite his anger and retaliation. Chinese ethnic minorities, however, tell animal stories to pass on their life experiences or to illustrate philosophical points. "A Golden Deer," from the Hezhen, teaches us to trust whom we love; "A Muntjac and a Leopard," from the Achang, tells us not to do what we would not want others to do to us; "The Jingpo's "Lions Ask a Yellow Ant for Help" advises against despising those we think are unimportant; "A Goat and a Wolf," from the Xibe, illustrates how wisdom can help fend off a grave danger; "A Lion and a Wild Goose," from the Uygur, cautions against greed and ungratefulness; and "A Bear and a Leopard" from the Gaoshan illustrates a situation in which a good-humored joke may get out of hand.

A GOLDEN DEER

This is a tale from the Hezhen, one of the smallest Chinese ethnic minorities. Its 4,640 (China, 2002) people primarily live in Northeastern China. Only at the turn of the twentieth century did they part with their primitive lifestyle of fishing and hunting. Like the Inuit people in North America, they used to wear clothes made of fish skins.

*O*n a wintry day a long, long time ago, a young hunter found a doe in the snow. Wounded in the leg, she was unable to run. Seeing tears trickle from her begging eyes, the young hunter felt compassion. He applied a bone-healing ointment to her wound and bandaged it with shreds of cloth torn from his clothes. Then he fed her some dried fish and meat, provisions he had brought for his hunting. In a short time, the doe regained enough strength to rise to her feet, although she was still too feeble to run. She stumbled around the young hunter three times before limping away toward the forest.

One day, jaundice struck the young hunter and confined him to bed. Gaunt and listless, he was on the verge of death. He had just given up hope when a beautiful young woman came to him. "Brother Hunter, I heard you were sick, so I'm here to treat you," she said as she sat at his bedside.

With great effort, the young hunter opened his eyes and peered at her. With what strength he had left, he muttered, "I feel really sick. I'm afraid I'll give up the ghost any moment."

"Don't you worry," said the young woman. "I've brought you a medicine that can raise the dead. After you take it, you'll recover soon." With that, she produced a mirror and a pitch-black stalk from a red cloth parcel she had brought with her. Then she went on, "This is the herb of resuscitation. Take it and you'll be free from and immune to any disease."

The young hunter took the herb, half believing and half doubting. But, as the young woman had promised, the herb sent a surge of warmth through his body. Sweating all over, he was seized with a sense of relief and then a burst of energy.

"So, how do you feel, Brother Hunter?" asked the young woman.

The hunter thanked her profusely and said, "If I can't repay you in this world, I'll become your servant in the next."

"Oh, no," said the young woman. "I want nothing from you." Then pausing and blushing, she finally summoned enough courage to say, "Instead, I want to be your wife."

Happily surprised, the young hunter accepted her proposal wholeheartedly. They lived happily by honest labor. While the husband hunted in the mountains, the wife cured animal hides and attended to the chores at home. They always had a surplus of meat from their game and a sufficient supply of millet and other daily necessities, which they traded their processed leather for.

Three years went by quickly. They gave birth to a precocious son, who started walking and talking even before he was one year old.

One winter day, the hunter ran into a female shaman priest on his way back from a market. Eyeing him from head to toe, she blurted out, "You're possessed!"

"By what?"

"An evil spirit in your home."

"It can't be! I've got nobody at home but my lovely wife and son. Where on earth does this bogey come from?"

The shaman priest danced and chanted ceremoniously, her waist bells chiming rhythmically. After a while, she said, "My guardian divinity told me that your wife is a doe."

"How come?" asked the incredulous hunter.

"If you don't trust me," said the priest, "then look in your fish barn, and there you'll find a deer hide belonging to your wife. You must burn it to get you and your son out of harm's way."

When the hunter returned home, he rummaged in his fish barn and, sure enough, found the doeskin. Immediately, he built a fire in the courtyard and threw it into it.

At the time, his wife was sewing in the bedroom. Instantly, she felt sharp pain all over her body. She dashed out, salvaged the hide, and stamped out the fire. But it was too late. The hide was seriously damaged already.

"Now that you've hurt me so badly, I've no reason to stay."

"So you really are a doe?"

"I was, and now I am," said she. "To thank you for saving my life, I came to save yours. Since then, I've become your wife and the mother of your son. See what you did to me. By burning the hide, you nearly killed me. Well, I've no choice but to leave."

As she admonished her foolish husband, she took the mirror and held it up in front of his face. The hunter immediately felt a spasm of queasiness and vomited up the stalk that had saved his life. She picked it up, stowed it in the red-cloth parcel, and, carrying the partly charred deer hide under her arm, went off in a huff, not looking back even once.

Their young son, crying bitterly, asked his father to get his mother back. Picking him up and holding him in his arms, the hunter set out to pursue his wife. He traced her to the foot of the mountain, only to find her footprints turn into those of deer hooves. Then he heard a doe moaning with tremendous grief in the distance.

The hunter deeply regretted his folly, but to no avail. Before long, he died of his original illness. The doe returned and took their son away with her. Eventually, she nurtured him into a young hunter like his father.

Drawing by Sarah Martin, fine arts student, WKU

A MUNTJAC AND A LEOPARD

This tale is well known to the Achang, an ethnic minority of 33,900 (China, 2002) people living in Yunnan. Muntjacs are small deer found in Southeast Asia. Because they cry like dogs, they are nicknamed "barking deer."

*A*long time ago, muntjacs (barking deer) made their living by farming. At the beginning of each season, they prepared their fields by weeding them. Leopards, carnivores that they were, had to do the same to compensate for the lack of prey from time to time.

One day, a muntjac and a leopard ran into each other. Strangely, although they were natural enemies, the leopard had no intention of hurting the muntjac, and the latter didn't think of fleeing the other, either. Instead, they had a whim to weed each other's fields.

As a beast of prey, the leopard set the rules of the game: She made the muntjac work for her first. At the end of each day, the leopard would bring food back to the muntjac in compensation for his labor. The food, of course, was leftover meat of the animals that she hunted during the day. The herbivorous muntjac had to submit to the humiliation of feeding on what he hated to eat.

When it was the leopard's turn to weed the fields for the muntjac, the latter had to search for food to feed the former. The grass he brought back, however, outraged the leopard.

"You ungrateful brute!" she snarled. "How dare you feed me with grass while all I gave you was meat?"

"I'm sorry! You know I'm an herbivore and eat nothing but grass," replied the muntjac timidly.

"Then I'll have you for food!" said the leopard, and she arched her back and bared her teeth, ready to pounce on the poor muntjac, who begged profusely for mercy.

"Alright, go and find me meat or . . . ." Pointing at her sharp canine teeth in her wide-open mouth, the leopard stopped short of uttering the threat. But the muntjac got the message loud and clear. He dashed into the woods and embarked on the impossible mission, for he knew nothing about hunting and had never killed a single animal all his life.

As evening was closing in, fear crept upon the poor muntjac. If he returned empty-handed, he would become the leopard's meat himself. He was wandering helplessly and aimlessly in the woods as if in a trance, when he stumbled over something. To his relief, it turned out to be the decaying body of a small animal!

Before twilight gave in to darkness, the muntjac returned to the leopard. When she saw the odorous carcass, the big cat flew into a rage. She wanted to teach the ungrateful muntjac a big lesson. But the terrified muntjac, anticipating the retaliation, had already taken to his heels, leaving a trail of dust in his wake. The leopard chased him at full speed and, in no time, caught up with him. She was about to bear down upon him when a wild boar jumped between the two animals, shielding the muntjac behind his stout body.

The boar asked what had happened. After the panting leopard recounted her story, the boar passed his judgment, "The muntjac is innocent."

"What?" rumbled the indignant leopard "He wanted to poison me with rotten meat and you still think of him as innocent?"

"You forced him to hunt, didn't you?" asked the boar, who had decided to let the muntjac go.

"We worked for and fed each other. It's a fair game!"

With that, the leopard charged at the muntjac, who stood immobilized with terror. The boar tried his best to keep the furious leopard at bay. Unfortunately, in the struggle, the leopard was fatally wounded.

LIONS ASK A YELLOW ANT FOR HELP

This is a tale from the Jingpo, an ethnic minority of 132,100 (China, 2002) people indigenous to Yunnan. They didn't know how to write until the early 1950s, when the Chinese government helped them create an alphabetic script. Their folklore is hence primarily an oral tradition.

*L*ong ago, there lived in the forest a lion and a lioness, who claimed to be "King" and "Queen" of the jungle. They were as arrogant as all sovereigns can be, showing no respect for any member of their animal kingdom. They especially despised smaller creatures like insects.

One morning the couple caught a big elk between them. They were beside themselves with joy because, after a few days of hunger, they could finally enjoy a good meal. They took the elk back to their den, where they tore the carcass up with their sharp teeth. The lioness got hold of a large piece of the poor animal's body, but it was attached tenaciously to a bone. She shook the body hard while crushing the bone with her powerful jaws, trying to rip the meat from it. But a freak accident happened. Her violent movements catapulted a big splinter of the bone into the air and, as it happened, it flew straight into the ear of the lion, who had been gnawing at what was left of the elk's body beside her. Immediately he fell to the ground, writhing and howling with excruciating pain. The lioness was stunned and felt terribly sorry. She tried every possible means to get the bone fragment out. She scratched the base of his ear, licked its outer part, and poked about inside it, but to no avail. Unfortunately, the bone was lodged too deep in the ear to retrieve it.

Dusk fell. The royal couple were exhausted, the lion from his agonizing struggles and the lioness from her panicky efforts to free him from his suffering.

"We can't go on like this. It gets nowhere," the lioness said despondently.

"What do you think we can do?" the lion asked hopelessly and painfully.

"Well," the lioness faltered, "since we are at our wit's end, how about sending for the biggest animals to see if they can help?"

"Ask them for help?" The proud King would have flatly rejected the proposal but for the unbearable pain. He said resignedly, "Fine!"

The Queen called for the largest animals she could find in the jungle. First came the elephant, followed by the bear, the tiger, the leopard, and the boar, in that order. They tried all they could—fishing with the trunk, licking with the tongue, scratching with the paw, and prying with the tusk—but none could get the bone out of the lion's ear.

When all the guests had departed, the silence of despair reigned in the den. The anguish of the lion was tightening its grip, depriving him of his desire to eat and sleep. The lioness fared no better because she was tormented by guilt and anxiety. Pacing around her partner with a heavy heart, she kept saying, "What shall we do? What shall we do? Who else can help us then?" She paced and paced, then suddenly she halted.

"I've got it!"

"You've got what?" the weary lion asked.

"We've always been looking down upon our neighbors, especially the small ones. Why can't we try the yellow ant?"

"Do whatever you can to get rid of my pain!"

The tiny yellow ant was summoned. It took him a few days and a tough climb over a mountain to reach the den. When he learned of the lion King's condition, he told the couple not to worry.

"I can get the bone out easily," he said confidently.

"How can you?" Apparently the lion was unconvinced, "Even the elephant and the wild boar could do nothing to help. What makes a tiny ant like you think you can do what you promise?"

The yellow ant smiled but said nothing. The next moment, he was in the lion's ear, where he soon found the bone splinter. He started gnawing at it nonstop. Hours later, he had reduced the bone to a heap of tiny bits and pieces. He then slipped them out one by one. The next morning, the yellow ant emerged with the last bit of the bone, purging the lion King of his nuisance once and for all.

The royal couple's gratitude was beyond words. After the yellow ant had left, the King said to his Queen, "Any one, whether a king or a pauper, should treat others like equals. Take me, for example. I am a powerful King all right, but I can't even deal with a piece of bone in my ear. And neither can you, my Queen, nor the other big animals in our kingdom. Who could imagine that help should come from such a small and unpromising creature as the yellow ant?"

Courtesy of Sarah Martin, WKU student

A GOAT AND A WOLF

This is a folktale of the ethnic Xibe, who have a population of 188,800 (China, 2002). There are two major Xibe communities living more than 2,000 kilometers (1,243 miles) apart in North China. Interestingly, although the Xibe in Northeastern China have mostly abandoned their mother tongue, those who have migrated to the northwest have become the only significant Manchu-speaking population in the country.

A hungry wolf was looking for food when he caught sight of a plump goat grazing on a hillside. He rejoiced at the sumptuous meal lying in front of him. Instead of attacking the goat right away, however, the wolf had a whimsical idea. He wanted to know more about his victim before gobbling him up.

"Brother Goat, what are the things that grow on your head?" asked the wolf, gesturing with his nose at the goat's spiraling horns.

"They are tailor-made swords for piercing through the bellies of wolves," the clever and intrepid goat answered.

These strange "swords" struck great fear into the wolf. Still, he asked tentatively, referring to the goat's long beard, "What's that growing under your chin?"

Glowering at the wolf, the goat answered gruffly while stroking his beard with his cloven hoof, "You mean this? It's a napkin. I use it to wipe my mouth after eating a wolf."

At this, the wolf began to quiver. The goat, on the other hand, kept glaring at the faltering wolf, his chest heaving heavily with indignation at the beast's annoying questions.

The wolf couldn't resist his curiosity despite his fear. Plucking up his courage, he inquired of the puffing goat, "How come your chest goes up and down like that when you are angry?"

"Well," throwing out his chest, the goat bluffed, "I've got three wolf-eating hounds in my belly. Whenever I'm mad, they all run about and kick around in it. Since I'm now in a bad mood, they can burst out of my throat and get at you any moment!" With that, the goat sprang as if to charge at the wolf.

Frightened out of his wits, the wolf turned and sped away. In his hurry, he crashed into a tree stump invisible among the grass and crushed his skull, never to rise again.

A LION AND A WILD GOOSE

This is a popular tale among the Uygur. The 8,399,400 (China, 2002) Uygur primarily inhabit the Xinjiang Uygur Autonomous Region in Northwestern China. Scholars find the plot of this tale very similar to "The Rebirth of the Bird of Wisdom," a Buddhist scripture story from India. They conclude that this tale may have been the result of Indian influence (Wang and Fuxue, 2005).

A lion stole a fish from a fisherman and gulped it down without the fisherman noticing. But the lion was in such a hurry that a fish bone was stuck in his throat. He could neither spit it out nor swallow it. The more he tried to do either, the more it hurt, until his throat began to bleed.

The lion was at a loss what to do, so he cast about for a doctor. Before long, he came across a wild goose and begged him, "Brother Goose, could you please help me get rid of my pain? I'll never forget your kindness."

"Sir," said the wild goose, startled, "I've never given medical treatment to anyone because I don't know medicine at all."

"Please, Brother," begged the lion, who began feeling anxious, "You are the only one who can relieve me from my anguish. Please help me . . . ."

"Er . . . ," the wild goose hesitated. Having no alternative, he asked, "Okay, first tell me what's wrong with you."

Opening his big mouth as he raised its head, the lion muttered, "Here, do you see it? A fish bone's caught in my throat. It hurts so much that I really don't know what to do. I'll be obliged if you can probe my throat with your long beak and take the bone out."

Although distrustful of the beast, the wild goose didn't have the courage to say no. He gingerly placed his long neck into the lion's big mouth and delved into the depths of the lion's throat with his beak. Soon he pulled the bone out.

The lion gave a great sigh of relief. Licking his mouth with content, he began, "I'm very grateful for what you've done for me, Brother Goose. But if you really want to help me, you must make me completely satisfied. You know, the fish bone prevented me from eating for a long time. You've got to figure out how to feed me."

"Brother Lion, how can I feed you? I've already freed you from your pain, haven't I?"

"Stop your nonsense," roared the lion, "I can't believe you have the guts to mention what you did to me without remorse. You insulted me by putting your dirty beak into my mouth, and I must eat you up."

"Don't do this to me, Brother Lion," the terrified wild goose pleaded. "I placed my beak in your mouth because you asked me to."

"Shut up," snarled the lion, "I asked you to free me from my suffering, but you added to my pain and even caused my throat to bleed. You must pay for your criminal act."

Before the wild goose could defend himself, the lion pounced on him, saying, "I don't have the time to bicker with you. I can't resist the temptation of your juicy meat." With that, the lion gobbled up the poor goose. Ever since, there has been the proverb "repay kindness with enmity (bite the hand that feeds one)."

A BEAR AND A LEOPARD

This is a folktale from the Gaoshan (mountain people), known in Taiwan as Yuanzhumin (original inhabitants). The Chinese 2000 Census (China, 2002) recorded 4,500 Gaoshan people on the mainland, and a census done by the Taiwanese authorities in the late 1990s registered 345,000 on the island. It has twelve branches speaking more than twenty different dialects of the South Island linguistic family. For more tales from Taiwan, read Tales from the Taiwanese, *retold by Gary Marvin Davison, also in the World Folklore Series.*

*B*oth the leopard and the bear had once worn snow-white furs. One day they bumped into each other and soon became good friends. Having nothing to do, they thought of painting each other for fun. The bear started first. He marked the leopard with stripes of white alternating with black. When the bear had finished painting one side of the leopard, he took her to a nearby spring so that she could look into the reflecting water. The leopard was very pleased with the result and impressed with the bear's creativity as well.

Feeling extremely flattered, the bear worked even harder. He painted and painted until he was so tired that he dropped to the ground fast asleep. Seeing this, a mischievous idea dawned upon the extrovert and fun-loving leopard. "Let me play a joke on the silly bear," she said to herself.

She found some soot in a nearby village and rubbed it gently and evenly into the fur of the slumbering bear. When he woke up and glanced into the spring water, he was taken aback. In the reflection was a strange black monster he had never seen before. When he realized that the monster was none other than himself and that the leopard was behind this horrible practical joke, he became extremely angry with her. After he tried to wash the soot off in the water and failed, his anger escalated. He charged at the leopard in an attempt to kill her.

"Wait! Let me tell you what happened." The leopard tried to offer an explanation to calm the seething bear while apologizing profusely.

"Sorry! I'm terribly sorry! I really didn't mean it. I goofed up because I was clumsy. I'm desperate to atone for my sinful mistake. How about my catching some deer for you? I'll send you the meat without delay."

"Hmmm," the bear hesitated. Finally his anger gave way to his grumbling stomach, and he said, "I do feel hungry now. Go and get me a deer."

"Thank you for pardoning me! I'll be right back."

"Wait!" The leopard was about to run off when the bear stopped her, saying, "You have to feed me all the time from now on or suffer the consequences."

"Yes, sir! I'll do what it takes to atone for what I did to you."

Leopards in the forest today still bury the carcasses of the deer they have caught so that bears can sniff them out. What's more, the leopard's growl is still believed to be her regretful lament for her past tomfoolery.

Moral Tales

Tales in this group also teach lessons, but as in most stories, their characters are humans instead of animals. "A Clever Man" from the Russ beats a king who thought himself cleverer. The lonely "Son of a Horse" from the Salar longs for brotherhood but runs into unfaithful companions instead. As the story "Three Brothers" from the Tatar teaches, only the self is the master of one's fate. "Three Neighbors" from the Bonan find unity to be the best defense against an adversary. The cruel stepmother of a Dongxiang girl in "A Feathered Flying Garment" reaps evil consequences in the end. "A Foolish King" of the Uzbek gets himself killed because of his stupidity. Finally, the Lahu "Man with Only a Head" finds his true love and learns how to trust her.

A CLEVER MAN

This is a tale from the Russ, or Chinese Russians. The 15,609 (China, 2002) Russ primarily inhabit Northwestern Xinjiang, Northern Heilongjiang, and Northeastern Inner Mongolia. Descendants of Russians and Russian Chinese immigrants in the eighteenth century, they speak and write in Russian with a hint of Chinese, Uygur, and Kazak influences. Tales of the Russ are very humorous, as is evident in the following story.

*T*here was once in Russia a king, who thought of himself as the cleverest man in the world. He claimed that nobody could cheat him. One day, he heard that a clever man had come to town and that he was able to make rich people give up their money, after which he would distribute it among poor people.

Skeptical of the hearsay, the king sent a minister to investigate. He came back and reported that the rumor was true. At this, the king became very jealous and angry. So he ordered the minister to bring the clever man into his presence. When he saw the clever man, the king said, "I take great pride in my intelligence, and no one has ever challenged it. Do you think you can make me surrender my money to you?"

"Your Majesty, now that I have pawned all my tools to others," said the clever man, "I can't even con the most foolish in the world anymore. How can I trick you, the wisest king?"

"Why don't you redeem your tools?" asked the king.

"How can I," said the clever man, putting on an air of helplessness. "Since I don't even have a single penny in my pocket, how do you expect me to get my tools back?"

"How much do you need to get them back?"

"200 solid gold coins."

To prove that he was not gullible, the king demanded that the minister give the clever man 200 gold coins. He then urged, "Hurry! Go and redeem your tools immediately!"

Taking the money, the clever man bowed to the king as a token of thanks and left. The ministers couldn't help chuckling, which enraged the king.

"What are you laughing at?"

"Your Majesty," one of them said, trembling with fear, "you've already given your money to him. You can't expect him to be back again, for his tool is none other than his brain."

THE SON OF A HORSE

This is a tale from the Salar, one of the ten Muslim ethnic minorities in China. With a population of 104,500 (China, 2002), the Salars inhabit parts of Qinghai, Gansu, and Xinjiang.

A long, long time ago, there was a family that kept a black mare. One morning, its owner went to feed her in the stable and found her in labor. To their astonishment, she gave birth to a boy instead of a foal. The owner took the baby and carried him to the mosque in the village. The imam gave the baby boy the name Ma Shengbao, or "Baby Born of a Horse." The horse owner then adopted the boy as his own son.

Ma Shengbao soon grew up. He learned not only kung fu but also the art of archery. One day, he said to his adopted parents, "I feel very lonely because I've got no brothers. I'll go and look for one." The understanding parents consented.

The next day he set out, carrying his bow and arrows. On his way, when he found a tree giving off smoke, he shot an arrow at it. With that, a man jumped out of its crevice, saying, "If you're a passerby, go away. If you're looking for someone, come in. Your arrow's broken my only pot."

"I'm looking for a relative," answered Ma Shengbao.

"Come in then," said the man from the tree, "but I have no brothers."

Ma Shengbao entered, and they became sworn brothers. The next day, they set out together, and after awhile they saw a rock emitting smoke. Ma Shengbao launched an arrow at the rock, which cracked. Out leapt a man from the fissure, saying, "If you're a passerby, go away. But if you're looking for someone, come in. Your arrow's broken my only pot."

"We're looking for a relative," Ma Shengbao and the man from the tree answered in unison.

"Come in then," said the man from the stone, "but I have no brothers."

In the stone, the three became brothers on oath. They started calling one another in the order of their seniority: The man from the tree was regarded as Big Brother because he was the oldest. Since Ma Shengbao was the youngest of all, he was called Little Brother. The man from the stone naturally became Second Brother.

As they lived and hunted together, strange things began to happen. Each time they returned home, they found their meals cooked and spread on the table piping hot. So they talked about discovering the source of this mystery. They decided to go out hunting by turns and leave one of them behind on watch for what would come to pass.

The next day, Big Brother was on the lookout at home. He was hiding in a corner when three doves flew into their shed. They plucked their wings off, hung them up, and began to chatter.

"Coo, coo, here's flour," one said.

"Coo, coo, here's cooking oil," said another.

With that, they transformed into three young women and set about cooking. After they finished, they put on their wings and flew away. Big Brother did nothing when the strange phenomenon happened, nor did he say anything to his brothers afterward.

The third day, Second Brother remained and saw the same dove fairies. Like Big Brother, he acted as if nothing had occurred.

When Ma Shengbao's turn came, however, he stole the wings and burned them so that the young women couldn't take off any more. To his pleasant surprise, instead of protesting, they simply decided to stay.

One of them told Ma Shengbao, "If you and your brothers want us to be your sisters, it's fine with us."

"If you want us to be your wives," said another, "we'd be glad to."

Then the first introduced herself and her sisters, "This is Ayi Ana. I'm Yulutusi Ana, and this is Guni Ana."

Guni Ana was the most beautiful of the three, but she didn't like a man to take her as his wife merely because of her looks. While the other two sisters were talking, she had secretly smeared her face with soot so that she appeared unattractive.

When the other two brothers returned, Ma Shengbao told them everything. They picked Ayi Ana and Yulutusi Ana, leaving the "ugly" Guni Ana to Ma Shengbao. But soon they learned the truth and began to regret their decisions.

One day, as the three wives were ready to cook, a chicken happened to flutter into the hearth and snuffed out the fire in it. They had to go out to look for something like a live coal or stalk to start a fire. When they passed by a big rock, they noticed smoke threading out from its crack. They pushed on it, and a door opened into the rock, revealing a cave. They went in, only to run into a devil. Although it was in the form of an old woman, it betrayed itself by its ominous look. By the time the women realized who she was, it was too late to run away. However, the devil showed no sign of harming them. Instead, she gave them a piece of live coal and a pouch of fruit and let them go.

As the three women stumbled back home, the fruit fell out of the pouch, one piece after another, through a hole. In fact, the devil had left it there intentionally so that she could trace the women to their residence by following the fruity trail. In the form of the same old woman, she began to visit the women every time the brothers were out hunting. She told the women that she was ridding them of the lice in their hair. In fact, she was sucking blood from their necks without their knowing it, causing them to weaken mysteriously. Puzzled at what was happening to their wives, the three brothers took turns hunting, leaving one at home to watch each time.

The next day, Big Brother stayed home, hiding from view. When he caught sight of the devil sucking blood from the wives, he was too scared to do anything. The same happened to Second Brother the following day.

When Ma Shengbao found the devil hurting their wives, he shot at it with his bow and arrow. The devil snatched Guni Ana and fled, leaving a trail of blood from her wound.

The three brothers traced the blood to the cave, which the devil had now turned into a deep vertical shaft for her protection. None except Ma Shengbao dared to venture into it. He asked the other two brothers to tie a rope to his waist and hold the other end in their hands while he climbed down. He told them to drag him out if he was in danger.

At the bottom of the cave, Ma Shengbao saw his wife, Guni Ana, alone. She told him that the devil had gone to another cave and would return any moment, and then hid him inside the cold hearth. Upon her return, the devil claimed that she smelled unfamiliar human flesh. Guni Ana reasoned that since she ate humans often, the scent must have stayed with her. While Guni Ana was trying to convince the devil, a crow that had snuck into the cave after Ma Shengbao gave away his hiding place. At this, Ma Shengbao immediately shot out of the hearth to confront the devil. At the same time, Guni Ana poured a dustpan of beans under the feet of the devil to make it difficult for her to stand firm when she tried to charge at Ma Shengbao. Taking advantage of the opportunity, Ma Shengbao shot an arrow at the devil, and she crashed to the ground. However, before the couple could celebrate their victory, the devil sprang up to attack them again. Guni Ana struck her a heavy blow in the face and finsihed her off.

Ma Shengbao then asked his brothers to pull his wife Guni Ana out of the pit first, along with large amounts of the devil's treasure. When they had finished, however, the two brothers dropped the rope into the cave and went away with the riches and the struggling Guni Ana. They left Ma Shengbao yelling helplessly in the pit. He paced back and forth until he was exhausted and went to sleep. When he woke up, he saw a big serpent attacking a young eagle. He struck the snake on its head and killed it. The young eagle soared out of the shaft into the sky, where it circled a few times. Then, instead of flying away, it suddenly dived back into the cave and alighted on Ma Shengbao's shoulder. When it learned that he was the victim of his brothers' treachery, it lifted him up, carried him out of the cave, and took him to its parents on a big tree. Before they could attack him, the young eagle told them what had happened in the pit. Gratefully, the eagle mother offered to carry him home, but asked him to feed her a hundred sparrows on the way.

Ma Shengbao managed to capture ninety-nine sparrows but gave the impression that he had gotten a hundred, for he desperately wanted to get back home. Ma Shengbao fed a sparrow to the eagle carrying him on its back at intervals of a few miles until he exhausted his supply. The eagle had yet to finish the last leg of the long journey, and she kept asking him for the hundredth sparrow. In desperation, Ma Shengbao cut a piece of flesh from his leg and gave it to the eagle. When the big bird alighted and let him go, she saw him limping.

Only then did she realize what had happened. The eagle disapproved of Ma Shengbao's recklessness, saying that she would have transported him to his destination anyway if he had told her the truth.

Ma Shengbao saw the eagle off and hobbled toward his home. Before he reached it, he became too tired and sore to continue. He found a place near a well, took off his vest, and was about to lie down to rest when he spotted a haggard young woman staggering toward him, a water jar on her shoulder. Apparently she was coming to the well to fetch water. Catching sight of a familiar birthmark on his chest, the woman instantly recognized him as none other than her husband. She told the stunned Ma Shengbao she was Guni Ana. When asked why she was so wan and sallow, she complained of her suffering at the hands of his two brothers.

When Ma Shengbao arrived home, followed by his wife Guni Ana, Big Brother and Second Brother were practicing martial arts in the courtyard. Seeing a tattered man approaching them, they jested with him and challenged him to a fight. Ma Shengbao beat them hands down. Embarrassed, they fled with their wives and were never heard from again. Ma Shengbao reunited with Guni Ana, and they lived happily thereafter.

THREE BROTHERS

This is a tale from the Tatar. About 4,900 (China, 2002) Chinese Tatars inhabit part of the Xinjiang Uygur Autonomous Region. They speak a dialect of the Altai linguistic family and primarily use Chinese, Uygur, or Sak as their writing systems.

Long ago, there were three Tatar brothers who had never achieved anything in their lives. From time to time they sighed dejectedly about this. One day, however, good luck suddenly befell them. To help improve their livelihood, a fairy of good fortune had decided to lend them a helping hand. On this day, the invisible fairy snuck into the three brothers' home without their knowledge.

The eldest brother was a farmer, so the fairy helped him reap a bumper harvest. The second brother was a fisher, so she caused him to catch a great amount of fish. Unlike his brothers, the third could do nothing but gamble. In order to teach him a lesson, the fairy first helped him win a big fortune.

After what she had done, the fairy of good fortune left. Back in her remote abode, she kept a close watch on the brothers, expecting them to make good use of her kindness.

The first and second brothers lived up to her expectations, working hard without idling away a minute of their time. As a result, their lives improved with each passing day. The third brother, however, never changed his habit of gambling. Before long he had squandered all the wealth the fairy had helped him win. With nothing left, his only option was to go begging.

THREE NEIGHBORS

This is a tale from the Bonan, one of the ten Muslim ethnic minorities of China. Most of its 16,500 people (China, 2002) live in Gansu. The Bonan speak a tongue of the Altai language family similar to Mongolian and have no written script.

*T*here was once a tiny, picturesque village called Dahejia by the Yellow River. It had only three families, who lived in harmony for generations. United as one, they stood as firm as a rock against their adversaries.

A brother with supernatural powers headed each of the three families. The head of the family in the east of the village was known as Ears in the Wind. He had magic hearing, capable of catching the slightest sound in the distance. The head of the family in the west of the village was called Eyes through the Mountain. He had the uncanny power to see faraway objects, such as deer drinking on the other side of the mountain. The head of the family in the north of the village was nicknamed Jack of All Trades. He was capable of making all kinds of crafts, even a ladder long enough to reach the stars.

In the South Mountain there lived a Prince of the Devils, who was jealous of the unity and harmony enjoyed by the three families. He tried to separate and conquer them by various means, but he had never succeeded because they fought him in a concerted effort each time.

One day Prince of the Devils came up with an insidious idea. He called in God of the Yellow River and ordered him to raise the water level to inundate Dahejia for three days. However, big brother Ears in the Wind had overheard their conversation and told the other brothers about the Prince's plot.

"If we have a couple of whole cowhides, then we'll have nothing to worry about," said the third brother, Jack of All Trades.

"Let me take a look," said the second brother, Eyes through the Mountain. He swept around with his extraordinary eyesight and said, "Ha, I saw butchers slaughtering their cows on the back of the snow-clad mountain. They are hanging up the carcasses and throwing away the hides."

Jack of All Trades said, "I'll go and buy them."

Soon he came back with the hides and inflated them so they became floats. The brothers constructed a raft with logs and planks and attached the leather floats to it. This type of vessel is still in use today on the Yellow River.

The next day, God of the Yellow River flooded the village, but the three families were safe and sound on the raft, very much to the dismay of Prince of the Devils.

The Prince would not take his defeat lying down. When summer came, he summoned Goddess of Plague and demanded that she open her gourd of epidemics. Once again Ears in the Wind overheard their scheme and warned the other brothers about it.

"What shall we do?" he asked.

"Don't worry," said Jack of All Trades. "If we can find some mugwort plants, then they can't do any harm to us."

"Let me take a look," said big brother Eyes through the Mountain, and he spotted a great amount of mugwort plants on the top of Taizi Mountain on the other side of the Yellow River. The third brother, Jack of All Trades, again volunteered to fetch them. Crossing the river on the cowhide raft, he climbed up to the mountaintop and harvested as much of the mugwort as he could. Back in the village, he found the other brothers busy digging up a great amount of red-skinned garlic from their gardens. They were doing their share of getting prepared for the onslaught of the plague.

By the time the plague reached their village, the three families had set fire to the mugwort plants outside their houses, and they gave off enough smoke to repel the deadly disease. Inside their houses, they plugged their ears and noses with garlic and bathed again and again. This made them immune to the pestilence.

Frustrated, Prince of the Devils racked his demoniac brain for days, trying to find another approach to defeat the three families. Finally he came to realize that tactics could be more effective than force. He sent for a bird called *chijiaozi*, known for its big mouth, and made it sow discord among the families.

"Go and separate them with your glib tongue," he demanded. "So long as they are not united, I'll be able to defeat them one by one."

That evening, *chijiaozi* landed on the eaves of Ears in the Wind's house and began to sing in its croaky voice:

> *Heh, heh, heh, ho, ho, ho,*
> *Hark, Brother Ears in the Wind*
> *That's more capable than Heaven.*
> *Without the powerful ears you have,*
> *Flooded would have been the others.*

At the time, Ears in the Wind had just returned home with the firewood he had collected. He picked up a piece and drove the garrulous bird away with a single swipe.

The next evening, *chijiaozi* alighted on a peach tree in the courtyard of the second brother's family. At the top of its raucous voice, it sang:

> *Heh, heh, heh, ho, ho, ho,*
> *Hark, Brother Eyes through the Mountain*
> *That's more capable than Heaven.*
> *Without the powerful eyes you have,*
> *Died of plague would have been the others.*

At the time, Eyes through the Mountain was about to say his prayers. Annoyed by the bird's clamor, he picked up a cobblestone and threw it at the tale-telling bird.

Having survived two attacks, the treacherous bird wanted to make a last try before calling it quits. On the third evening, it stopped at the doorstep of the third brother and began to sing in a hoarse voice:

> *Heh, heh, heh, ho, ho, ho,*
> *Hark, Brother Jack of All Trades*
> *That's more capable than Heaven.*
> *Without the deft hands you have,*
> *Gone are all your two neighbors!*

The third brother was washing his feet in the courtyard. Unfortunately, he concurred with what *chijiaozi* said and nodded. Seeing that he had taken the bait, the bird went all out with its spiteful song:

> *Heh, heh, heh, ho, ho, ho,*
> *Hark, Brother Jack of All Trades.*
> *You treat your brothers with sincerity,*
> *But unpleasant words they say in return:*
> *"A good-for-nothing he's always been,*
> *And, in fact, he's but blind and deaf.*
> *Without the hard work we have done,*
> *Nothing would he have accomplished."*

Hearing this, the third brother grew so angry that he kicked away the water basin under his feet and vowed not to befriend the other two families any more.

Encouraged by its success, *chijiaozi* came every night to play the three families against one another until a squabble started among them. In the end, they quarreled so much that Jack of All Trades and his family relocated to the foot of the Taizi Mountain, Eyes through the Mountain and his family moved to Sanherjia, and Ears in the Wind and his family remained in the village.

Prince of the Devils then mobilized the demons of all disasters, including wind, drought, thunder, and flood, to attack the brothers repeatedly. Without their unity, they succumbed to the torment one by one. On their deathbeds, each called in his sons and daughters and asked them to seek harmony and unity with the other families. Their generations thereafter heeded their advice and have thus survived unto this day as three ethnic groups—the one that inhabits Dahejia is Bonan, the one that lives at the foot of the Taizi Mountain is Dongxiang, and the one that populates Sanherjia is Tujia.

To this day, the three ethnic peoples still resent the song of the *chijiaozi* bird, treating it as a bad omen.

A FEATHERED FLYING GARMENT

This is a tale from the Dongxiang, one of the ten Chinese Muslim ethnic minorities. Its 513,800 (China, 2002) people live in Gansu, Ningxia, Qinghai, and Xinjiang.

*O*nce upon a time, there was a girl named Fatuman, who lost her mother at an early age and had to live with her stepmother. Cruel and ill-minded, the stepmother tormented the girl by every possible means. The clever Fatuman, however, headed off each episode of mistreatment by accomplishing her assignments to perfection, much to the frustration of her fault-finding stepmother. She considered Fatuman an eyesore and wanted to get her as far out of her sight as possible.

When Fatuman was thirteen, the dark-minded stepmother sold her to a black-bearded man as his wife for fifty silver nuggets. The man was coming to get her in three days.

In the meantime, the stepmother locked Fatuman in her room. Like a fawn caught in a snare, the helpless girl was scared. She wished she were one of the white doves she saw through the window flying freely in the sky. Following them with her eyes, she began to sing,

> *White dove, flying dove,*
> *How envious of you I am!*
> *I wish I had a pair of wings,*
> *So I can fly freely high above.*

She sang herself to sleep, and in her dream, she saw a flock of white doves land by her bed.

"Hi," the doves cooed, "We are here to give you something so you can make a garment. When in danger, put it on, and it will not only keep you out of harm's way but also give you freedom and happiness." With that, they all plucked a few feathers from their bodies and piled them on her bedside before taking off.

The flapping of their wings woke Fatuman up. When she opened her eyes, she saw the white feathers heaped on her bed. She was very happy. Lighting an oil lamp, she set to work to make the garment as the doves had told her to in her dream. She finished it with her dexterous hands before daybreak.

On the third day, the black-bearded man came to pick up Fatuman. Terrified, she buttressed the door with a pole and holed up in a corner of the room, not knowing what would be in store for her.

Her stepmother put on a smiling face and attempted to lure her out with sweet talk, "Honey, open the door."

"I need to dress myself up."

After awhile, the stepmother came again and asked, "Are you done?"

"No, I'm combing my hair now."

In another few minutes, the stepmother came again, "Fatuman, are you finished?"

"I'm washing my face now."

In still another moment, the stepmother, beginning to lose her patience, inquired, "You rascal, haven't you finished dressing up?"

"I'm just putting on my costume."

This time, the stepmother wouldn't wait any longer. She told the black-bearded man to kick the door open, and both stormed into the room. Right at that moment, Fatuman had put on the white-feathered garment and turned into a white dove. She flapped her wings, darted out of the open door, and soared into the clear sky. After circling above her house a few times, she raced into the distance and disappeared.

Fatuman flew and flew until the sun was setting. She alighted in a tree by the roadside near a highland. She was so sad that she couldn't help singing,

> *Coo, coo; coo, coo,*
> *My stepmother is unkind,*
> *None loves me in the world,*
> *Not a dwelling I can find.*

As she sang, tears streamed out of her eyes and dripped down the tree, catching the attention of an old man underneath. He sang in response, hoping to alleviate her sorrow,

> *White dove, oh, white dove,*
> *Cry you not poor little child,*
> *My house is now your home,*
> *Never again will you be exiled.*

The old man was selling tea to passersby, and outside his teahouse, a table was laid with three kettles—of gold, copper, and iron. He poured tea into a little jade cup from the gold kettle and invited Fatuman to drink. The old man's kindness and hospitality drove away all her fear. Besides, after a day's travel in the air, she was very thirsty. She flew down from the tree and drank from the gold cup. Immediately, she felt a shudder. Before she knew it, the old man had taken the white-feathered garment from her. Instantly she resumed her human self. She then became the old man's helper. He treated her like a granddaughter. Her "grandpa," as Fatuman called the old man, told her about the secrets of the mysterious kettles: The gold one was godly; the copper, human; and the iron, devilish.

One day, Fatuman was going to a well to fetch water, when all of a sudden she caught sight of her stepmother and the black-bearded man coming up the highland. Their appearance rekindled her fear, and she scurried back home as fast as her slender legs could carry her. Panting and heaving, she told her grandpa they were approaching and intended to capture her.

"Don't be afraid, honey," said the old man. "I'll deal with them."

As the stepmother and the black-bearded man clambered up the hill and approached the old man, they asked, "Grandpa, have you seen a runaway girl coming this way?"

"No," answered the old man, "I only saw a little white dove flying into my teahouse, fleeing from persecution."

"That's my daughter!" the excited stepmother blurted out.

"Yes, that's her, my wife," echoed the black-bearded man.

"Please return her to us," they pleaded in unison.

"No rush! No rush!" The old man chuckled, "You've come all the way in such hot weather, so you must be thirsty. Here, have some tea before we get down to business."

With that, he poured two cups of tea from the devilish iron kettle. After a few sips the two were rolling on the ground and instantaneously changed into ugly birds, fluttering and tumbling under the tea table. With a wave of his hand, the old man scared the birds away. Then he said to Fatuman with mirth, "My child, now that they've fled to the tree, you'll have nothing to fear any more."

No sooner had Fatuman come out from hiding than the two birds crowed to her,

Back, back, you bad girl,
Back, back, you bad girl.

Annoyed, Fatuman asked her grandpa to shoo them away, which he did. But the birds returned in a while and resumed their clamor,

Back, back, you bad girl,
Back, back, you bad girl.

"Grandpa, they are back and drive me crazy. Please chase them off so they'll never return," entreated Fatuman.

Her grandpa was baking cakes at the time. He pulled off a piece of dough and threw it at the birds. The dough, however, transformed into a dove as it flew and pounced on its targets. The terrified gray birds took flight just in time. They were so fearful of the dove that they have never returned to bother Fatuman since.

To this day, the gray birds, now known as *xunrenniao* (birds looking for people), can still be heard in the woods crowing,

> *Back, back, you bad girl,*
> *Back, back, you bad girl.*

Upon hearing this, doves, their natural enemies, will spring up to chase them.

A FOOLISH KING

This is a folktale from the Uzbek, one of the ten Muslim ethnic groups in China. The 12,400 Uzbeks (China, 2002) are scattered in different parts of Xinjiang. Uzbeks are known for their jokes. The following is one of them.

*O*nce there was a penniless man, whose tattered house collapsed. He saved some money through hard labor and started to build a new one. Before he had half of the thatched roof plastered with mud, his money ran out. He had to dismiss the plasterer and thatcher he had hired, saying, "I'll call you back to finish the other half when I can afford it." Then he moved into the unfinished house.

One day a thief came by, thinking that the owner must be wealthy enough to build a house from scratch. "I need to pay him a visit," he said to himself.

At midnight, the thief snuck up to the roof and happened to land on the section not yet fortified with mud. He had moved only a few steps before crashing into the room on top of the poor man, who was asleep. The sudden impact scared the poor man out of his wits and sent him scurrying out of the room. The thief quickly rummaged it but had to leave frustrated because he found nothing that was worth his effort and pain.

The next day the thief went to the king to sue the poor man. He complained, "Your Majesty! I'm a robber. Last night, I went to steal from a poor man, but who would have thought that his roof should be a mere mat of straw, and I fell through into his room, nearly breaking my legs."

"Well, do you have any demands of the man who owns that house?" the king asked.

"You've got to punish him," the thief pleaded.

The king ordered his guards to summon the poor man to his court. Pointing at the robber, the king asked, "Is it true that this man dropped into your room from the roof?"

"Yes, Your Majesty," the poor man answered. "If he had not fallen on me, he would have broken his legs."

"No matter what happened that night, one thing was for sure: That man fell from your roof. You deserve death by hanging."

"Oh, have mercy, Your Majesty!" The poor man, dumbfounded, pleaded while crying, "I'm innocent. It's the thief that should be punished."

"Shut up!" demanded the king.

Seeing that the king was hopelessly unreasonable and fearing the prospect of having his neck put in the noose, the poor man tried to find a scapegoat. He argued, "Your Majesty, the thief dropped because the plasterer left his work unfinished. How can I be blamed for his sloppiness?"

Then the king ordered the poor man to be released and the plasterer to be brought to him. The hangmen were about to send the plasterer to the gallows when he cried out, "I have to tell the king that I am wronged."

The king stayed his execution and asked about his grievance. The plasterer told him that it was the thatcher who had failed to put enough straw on the roof and caused the accident. The king then had the plasterer released and the thatcher arrested.

"So you were the one that thatched the roof?" the king asked.

"Yes, I did, Your Majesty."

"Then you take the consequence." Turning to the executioners, the king ordered, "Hang him!"

"This is unfair, Your Majesty!" The thatcher cried out. "I used to do a very good job. I've been sloppy these days because the pigeons flying above me distracted my attention."

At this, the king set the thatcher free and had the pigeon keeper captured and condemned him to death by the noose.

"Keeping pigeons is not a crime, Your Majesty! What's the benefit of killing a commoner like me?" reasoned the pigeon keeper. "Wouldn't it be better if you put the robber to death to make your kingdom peaceful and your people secure?"

"Huh," pondered the king, "what you say makes sense. Apparently the culprit is the robber." Turning to his guards and hangmen, he decreed that the robber be found and executed.

The robber was apprehended again and brought to the gallows. However, he was too tall to fit. When the hangman asked the king what to do, he was irritated, "You fool! How can you bother me with such a simple question! If the robber is too tall, why can't you find a short person instead?"

At that, the hangman found him a short man in the street. He was going to a market known locally as bazaar, a sack on his back. When he was taken to the scaffold, the short man claimed that it was an injustice to kill him, for he had done nothing wrong. He added, "I'm only an honest merchant transporting goods for sale over the mountains."

"You're really dumb!" jeered the king. "You think I truly care who's guilty? No! My only concern is to punish someone when a crime is committed. Since the robber is too tall to be hanged, you are the right size to take his place. This is your poor fate, and you have to face it."

"Your Majesty, how can you penalize me for another man's offense?" the short man argued. He then offered the king a solution: "Why don't you dig a pit beneath the tall robber so his feet won't touch the ground?"

The short man's suggestion set the king thinking for a while. Then he looked around and commented, "The short man's right." He then ordered a pit to be dug and the robber to be hanged.

This time, the robber didn't show the slightest sign of fear and reluctance. Instead, he looked happy and impatient, urging the hangman to work harder and faster, saying that he wanted to die sooner.

"Why on earth are you in such a hurry?" the king was baffled.

"Because the King of Heaven has just passed away," the robber said, trying to make up a story to save his neck. "He left a will, saying whoever went to heaven first would become his successor. I want to succeed to his throne ahead of anyone else, and I'm really anxious. Hang me now. Don't waste my time!"

Hearing this, the king thought, "Since I'm a king on earth, I must rule over heaven as well." He then told the hangman to put his neck in the noose instead of the robber's. The hangman followed his order to the letter.

A MAN WITH ONLY A HEAD

This is a folktale from the Lahu, one of the sixteen aboriginal ethnic groups of Yunnan Province, with a population of 453,700 (China, 2002).

A long time ago, there was a widow who lived in a village on the waist of a mountain, surrounded by bamboo groves. Because she was childless, she had to do every bit of the farming herself.

One day she was mowing grass on the mountain under the scorching sun. She was so thirsty that she longed for water. She looked around but found none. As she cast about, she came down to the foot of the mountain. There she caught sight of a puddle. She thanked the omnipotent deity Esha for not letting her die of thirst.

As she came near the water, she found it was formed by the footprint of a giant elephant. Desperate, she drank to her heart's content, disregarding its poor sanitary condition. Strangely, it tasted better than any of the clear water she had had before, and it was very rejuvenating. But she could have never imagined that the water would get her pregnant!

For a widow to conceive a child was unacceptable to society. Consequently, after much gossiping among the villagers, they banished her from the community, and she had to relocate to a rickety shed on the fringe of the village.

Three months later, she was in labor. When the child was born, the widow was first terrified and then saddened, for it was nothing but a head, having no trunk or limbs. But, after all it was her son, so she reared him with motherly care and yet a heavy heart.

As the years went by, the head began to mature. One day, he said,

"Mom, I can help you now. I can open up the land, plow it, and farm it."

"How?" said his mother, perplexed, "since you don't have hands and feet."

"Don't you worry, mom," said the head boy. "You'll find out what I can do today. Put me in a bag and hang it on a tree. Then you may go back home to cook. After you finish, come to pick me up."

Though incredulous, the mother did what her son had asked her and went home. She was back before sunset, to find that the land had been prepared.

"How did you do it?" asked his mother.

The head boy, however, didn't say a word. Instead, he insisted that his mother take him home.

The next day, the same miracle happened: The head boy had tilled the land when his mother came to get him. Again, he refused to answer his mother's query. After that, his mother carried him to the fields every morning and picked him up at sunset, questioning him no more. In due course, the seeds germinated and grew into crops. Things were getting better and better for the mother and son.

One day a war broke out between Payayi, a heavenly god next in importance to the supreme deity Esha, and Payana, who was in charge of the underworld. Seeing that he could by no means beat his opponent, Payayi was desperate. He asked the Lahus to help him, promising to marry one of his seven daughters to the one who could defeat his enemy.

"If what he said is true, I can help," the head boy said to his mother, and urged her to let Payayi know of his intent.

"Nonsense," said his mother. "Even if you could win, do you think Payayi's daughter will marry you?"

But the head boy's words eventually reached Payayi, who sent for him and introduced him to the Lahus.

"It's a great day today because this head boy will fight with us against our common enemy." With that, Payayi put him in a bag, placed him on his horse, and led his army to the battlefield.

Since the head boy's departure, his mother had been worrying about his safety. Eventually she cried herself blind.

In the meantime, the wicked Payana, in the form of a vulture, had kidnapped Payayi's youngest daughter, Nala. The bad news stunned and demoralized Payayi. For a while, he didn't know what to do. Suddenly he remembered the head boy on the back of his horse and let him out of the bag.

The head boy dashed towards the enemy at the speed of light. His close combat with Payana kicked up black clouds that dimmed the sky and filled the air with terrifying rumblings. Finally, as the clouds dissipated and the sounds quieted down, the head boy emerged triumphant. With him was Payayi's beautiful daughter Nala, whom he had rescued from Payana.

Back home, Payayi talked with his daughters about honoring his promise to marry one of them to the head boy, who had helped him defeat his enemy. All felt disgusted except his youngest daughter, Nala.

"I will marry him," she said. "not only because our father needs to keep his promise, but also because I owe my life to him."

"Don't be silly," her sisters said. "How can you live with a man that's nothing but a mere head? To marry him is to ruin your life!"

"Thank you for your concern," responded Nala. "But I've made up my mind."

After their marriage, the newlyweds went back to the head boy's home, where his blind mother was expecting them. The head boy was very sad at his mother's loss of eyesight. Nala comforted him by vowing to take good care of her.

A Man with Only a Head

One day, Nala was going to shop in a nearby market and told the head boy that she would be back in no time. The head boy appeared to agree, but in fact he had a secret agenda. No sooner had Nala left than a full human figure slipped out of the head and trailed her. Then he arrived at the market in advance so as to watch her every move. After she finished shopping, he accosted her, "Hey, pretty girl! Do I look handsome to you?"

"Yes, you are handsome," said the unknowing Nala, "but I am married."

Assured that his wife was faithful, the head boy went back home ahead of her and slipped back into the head. When he heard her footsteps, he greeted her, "So you're back. Did you come across anyone on your way back?"

"Yes?"

"A handsome young man, right?"

"So?" Nala was baffled.

"He flirted with you, didn't he?"

"Yes, he did!" She was even more confounded.

"And you accepted it?"

"No! What's the matter with you today?" Nala began to lose her patience, "You are the one I love. When I have you as my husband, I can't love anyone else."

Satisfied with his wife's answer, the head boy stopped questioning her. On the next market day, however, he followed his wife again, and found nothing abnormal.

When another market day arrived, he decided to test her for the last time. He tagged along without her knowing, as before. This time, he went a little further: He pretended to harass her in the form of the same handsome young man.

"I told you I am married. Why are you still pestering me?"

"I can't help it because I like you."

"Let me tell you this: Next time you do this to me, I'll alert my husband. Then you'll know how he deals with you."

The young man made a face and left. When he got home, however, he could no longer find the head where he had been residing. It turned out that his blind mother had accidentally swept it into the hearth, where it was burned to ashes. When Nala returned home, she was alarmed to see the young man who had humiliated her in the marketplace. When he explained everything, her joy knew no bounds. She felt vindicated and rewarded.

After they learned that the head boy was in fact a normal, handsome young man, Nala's six sisters became envious and wanted to marry him all together. Nala found it difficult to say no to her sisters, but her husband thought otherwise.

"I must thank you all for your interest in me," he said to them. "But I've never loved you. I love Nala only because she has been faithful to me. We're already very happy, so we don't need you at all."

Hearing that, the ashamed sisters left, never to return. The couple loved each other all the more and lived happily thereafter with the aging mother.

Tales of Deities, Immortals, and Legendary Figures

Each of the Chinese ethnic minorities worships a number of gods, supernatural beings that never die, or heroes and heroines alleged to exist in history. Despite the varied nature of their divinity, they all have one thing in common: their unselfish devotion to the welfare of others. The region where the Sui live was "Blessed by Nine Immortals." Deities like "Zhang Guolao and Li Guolao" saved the Tujia from scorching suns. "Sax—Mother of the Dongs" led a valiant though failed revolt against oppression. "Liu Sanjie—A Fearless Folk Song Singer" of the Zhuang taught her foes a good lesson before they could get her. A She hero delivered his people from darkness, as related in "The Eyes of Heaven Reopened." The Maonan god "Tan Sanjiu" never quit trying to create a better world despite repeated frustrations. A Daur "Ginseng Boy" emancipated the debilitated serfs. Not all deities and heroes succeeded, but their deeds are remembered forever.

BLESSED BY NINE IMMORTALS

This tale is from the Sui. The 406,900 (China, 2002) Sui people live primarily in Guizhou and Guangxi. In the Sandu Sui Autonomous County in Guizhou, there is a Jiuqian Mountain. "Jiuqian" is local dialect for the Mandarin jiuxian, *or nine immortals, which are comparable to the* baxian *(eight immortals) in a tale from the Han Chinese.* The following story tells how the Jiuqian Mountain came to be.*

*O*nce upon a time, there was a land of a hundred square miles in what is known today as the Jiuqian region. It was densely covered with trees and grass, in which beasts and reptiles ran wild. Humans had never ventured to inhabit it since their creation.

One day, there came from the south a couple, the man named Gulong and the woman Zhahua. Gulong was diligent and courageous; Zhahua was clever and deft. They saw in this wilderness a big opportunity to create a better life for humans to come. So they built themselves a shed and settled down. Determined to turn the wasteland into a productive place for their children and grandchildren, they set to work to weed the land and hunt the wild animals and reptiles running amok. They worked tirelessly and fearlessly, day and night.

To their dismay, no matter how hard they worked, all their efforts were fruitless. The harder they tried to clear the weeds, the thicker and taller they grew. No sooner had they reclaimed a plot than it reverted to its original status. There seemed to be no hope at all. Disheartened, Zhahua said to her husband, "I'm afraid that Heaven doesn't want us to live here. Let's find another place."

"Our persistence and determination will eventually change Heaven's mind," said Gulong in an effort to conciliate his wife. "Let's hang in and work harder."

At this, Zhahua felt ashamed of her frailty. She went back to their shed and cried herself to sleep. In her dreams, she found herself in a wonderland, where pine trees stood tall, streams ran giggling, flowers bloomed in full, and hogs and cranes sang here and there. Then, in front of a crag in a wood of tall trees intertwined with vines, she saw nine white-haired and ruddy-faced immortals. Clustered around a stone table, some were playing chess while others were watching and chatting. Zhahua overheard their conversation.

One said, "I can't bear seeing Gulong and Zhahua bullied by the mud fish repeatedly."

The next contended, "The two goddesses of creation are to blame—the greedy Yahuani and the sleepy Yahuasa."

Another suggested, "We've got to guide the couple to the goddesses."

Still another added, "Tell them to find the goddesses at the Dragon Cave beside the deep pool."

Just then, Zhahua woke up. She rushed out to tell Gulong of her odd dream, but he told her he had had the same experience when he dozed off after she had left him. They decided to find the two goddesses and ask them to help subdue the mud fish demon that had made their labor futile.

After praying to heaven, earth, and their ancestors, as tradition dictated, they departed, bringing with them glutinous-rice cakes, a drum, a *hulusi* (pipe instrument made of a gourd), and a *suona* (Chinese horn). They trudged on for eighty-one days and nights. Along the way, they fought off numerous wild beasts and braved a variety of inclement weather. Their clothes were torn by twigs and their shoes worn by gravel. After passing through a ninety-mile-long brushwood of thistles and thorns and climbing up the nine-thousand-foot tall Mountain of the Moon, they finally reached the cave where the goddesses lived.

Gulong and Zhahua tiptoed into the cave. There they found two old women, one fast asleep and the other eating. Neither, however, noticed their intrusion. The couple was so happy to see the goddesses that they couldn't help playing the *hulusi* and *suona* and beating the drum, which startled the goddesses. When they saw the couple, they relaxed and invited them in. Zhahua immediately built a fire and began to toast the rice cakes she had brought with her. Gulong played his *hulusi* and *suona* again. When the cakes were ready, Gulong and Zhahua dropped to their knees and presented them to the goddesses. Then they told them about the mud fish demon and pleaded, "Please help us with your magic power!"

Convinced, the goddesses took the couple back to their homeland, riding on their magic cranes. Goddess Yahuasa set a magic fire to the brushwood and Goddess Yahuani used her magic hoe to till the reclaimed land. Gulong and Zhahua farmed it and had a bumper harvest that year. They decided to dedicate rice cakes to the goddesses and play drum and *hulusi* pipes to them as a token of thanks. And this has since become a tradition among the Sui people.

Later, Gulong and Zhahua gave birth to a son and a daughter, and named them Ayang and Ayue. Every day, they brought their children to the fields with them and let them play by themselves while they worked. Their life was modest but happy.

However, the mud fish demon wouldn't surrender. Soon it mobilized a calamitous hail storm, each hailstone as big as a buffalo's head. The hail destroyed Gulong and Zhahua's crops and demolished their house, but they wouldn't yield to the demon's atrocity. They relocated to a cave and set about salvaging their crops in the fields. Unfortunately, Gulong died of exhaustion a few days later. Zhahua refused to let the tragedy strike her down. She continued working while taking care of her children.

Finally, the nine immortals were so touched that they descended from heaven to assist Zhahua. Each used his unique magic skill and subdued the mud fish monster so that it fled into the mud and has never since dared to surface.

Years later, the children Ayang and Ayue each raised a family, which multiplied subsequently. With the help of the nine immortals, the families constructed canals, planted trees, built houses and barns, and set up mills to brew wine and press oil. Year after year and generation after generation, the descendants of Gulong and Zhahua built their homeland into a productive and beautiful one.

The nine immortals didn't return to heaven. Instead, they found it so hard to tear themselves away from this wonderful world of humans that they turned into nine hills and stayed, watching and guarding the Sui people forever. They came to be known as the Jiuqian (Nine Immortals) Mountain.

Courtesy of Dai Yuru and Yunnan Fine Arts Publishing House

---

* For details, see Haiwang Yuan, "Eight Immortals Crossing the Sea," in *The Magic Lotus Lantern and Other Tales from the Han Chinese* (Libraries Unlimited, 2006), 127–131.

ZHANG GUOLAO AND LI GUOLAO

This is a myth from the Tujia, whose 8,028,133 (China, 2002) people live in the Wuyi mountainous region adjoining Hunan, Sichuan, and Chongqing in Southern and Southwestern China. The main characters in this Tujia myth have an apparent connection to those in the famous Han Chinese tale "Eight Immortals Crossing the Sea." *

A long, long time ago, there were two creators: Zhang Guolao and Li Guolao. No sooner had they created the sky and the earth than a deluge struck and inundated the entire world for seven days and nights. As a result, the sky was torn into parts. Then the two creators reconstructed the sky and the earth, beating back the flood in the process.

However, the earth had become so sodden that nothing could grow in it any more. So Zhang Guolao and Li Guolao called in twelve suns to dry the earth, but their concerted heat nearly scorched it. Seeing this, a clever frog looked up and said, "This won't do! They are too many!" With that, he climbed up to a treetop, opened his big mouth, and started swallowing the suns.

The frog had already gulped eleven of the suns when Zhang Guolao hit the tree hard with his cane and caused it to bend. The frog was thrown off the tree and has never since been able to eat the sun, which has remained in the sky until today.

---

* For details, see Haiwang Yuan, "Eight Immortals Crossing the Sea," in *The Magic Lotus Lantern and Other Tales from the Han Chinese* (Libraries Unlimited, 2006), 127–131.

SAX—MOTHER OF THE DONGS

This is a legend from the Dong. Most of the 2,960,300 Dong (China, 2002) live in the provinces of Guizhou, Hunan, and Guangxi. The Dong worship Sax (also known as Sama, Sasui, and Saxiang), or "Great Grandmother." There is an altar or temple dedicated to this heroic deity in every Dong community, and they all celebrate a Sax festival every spring. The tale gives a glimpse of how the Han Chinese used to oppress the ethnic minorities.

There was once a poor man named Danggong in Wuzhou, Guangxi, who died at the hands of a rich bully and left his pregnant wife behind. After she gave birth to her son, she drowned herself in a river, in the hope of joining her husband in the other world. The orphaned baby boy was picked up by a Dong family named Wu, who made their living by fishing. They named him Wu Dunang ("*nang*" means "younger brother" in the Dong dialect). They attended to Dunang as they did their own son, Duqiang. As time went by, Dunang and Duqiang grew to be young men of great strength, and they learned martial arts from the elders.

One day, the region was hit by a big flood. Li Congshun, a rich Han man, tried to profit from the disaster by stealing land from the Dong. He could do so not only because he had money, but also because he was powerful; his son Li Dinglang was a magistrate of a town not far away.

Led by the brothers Dunang and Duqiang, the Dong revolted. Duqiang was killed in a battle, and soon their parents died of grief. The Dong had to move south along a river, fleeing from the persecution by the Li family. Bringing up the rear, Dunang found a young woman tagging along. Suddenly she fell and passed out, apparently from fatigue and starvation. After Dunang brought her back to life with water and food, the young woman told him her name was Yangxiang. Orphaned at an early age, she and her elder brother had been following the Dong to the south but somehow were separated from each other. She had been begging her way here, hoping to find her brother. The sympathetic Dunang decided to help her, and they resumed the journey together. When the Dong reached and settled in the south, Dunang and Yangxiang became husband and wife.

Though a loving couple, they remained childless for a decade. One night, the couple had the same dream, in which a bright star fell upon the roof of their house, followed by a white-haired grandma, who led a young girl to their home. Before long, Yangxiang gave birth to a baby girl and named her Biben, or "the girl who had flown to them." Biben began to learn martial arts at five, and as she grew, she became not only pretty, but also a skillful kung fu master. Her parents nicknamed her Xingni, meaning "fairy" in the Dong dialect, for they believed that she was the incarnation of Chang'e, the Moon Goddess.*

By then the Han Chinese, with Li Congshun in the lead, had caught up with the Dong in the south. The Dong again fell under their oppression and exploitation. Xingni's parents had to farm for Li Congshun because he had taken all the arable land in the region. One day Li attempted to assault her mother, Yangxiang. When her father, Dunang, came to her rescue, Li's henchmen attacked and killed him. Yangxiang grieved to death soon after, and Xingni barely escaped, with the help of an old man.

Climbing over several mountains, Xingni came to a flatland on a hill. She was about to sit and rest after days of trudging and plodding, when all of sudden a tiger swooped out of the woods. As she dodged its initial attack, the beast turned around and sprang to pounce upon her again, roaring and snarling. With all her might, Xingni clutched the beast in her arms, her head forcefully against its chin so it couldn't bite her with its wide-open mouth. She wrestled with the tiger, the two rolling in a tangle, neither able to get the upper hand of the other. Just then, an arrow came whistling and went straight into the tiger's eye. Giving a thunderous growl of pain, the beast let loose of Xingni and jerked back for a few steps before it dropped dead.

"What's your name, Sister?" asked a stout young man, who had launched the arrow that killed the tiger. "Why are you here alone?"

"My name's Xingni," she answered. "After my parents' death, I've been looking for my uncle, that is, my mother's brother."

"I'm Shidao," the young hunter introduced himself. "I lost my parents when I was young. I live in the Liujia village at the foot of the hill." With that, he led Xingni to his home, carrying the tiger's body on his back.

An elderly man came to visit Shidao. When he learned Xingni's name, he asked what her mother's name was.

"Yangxiang," she answered.

"My poor child, I'm your Uncle Jiuku."

Xingni threw herself into his arms and wept heartily. When she calmed down, Uncle Jiuku took her home and settled her there. The young hunter Shidao often came to see her, sharing his knowledge of archery with her, and she shared her martial arts with him. Eventually, they fell in love and got married.

One day the Dong were having a singing party, at which Xingni was selected the leading singer. The Dong were enjoying themselves when Li Congshun and his armed men arrived. He came to pick a pretty girl to become his seventh concubine. He was surprised to come across Xingni here, and he immediately took her to his mansion. Soon Uncle Jiuku and her husband Shidao rescued her. Anticipating Li Congshun's retaliation, Uncle Jiuku asked Xingni and Shidao to flee to a faraway place.

After tramping over nine mountains, Xingni and her husband came to a village at dusk. They didn't venture into the village for fear that they would be tracked down by Li Congshun and his men. So they hid in a nearby wood until the next morning. When they approached the village, they ran into an elderly woman, and asked her what village this was and if there were any villagers related to the Li family in it.

"This is Shiluo village, and my name is Satianpa," the elderly woman told them. Pausing a little, she went on, "All the villagers are as good as you are, and you'll be okay."

Leading them a few yards farther, she added, "Though my home is small, you are welcome to live with me."

"Thank you so much, granny," said the couple, "but this may cause you and your family trouble."

"No trouble at all," said the elderly woman. "I live alone. I've no one else in my family."

The couple stayed with her and treated her like their parent. Later, the couple gave birth to two daughters, one called Jiaju and the other Jiamei. Xingni taught them to sing and Shidao instructed them in martial arts.

Shiluo village did not have enough water for all the people, so Xingni and her husband set about helping the villagers to expand the well in front of the village into a pond so it could collect rainwater. As they dug, they found two swords wedged firmly in a crevice at the rocky bottom of the well. The villagers tried to pull them out, but failed. When Xingni and her husband gave it a try, they removed them with little effort. The blades of the swords were very sharp, each with the words "Sword of Nine Dragons" engraved on it. Hence the villagers named the large body of water they had created "Nine Dragon Pond." The pond not only had water but also plenty of fish.

Xingni and her husband opened up wasteland for themselves as well as their fellow villagers with the swords. In time, both arable lands and fishing ponds multiplied. Since they had more than they needed, they started inviting people outside their village to share with them, and in so doing, they unwittingly invited trouble as well.

Word of Shiluo village soon reached Li Congshun. One day he came with scores of armed men, called the villagers together, and said to them, "The entire mountain, including your village, the well, and the swords—all belong to me. By changing the well into a pond and removing the swords from it, you hurt my family's dragon vein. You must restore the well to its original condition and the swords back to its bottom. Besides, you must pay me indemnity for what you've done. You must turn in two thousand baskets of fish and ten thousand pounds of grain each year."

The villagers held back their anger without daring to speak out. Satianpa, the granny who had adopted Xingni and her husband Shidao, however, stood up against the bully Li Congshun. She argued, "Our Shiluo village used to belong to the Miaos. They left it to us because they didn't like its *fengshui* (geographic location in connection with their luck).

You have just arrived here. How can you claim the village to be yours? If we give so much of our fish and grain to you, what's left for us?"

Upon hearing the protest, Li Congshun kicked Satianpa hard in the chest and killed her. Then he and his men fled before the enraged villagers could engulf them.

Xingni and the villagers vowed to avenge Satianpa. They were fed up with the Li family's tyranny, and it was high time they vented their pent-up anger. Swords in hand, Xingni and Shidao led the villagers to Danyang village, where Li Congshun's new mansion was located. Before Li Congshun could escape, Xingni cut him down with her sword. Then she asked the villagers to build fortifications outside the village, knowing that Magistrate Li Dinglang would not forgive his father's slaying. Sure enough, he ordered his 8,000-strong army to attack Danyang village. They were about to storm into it when heaven seemed to collapse. Drums thundered and gongs boomed. Logs and stones came crashing down. The unwary soldiers were so terrified that they scampered in all directions. In the confusion, many of them fell into the traps that Xingni and the villagers had laid for them. Only half of the troops got away.

Magistrate Li Dinglang sent a messenger to the capital to lie to the emperor about the Dong rebellion. The emperor gave him 80,000 soldiers as reinforcements. The war dragged on for nine years and nine months, until the land was laid barren and food was in short supply. The villagers had to fill their stomachs with bark and weeds.

What's more, Li Dinglang dispatched a spy into the rebels' camp, where he managed to stain the powerful swords with wolf's blood, which rendered them useless. Consequently, defeat began to dog Xingni and her husband Shidao. They lost one battle after another, and the number of Dong fighters diminished sharply. The Dong had to retreat to a strategic location deep in a mountain, where they hoped they could hold their ground. Li Dinglang and his army followed them closely and surrounded the mountain in an attempt to wipe them out. As the encirclement tightened, a fierce battle ensued. Xingni's husband Shidao died in action. Xingni and the survivors had to retreat to the mountaintop. There, after several bloody battles, only Xingni and her two daughters were left. Xingni then told them to stand on the summit as bait while she hid behind a boulder close by. Li Dinglang had barely gotten hold of the girls when the mother sprang out and halved him with a single slash.

As the enemies closed in and forced Xingni and her daughters to the edge of the cliff, Xingni held their little hands in hers and said to them in grief and indignation, "If we die, we'll do so on our territory and be buried in our water. We will never allow our bodies to be dragged to the enemy's land."

Looking up at their mother, the daughters said with stoical calmness, "We're with you live or dead!"

With that, the three threw themselves off the cliff and down into the river running through the valley. The Dong believe to this day that they were saved by an elderly man and died natural deaths later.

Dong "wind and rain bridge"

---

* See the tale "The Origin of the Mid-Autumn Festival," in Haiwang Yuan, *The Magic Lotus Lantern and Other Tales from the Han Chinese* (Libraries Unlimited, 2006).

LIU SANJIE—A FEARLESS FOLK SONG SINGER

The Zhuang, with a population of 16,178,800 (China, 2002), is the largest ethnic mi-nority in China. The Zhuang primarily live in Guangxi, Guangdong, and Yunnan. This oral tradition has found its way into the romances, dramas, and county annals of the Miao, Yao, Buyei, Mulao, and Han due to cultural diffusion (the spread of different cultures into each other's societies). The Zhuang version became known nationwide thanks to a famous movie produced in 1961.

A melodious song broke the silence of a serene morning on a green river. The song came from a beautiful young woman on a fishing boat. She was Liu Sanjie, literally "Third Sister of the Liu Family." Orphaned at an early age, she was raised by her brother Liu Er, who was honest but shy and timid, so much so that everyone thought him too much of a pushover. Liu Sanjie, on the contrary, was smart and courageous. She was known to use her taunting songs to castigate those whom she considered abusive and bullying. She was therefore very popular among average Zhuang people but hated by those lording over them.

Now, Liu Sanjie and her brother Liu Er had to flee from their homeland. She had been involved in a singing duel with a local despot in her hometown. The despot had died of a heart attack during the contest, in which Liu Sanjie relentlessly reprimanded him with her sarcastic songs for his evil doing. Blaming his death on Liu Sanjie, the tyrant's family bribed the local authorities to make her pay for his life. Liu Sanjie and her brother were on their way by boat to their grandmother's village to seek refuge.

When she and her brother landed, they were caught in a dispute between a bully and a young fisherman. It turned out that the bully was Mo Fu, a servile follower of the tyrannical village head, named Mo Huairen. Mo Fu claimed that since the river belonged to his master, everything caught from it was to be taxed. A young man stepped out of the crowd, which was choked with silent fury, and reasoned with the henchman, saying that the rivers and mountains belonged to none but the villagers at large. When challenged to a physical fight, the young man simply threw Mo Fu to the ground, amid cheers from the villagers, who now

---

vented their pent-up anger. Liu Sanjie learned that the young man's name was Li Xiaoniu and felt drawn to him.

As Liu Sanjie and the villagers were laughing at the embarrassment of Mo Fu, Mo Huiren's steward Mo Jincai came along. Brandishing his fist at the fisherman and his defender, Mo Jincai fumed, "Every fish in the water and every tree on the mountain in the area belongs to our master Mo Huiren. He certainly owns whatever you get from them! If you dare to challenge his authority, he'll prevent you from using them at all!"

At this, Liu Sanjie could no longer remain silent. She sang:

> *Since nature is the Creator's offspring,*
> *To us all, what it offers is belonging.*
> *Those who love fish board your boats;*
> *Those who like pheasants draw your bows.*

Finding it hard to rebut Liu Sanjie, both Mo Fu and Mo Jincai took to their heels, frustrated and humiliated. Liu Sanjie's reputation for repelling two bullies with a single song spread in the village. Villagers flocked to her to learn how to sing.

Sanjie enjoyed *duige* with her peers from the village while picking tea leaves in the tea plantation. In *duige*, two parties sing alternatively, like a conversation. When challenged to a *duige*, Liu Sanjie started metaphorically,

> *Sing to your heart's content,*
> *Row till your muscles relent,*
> *Barge poles in your hands, oars in mine,*
> *I'll race you anywhere to the finish line.*

The young women responded with a salvo of tough questions:

> *What crop has seeds on the top?*
> *What crop has seeds at the waist?*
> *What crop has seeds in pairs?*
> *What crop has seeds harvested by caning?*

Without hesitation, Liu Sanjie gave the answer:

> *Sorghum has seeds on the top,*
> *Corn has seeds at the waist,*
> *Beans have pods in pairs,*
> *And sesame seeds are harvested by caning.*

The girls admired Liu Sanjie's quick wit and continued the test of intellect:

> *What has a mouth but speaks not?*
> *What has no mouth but speaks a lot?*
> *What has feet but walks not?*
> *What is without feet but travels a lot?*

Liu Sanjie's response was prompt:

> *A puppet has a mouth but speaks not,*
> *A drum has no mouth but sounds a lot,*
> *A rich man has feet but hates to walk,*
> *A boat has no feet but travels a lot.*

The girls again thought highly of Liu Sanjie's quick thinking but wouldn't quit easily. They fired another series of questions at her:

> *What does somersaults on the water?*
> *What raises a high tower on the water?*
> *What extends an umbrella on the water?*
> *What lives in conjugal bliss on the water?*

Undeterred by the seemingly difficult inquires, Liu Sanjie replied readily:

> *Ducks do somersaults on the water,*
> *Boats raise decks of tower on the water,*
> *Lotus leaves extend umbrellas on the water,*
> *And mandarin ducks live in conjugal bliss on the water.*

The girls' pastime was interrupted abruptly by the arrival of Mo Jincai with a poster that read: "Real Estate of the Mo Family!" Planting it in the ground on the edge of the tea plantation, he arrogantly proclaimed, "You all listen carefully! This plantation has a new owner now! The village head Mo Huairen is going to use this piece of land as his ancestral burial ground. Get out of here and never return!"

The tea growers were enraged at Mo Huairen's blatant robbery. With Liu Sanjie in the lead, they were determined not to give in. Condemning the plunderous act of Mo Huairen, Liu Sanjie sang:

> *The plantation was once a sterile land,*
> *Where beasts and serpents rampant ran.*
> *It was the tea growers' labor of sweat*
> *That turned the poor land into fertile soil.*
> *Now the only source of their income,*

Each tea leaf bears witness to their toil,
Taking their plantation as you do
Makes you nothing but a greedy man!

"How dare you call my master a greedy man? You'll pay for your insolence!" Mo Jincai threatened. Not to be intimidated, Liu Sanjie went on scoffing,

With good reasons I even dare to curse the emperor,
I fear the least your master the brazen plunderer!

As the emboldened tea growers inched toward the steward, he recoiled. While retreating, he threatened that his master would deal with Liu Sanjie soon.

When he learned of his steward's mortification at the hands of a young woman, Mo Huairen flew into a rage. Slapping Mo Jincai in the face, he roared, "How could you allow a brat like her to stand up to my authority like that? You should have taught her a good lesson!"

"It could've led to a riot," argued the steward.

"Drive her away then!" The village head was apparently losing patience.

"But how can we let her off so easily?" The steward murmured, trying to find a way to get rid of Liu Sanjie. When his eyes fell upon a bird cage hanging from the ceiling, a sinister idea dawned upon him. He said, "How about making her a concubine of yours? Then she'll be confined in this mansion like that poor thing . . . ."

"And in time, she'll lose all the steam of her rebellious spirit," Mo Huairen chuckled, "Hum, that's a marvelous idea of yours! Go and get her!"

Meanwhile, Liu Sanjie and Li Xiaoniu, the young man who had defended the fishermen, had fallen in love. They were mending their fishing nets together when a matchmaker arrived. Sent by Mo Jincai, she came to propose marriage on behalf of the village head. Liu Sanjie dismissed the village head's intent as daydreaming and made the matchmaker an object of ridicule in her song:

You and your master are a match,
Like a spotted monkey with a boar,
Get yourself ready for the happy occasion,
I can't wait to marry you out of my door!

As the humiliated matchmaker was searching for words, Mo Huairen himself showed up. He had been too impatient to wait at home. Angry as he was at Liu Sanjie's bitter rejection, he tried to restrain his annoyance for fear that she might not take the bait. He began to lavish flattery after flattery upon her, against his will. Liu Sanjie knew only too well what this hypocrite was up to, and quickly came up with an idea: She challenged Mo Huairen to a *duige* contest.

"If you win," she said, "I will become your concubine willingly."

Mo Huairen had not expected the clever Liu Sanjie to be so gullible. He was confident he would win the contest hands down; for he could hire the best singers in the world with his money. He took the challenge readily and was about to leave with secret satisfaction when Liu Sanjie stopped him, saying, "If you lose, you are never to harass the villagers again."

"Fine!" Mo Huairen agreed, believing that she had no chance to win.

When the day for the singing duel arrived, the entire village turned out and gathered at the river, where important events were held regularly. Mo Huairen had hired three pedants, who claimed to know all the songs in the world. The books they brought with them filled a large part of the boat in which they traveled. Knowing that their opponent was but a country girl, they became more certain of their victory.

Equally confident, Liu Sanjie kicked off the contest by singing:

> *No matter how much you've read,*
> *If you can glide, then I can wing;*
> *I'm like a wasp above a tortoise head,*
> *Dare you stick it out and I will sting.*

After a few rounds, the mercenary pedantic scholars began to feel Liu Sanjie's strength, but they wouldn't take it lying down. Racking their brains and leafing through their books, they were looking frantically for songs that they hoped could help them turn the tables. Eventually, one of them seemed to have found a lifesaver and used it in his song:

> *Tell us, you smart girl, without delay:*
> *How many nails you can find in our boat,*
> *How much the mountains yonder weigh,*
> *How many grains there are in a basket of oats.*

However, the bright Liu Sanjie didn't hesitate and sang back with her answers:

> *You are right when you call me smart,*
> *I'll count the nails if you tear your boat apart,*
> *I'll weigh the mountains, lift them up if you can,*
> *Oats are measured by the gram not the grain.*

Another pedant stepped forward, hoping to silence Sanjie once and for all with a song he found in one of the books piled up behind him:

> *Flaunt not your cleverness anymore;*
> *Can you divide 300 dogs by four,*
> *Without leaving an odd number?*
> *I dare you to give a correct answer.*

Without even blinking, Liu Sanjie retorted:

> *Unleash ninety-nine dogs into the streets,*
> *Confine another ninety-nine in a house,*
> *Use another ninety-nine to guard the gate,*
> *Leaving you three the victims of my mockery!*

Disillusioned with the performance of the good-for-nothing pedants he had hired, Mo Huiren could not but join the battle in person. Shoving them aside, he stepped forward on the bow and hollered:

> *How much is your singing worth?*
> *A fabulous fortune I have by birth.*
> *With whatever it takes of my gold,*
> *Your songs I will forever withhold.*

Liu Sanjie chuckled contemptuously and retaliated:

> *You may be wealthy and powerful,*
> *Of plunder your money makes you capable,*
> *But my mouth you may never take away,*
> *With songs I'll fight you day by day.*

After the disastrous *duige* contest, the village head shut himself in his mansion, trying to find a way to avenge his humiliation. When he learned from the steward that the villagers were planning to celebrate Liu Sanjie's victory, he bribed the magistrate and obtained from him a decree to ban the villagers' gathering, charging Liu Sanjie with defying the authorities.

When news came that Mo Huairen had obtained help from the magistrate, Liu Er suggested that Liu Sanjie be absent from the party. Liu Sanjie wouldn't listen, and her fiancé Li Xiaoniu vowed to protect her. The party went on despite the ban. Wave after wave of singing sprang up with renewed intensity. With Liu Sanjie in the lead, the villagers chanted in chorus:

> *Our songs are loud and their messages clear:*
> *Imprisonment may rob us of our freedom dear,*
> *But our mouths you can never take away,*
> *Your ban will prove to be a wasted power play.*

The party over, the villagers began to worry about Liu Sanjie's safety. They knew Mo Huairen would definitely retaliate. Indeed, he managed to get the magistrate to send his men to get Liu Sanjie. The villagers urged her to keep out of harm's way temporarily. Liu Sanjie bid them farewell and embarked on a boat with Li Xiaoniu, while her brother Liu Er preferred staying behind. Liu Sanjie left a trail of songs as the couple drifted along the river. In no time, the songs spread throughout the region where the Zhuang people lived.

Courtesy of Dai Yuru and Yunnan Fine Arts Publishing House

THE EYE OF HEAVEN REOPENED

This is a myth from the She, who have a population of 709,600 (China, 2002). The She people are scattered in Fujian, Zhejiang, and Guangdong and speak a tongue of the Sino-Tibetan language family similar to Hakka, one of the Mandarin dialects.

*A*t the very beginning, the sky was blue and clear, and it was closer to the earth as well. The vault of heaven looked like a gigantic mirror of sapphire. In it, there was the reflection of mountains, trees, rivers, and plains on the earth.

One day, a burst of violent wind sprang up in the west, causing rivers to surge and dust to fly. The wind was raging for seven days and eight nights, when there appeared clusters of black clouds with a yellow skirt around each. As the clouds expanded, the sun began to lose its luster.

Everyone on earth was worried, fearing that it was the precursor of a calamity. Some went to fortune-tellers and others prayed at home—all asked the heavenly gods or Buddha to help them fend off the imminent disaster.

Despite what people did, the dark clouds kept rolling on and eventually filled the entire sky. It became pitch dark, rain began pouring down, and the entire world turned into one rumbling mass of chaos. People ran for their lives, but in their hurry-scurry, some were trampled to death. Many of those who survived eventually succumbed to starvation. The rest holed up in caves, where they made wild guesses about what had caused the ominous clouds.

At the time, there lived a mother and son in Dongfeng village at the foot of Phoenix Mountain. The son was a brave and strong hunter named Yongnan. Not long after they escaped into a cave, the mother died of an illness caused by the inclement wind and rain brought on by the clouds. After burying his mother, Yongnan was determined to rid his people of the disaster and bring light back to them. He racked his brain day and night, trying to find a way to disperse the clouds. He thought and thought until wrinkles crept up his forehead and gray hairs grew all over his head.

One day, Yongnan saw a long-bearded old man and asked him about the dark clouds. The old man seemed to turn a deaf ear to him. Yongnan then cried, tears dripping into the brows and beard of the old man, who then opened his mouth.

"In the far, far west," he said slowly, "there's a Double-dragon Mountain. Two nine-horned dragons of drought live on top of it. They have sharpened their magic power after 990 years of practice. They are vomiting billows of smoke at present. Soon they'll spit fire and lay dragon eggs. When that happens, the entire world will become a sea of fire, hot enough to melt stones."

Yongnan pledged to the old man that he would give up anything to get rid of the vicious nine-horned dragons of drought.

The old man said to him, "Courageous as you are, you need a magic weapon to accomplish the task."

"Where can I get one?" Yongnan asked.

After telling him where, the elder turned into a golden phoenix and disappeared with a puff. Following the old man's instructions, Yongnan managed to get a large piece of wood used for a doorsill and burned it three times. In its ashes, he found a sword of double blades. With it, Yongnan set out for the west to seek the two nine-horned dragons of drought.

On the way, he asked about the dragons' exact location. After trekking over ninety-nine hills and across ninety-nine rivers, he arrived at a place where he encountered a white-browed old woman. Seeing that she paid no attention to him, Yongnan wept again, and tears ran into her white brows. Holding out three fingers, the old woman started to talk, "I originally had three sons, each more capable than you are. Months ago, they went to fight the dragons, but none has returned."

Again, Yongnan promised that he would do anything to kill the malicious dragons. The old woman then pulled a hair out, turned it into a long band, and tied it around Yongnan's waist. As she did so, she warned Yongnan against untying it before he killed the dragons. "Or you'll be burned to ashes by the fire in the dragons' lair." With this, she turned into a golden phoenix and fluttered toward the west.

Yongnan resumed his journey. His steps were much lighter than before, and the wind passed whistling by, as if he were traveling in the air. Before long, he saw red lights shooting out from the horizon. When he came closer, a mountain with a barren peak blocked him. A few dozen yards from the mountain, there stood a big monument with the inscription on it, "Territory of Dragon Kings. No admission to men and animals!"

Seeing it, Yongnan felt both relieved and angry. He was relieved because he had finally found the whereabouts of the monstrous dragons. He was angry because he was reminded of all the sufferings these malicious beasts had inflicted upon his people. With a hard kick, he smashed the monument, its ashes dissipating in the air.

Dusting off the ashes that fell on his clothes, Yongnan headed for the mountain. Then a river of bubbling blood stopped him. Undeterred, Yongnan rolled up his pants and stepped into the sanguine fluid. As he set his feet in the river, the boiling hot blood first reached his knees and then his thighs. The burning he felt was as excruciating as would be caused by the bites of poisonous centipedes. Without fear, Yongnan pressed on. Strangely, the blood subsided quickly with each step forward, and soon the river revealed a bed of pebbles. After crossing it and clambering up to the mountaintop, Yongnan heard a harsh voice, "Caw, caw, caw. You're here to die!"

Looking up, Yongnan saw a raven standing on a stone column several dozen feet high. As big as a buffalo, the bird stared at him with its big yellow eyes. Yongnan gave the column a kick and it collapsed to its foundation, burying the raven under the rubble. When it struggled out, the raven told Yongnan that the dragons were on the top of Double-dragon Mountain. Begging for its life, it offered to show him the way. The trusting Yongnan relented, but the treacherous raven led him into a trap. He had walked only a few steps when his feet became snared in a web set by demonic serpents. Then a fiery snake with nine heads curled up his legs from the ground.

Above him, the raven crowed gloatingly, "Caw, caw, caw. The snake is going to pull your guts out, and I'll gouge out your eyes at the same time!"

The creepy and crawling snake on Yongnan's legs was about to reach his waist when the waistband he was wearing started to emit an intensely focused beam of light. It was so sharp that it cut off the snake's nine heads. Before the raven had a chance to flee, Yongnan wielded his double-headed sword, and whoosh, whoosh, whoosh slashed it into pieces. Untangling himself from the snake's dead body, Yongnan pressed on. In no time, he had reached the mountaintop.

"Ribbit, ribbit!" Suddenly, Yongnan heard a croak so loud that even the mountain quaked. He traced the sound to a humongous toad sitting languidly at the opening of a cave. When Yongnan asked it to make way for him, the toad refused. Glaring at him with its popping red eyes as big as baskets, it said in defiance,

"I'm the Toad King of the Mountain Front. I've gulped down a thousand dragon slayers. Who are you that dare . . . ?"

"Step aside, Toad. Make way so I can finish my task in time! Or I'll deal with you first," Yongnan cut the toad short and demanded.

"Hah, hah," the toad chuckled, but wouldn't budge an inch.

Before Yongnan let his sword fall, the toad drew a deep breath, blew up its cheeks, and let the air go abruptly. Tens of thousands of wasps burst out of the toad's big mouth and flocked around Yongnan, trying to sting him. As Yongnan brandished his double-bladed sword, the wasps lost their wings and fell, their bodies piling up in a mound. The toad then spewed forth innumerable poisoned arrows. With his sword, Yongnan bounced them back so they were thickly planted on the back of the toad. The amused Yongnan was about to finish the toad when it stuck out its forked tongue of ninety yards long, trying to clamp onto him. Dodging this sudden attack in time, Yongnan plunged his blades into the toad's tongue. The toad felt so much pain that it pulled it back. Taking advantage of the force of retraction, Yongnan let his sword go, and it went deep into the monster's mouth and finished it.

Yongnan removed his sword from the toad's body and entered the damp and eerie cave. Body parts were littered everywhere, reeking of rotten flesh. Yongnan didn't balk. Climbing over a stone wall blocking his path, he came to a totally different world. It was unspeakably bright and expansive. Soon he entered a bamboo forest, where he saw a pretty young woman. She told Yongnan she was the daughter of God of Phoenix Mountain, and her name was Ninan. She carried a two-headed hammer, just as Yongnan had his two-bladed sword. She told him she was the long-bearded old man and the white-browed old woman who had helped him. She said she wanted to assist him in his fight against the dragons. Together, they passed through the cave and arrived at the foot of Double-dragon Mountain.

The mountain had a single peak, flat on its top, as if surrounded by ninety-nine walls. Fire burning all over the mountain sent flames as high as 900 feet. The two nine-horned dragons of drought were perching on the mountaintop throwing up into the sky billow after billow of pitch-black smoke mixed with sparks of fire.

Seeing this, the indignant Yongnan couldn't resist the urge for vengeance. He was about to charge at the dragons when Ninan stopped him, saying, "The dragons are too powerful to fight with force only. Let's have a short break first and see what tactics we can come up with."

Then she produced a sparkling and bluish green pearl out of her headband, took a deep breath, and exhaled toward the mountain, casting the pearl to its summit. The trajectory of the pearl soaring up formed a dashing white light like that of a comet. Immediately before landing, the pearl increased in size and caught the attention of the dragons. Each of them tried to claim it as its own, and they got into a fierce fight. They were thus bounced back and forth between their mountain and another one nearby.

After watching them battling for a while, Ninan said to Yongnan, "Now it's time we get to the top."

The fire on the mountain hurt their feet like a million knives, but they were undaunted. After they took a few steps, however, there came a breath of cool wind from nowhere, and the fire was put out instantly. In its wake, a path of normal temperature appeared before them. Yongnan and Ninan reached the top of Double-dragon Mountain unscathed.

Only then did the dragons notice their invasion, too late. Before they could disengage from their battle and turn to attack, Ninan had repelled the smoke they spit, and Yongnan had jumped onto their heads and stuck his sword into them. Even when breathing their last breaths, the dragons were still tossing their tails vehemently in an attempt to lash their slayers. Having anticipated the death struggle, Ninan pounded the dragons' lower bodies with her two-headed hammer and broke their bones. The blood of one dragon streaming down the mountain has since painted its rocks burgundy. The blood of the other spattered on the tree leaves has since colored them bright red.

Looking up at the sky, Yongnan said to Ninan, "The dragons are dead alright, but the clouds are still there. If we don't disperse them, our people will be in the dark as before."

Smiling, Ninan pointed at Yongnan's waist and said, "Brother Yongnan, untie your five-colored waistband. Ride on it, and you'll be able to reach the sky and break up the clouds!"

Ninan then threw another pearl into the sky in the east, and there it remained, shedding a beam of sparkling and bluish green light. Untying his waistband, Yongnan flung it a few times before it became a rainbow. Upon it, Yongnan hurried to the sky. The two laughed heartily as they worked to drive away the dark clouds, and their laughter soon reached the earth.

Upon hearing it, people rushed out of their hiding places, torches still in hand. When they looked up, they saw the shining pearl in the sky and knew it was the herald of daybreak.

"Eye of Heaven is going to open," they said to one another.

People were looking up and waiting when, all of a sudden, a ray of bright, silvery light shone upon them through the pitch-dark clouds, almost dazzling their eyes. In its wake there came a deafening rumbling. A loud crack followed and tore the sky open, revealing the blue vault that people had missed so much. They were bursting with joy and started to sing, dance, and laugh. Tears of delight rolled down their bony cheeks as they shouted, "Look! Eye of Heaven is reopened! Eye of Heaven is reopened!"

The silvery light kept shooting across the sky and the rumble continued echoing in its wake. Meanwhile, the dark clouds were disintegrating into smaller clusters and scurried to the horizon. In the flashes, people spotted Yongnan and Ninan courageously driving the dark clouds away with their sword and hammer. At long last, the sky cleared again. Surprisingly, after the ordeal, the sky seemed much higher than before. It no longer resembled a large mirror capable of reflecting things on the ground.

The sun rose and cast its warmth onto the earth, and everything came back to life again. Yongnan and Ninan were sweating after days and nights of hard work. Ninan rubbed her forehead and tossed the beads of sweat off it. To her surprise, the beads all became stars. Curious, Yongnan did the same, and his perspiration also became stars.

Later, Yongnan and Ninan picked a lucky day and got married. It's believed that they are still living in the sky, helping people to look after the Eye of Heaven. To this day, when the sky is overcast, they will start driving away the clouds with their sword and hammer, until a rainbow emerges on the horizon. The rainbow is said to be Yongnan's waistband.

TAN SANJIU—A GOD OF PERSEVERANCE

This is a folktale from the Maonan. The 107,200 (China, 2002) Maonan people live primarily in Guizhou and Guangxi. The tale tells of their hero, Tan Sanjiu, who may not have been as successful as he wanted to be, but whose perseverance won the Maonan people's respect.

*T*he Maonan people had long been living in the mountains, where rivers were few and the water supply was inadequate. Drought was a constant threat. Tan Sanjiu wanted to create a lake large enough to hold a sea of water. So he set about leveling the mountains with a bamboo chopper. He worked nonstop day and night. He was so busy that he even begrudged going home to eat. Instead, he asked his wife to send him meals every day.

Seeing him chopping the mountains with a tool made of bamboo, she thought he was silly. But instead of saying anything about it, she let him have his way, until one day she could no longer contain herself. While he was burying himself in digging, she blurted out, "It's so foolish of you to hack the mountain with a chopper of bamboo!"

Tan Sanjiu was startled, and his shudder broke the bamboo chopper. Consequently, he wasn't able to flatten the mountain any more.

Undeterred by the incident, he decided to drive the mountain away altogether. While he was steering the rocks, his wife sent him food as usual, but made sure that she didn't utter a word to jeopardize his efforts. However, a stingy rich man and a corrupt official conspired to do just that. They hated to see him succeed. If he did, it would end their source of extra income, gained from hoarding grains or overtaxing the people under the pretext of fighting the drought.

One day, Tan Sanjiu was goading a large flock of rocks onward when the two vicious men's wives appeared. Sanjiu asked, "Have you seen a horde of cattle in front of me?"

The rich man's wife remained silent, waiting for the official's wife to answer, as their husbands had plotted. The official's wife finally responded with an incantation, "Cattle we didn't see, but we spied a lot of rocks."

At that, the rocks that Tan Sanjiu was herding stopped rolling. Despite the setback, he refused to give up. He went to seek help from the twelve dragons. He invited them to come and rain early the next morning when roosters began to crow.

But the rich man's wife had found out Tan Sanjiu's plan. At midnight, she slapped her fatty buttocks with a large palm fan to make a lot of noise. By doing so, she hoped to frighten the roosters perching in their roosts. Sure enough, the frightened birds began to crow all at once. Only two of the dragons were courageous enough to come. They have since become the Huan and the Eastern Rivers, draining the area that the Maonans inhabit.

GINSENG BOY

This is a tale from the Daur, who have a population of 132,400 (China, 2002). For historical reasons, the Daur live in two locations that are far apart: Inner Mongolia in Northern China and Xinjiang in the northwest.

*L*otus Lake used to drain into Deer-watering River to its south. The areas on both sides of the river were covered with forests and grasslands teeming with rare animals and birds. The fertile land nourished not only all kinds of flowers, but also ginseng and *lingzhi* (glossy ganodermas)—herbs that help the weak become strong and the sick recover faster.

Living in one of the forests was a couple, fugitive serfs of an oppressive prince. The husband was called Aoji and the wife was named after the medicinal herb *lingzhi*. While the husband hunted in the forest, the wife took care of the family chores at home.

After a year, they had a boy. Since Aoji had just found a big ginseng, they named the newborn "Ginseng Boy." When he grew to be eight years old, he began to demonstrate a talent for playing the flute. Whenever he did so, birds would stop singing, and fish would jump dancing out of the water. He was often seen riding on the back of a deer.

Aoji and Lingzhi never forgot their fellow serfs, still suffering on the prince's estate. Now that Ginseng Boy was old enough to help, they asked him to send their spare food and meat to the serfs. To get to the prince's estate, Ginseng Boy had to trek over Hala Mountain. But he never faltered. The food he sent kept many of the surfs alive. When he told his parents that the serfs looked haggard and skeletal, they had him take the serfs ginseng and *lingzhi*, which soon brought their health back.

Seeing his serfs look better, the cruel prince was very angry. He sent his chief steward to find out what had caused this to happen.

One day, Ginseng Boy came again, bringing with him fried millet and cooked meat, as well as the medicinal herbs. He was almost at the serfs' working site when the steward and his men in ambush rushed out and jumped at him. The boy gave the deer a spur, and it sprang to its feet, flew over the encirclement, and scampered away, carrying him to safety.

The wrathful prince made the serfs dig a number of pits to trap the boy when he came the next time. The serfs had no alternative but to pray secretly for the boy not to come. But

---

one night, under the cover of darkness, Ginseng Boy came again, bringing a great deal of food and medicinal herbs. He and his deer had just gone a few miles when they fell into the traps. The steward and his men lying in wait caught the boy and took him to the prince.

The prince coaxed him at first, hoping to get him to reveal the hideout of his parents. When Ginseng Boy refused to open his lips, the prince had him beaten black and blue while he was hung upside down from a crossbeam.

Aoji and Lingzhi were terribly worried by their boy's disappearance. For three days and nights, they stood at the riverside, expecting him to return. Affected by their emotions, flowers lowered their heads; birds moaned above them; fish lay quiet at the bottom of the waters; and deer wept as they clustered around. Aoji decided to go and look for him. He was about to set off when a flock of deer came galloping. As the dust settled, they saw their son riding the leading buck and their fellow serfs on the rest. It turned out that the serfs had rescued the Ginseng Boy and nurtured him back to health with the medicinal herbs he had brought them.

Aoji and Lingzhi settled the serfs on the fertile land by the river, and they started a new life of freedom. In time, the vicious prince learned of the secret wonderland. He surprised the serfs and enslaved them again. To teach them a lesson, he ordered Aoji and Lingzhi to be drowned in the lake. Then he and his crew hunted every day, driving the otherwise carefree birds and animals into the recesses of the forests and mountains.

Ginseng Boy had gone to the mountains to collect medicinal herbs and escaped the onslaught. Grieved by the news of his parents' death, he played his bamboo flute to find solace. The flute music, however, called in millions of deer. The terrified prince and his men began to flee. With Ginseng Boy in the lead, the horde of deer caught up and ran them over. Then the boy led the deer on a long march toward the east, where they were to find a new home.

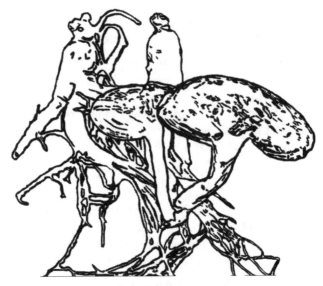

Ginseng and *lingzhi* (glossy ganoderma)

Magic Tales

The magic world may not be real, but magic stories mirror how people see and deal with reality, where hope and despair go hand in hand. "A Giant and a One-eyed Fairy" from the Derung became the first account of human mortality. The Lisu associate day and night with their ancient "Mother Who Drives the Sun." "Ah Dang Seeks the Seed of Fire" so his fellow Hui can have cooked food to eat. "The Toad General" of the Gin still cherishes a hope that the weak can eventually beat the strong. "Adventures of Aba Dani," a hero of Lhoba, reveals humankind's vulnerability to self-conceit. "Humans and a Gourd" illustrates the De'ang survival of many misfortunes.

A GIANT AND A ONE-EYED FAIRY

This is a tale from the Derung. The majority of the 7,400 (China, 2002) Derung people live in the Derung River Valley in Yunnan. The Derung are best known for their epics and mythologies.

A long, long time ago, a Derung hero named Tan Gapeng was born from the crotch of a tree with the blessing of a deity. Though he ate nothing, he grew very fast and soon became a giant, who was not only diligent but also capable of doing many things.

One day, Tan Gapeng cut down all the trees on a mountain with his chopper in an effort to open up arable land. But the next day, he was surprised to find the mountain reforested. At first he thought he had come to the wrong place. Then realizing that there was no other mountain nearby, he knew for sure this was where he had worked. He chopped the trees down again, only to see them standing tall the next morning. Overwhelmed with curiosity, he decided to investigate.

After hacking the trees down for a third time, he went back home. That evening, however, he didn't go to sleep. He snuck back to the mountain instead, a bow over his shoulder and a chopper in his hand. There he hid behind a big rock, waiting to see what in the world would happen. Soon a white-bearded, elderly man appeared from nowhere. The old man picked up the wood chunks and heaped them together. Then he blew on them three times. Immediately the chunks turned into tree trunks, rising with a swish one after another. In no time, branches and leaves emerged from them. Seeing this, Tan Gapeng was dumbfounded.

As soon as he had collected himself, he set out to shoot the old man with his bow and arrow. He was about to let the arrow go when the old man vanished. Before he realized what had happened, the old man was behind him. Tapping him on the shoulder, the old man said slowly, "Gapeng, I'm here to teach you a lesson because I'm your relative."

The white-bearded elder turned out to be the deity Meng Peng, who had blessed him when he was born. "I have two nieces, both pretty and kind-hearted. If you can accomplish the tasks I'm going to assign you, I'll let you marry one of them."

"Tell me what to do."

"The thick old tree over there, it's tall and slippery. See if you can climb up to its top."

Tan Gapeng climbed and clambered but couldn't make any progress. One of the old man's nieces, with one eye only, had already fallen in love with Tan Gapeng while watching him without his notice, so she came out of hiding and gave him a piece of gum stealthily. Rubbing it in his hands, Tan Gapeng reached the treetop with ease.

"That's great, my would-be nephew-in-law!" exclaimed the deity Meng Peng. Then setting free a large python, he asked, "Can you catch it?"

Tan Gapeng pounced upon the serpent and caught it by the key section of its body so that it became immobilized.

"You're awesome, my dear would-be nephew-in-law!" cried Meng Peng. As he said this, he produced a huge hive of wasps and hung it high in a tree. Turning to Tan Gapeng, he asked, "Do you think you can take it down?"

Tan Gapeng lit up a pipe of tobacco and drove the wasps away with the smoke he spat out. He then removed the hive with no effort.

"You're very smart, my would-be nephew-in-law!" With that, Meng Peng took Tan Gapeng to a big forest on a mountain and disappeared, leaving him alone and helpless. Apparently the deity hadn't finished testing him.

Lost and fatigued, Tan Gapeng was stumbling and groping in the dark when suddenly he spotted a gleam of light in the depth of the forest. He hurried toward it while trying to figure out why a residence should be in such a remote and lonely place. He began to feel nervous, but went on nevertheless. When he drew near, he saw a plank house, in which there lived a couple, a bear and a tiger, who were in the form of humans. They invited him in, fed him, and asked what they could do to help. The grateful Tan Gapeng told them what had happened to him and said he needed someone to show him his way home.

The bear and tiger couple talked about whether to send a tiger or a bear relative to be his guide. Finally, they decided upon a tiger named Ah Pu. Before they set off, the couple asked Tan Gapeng to be cautious with him. Eventually the tiger led Tan Gapeng back to his native soil. On his way home, an elderly man accosted him,

"You've had a pleasant outing, eh?"

"Well, it was a long journey full of distress."

"Then, how about coming to my home to take a break?"

"Where's your home, grandpa?"

"Not far from here," said the old man. "Just follow me."

Before long, they arrived at the old man's house. Two young women greeted them. They were, as the old man called them, Third and Fourth Sisters. Third Sister was slender and pretty, but Fourth Sister was heavier and plain-looking. What's more, she had only one eye, and for that she was called One-eyed Fairy. Tan Gapeng immediately recognized her: She was the one who had helped him climb the slippery tree. He picked her as his wife. In fact, that was what the old man, who was the deity Meng Peng in disguise, had intended.

Tan Gapeng decided to take his wife home. Before their departure, Meng Peng gave the single-eyed bride a bamboo tube and told her not to open it until they reached their destination. On their way, however, they were overcome by curiosity and opened the tube to see what was buzzing inside it. Out flew a large swarm of bees, and they made for the cliffs and trees immediately. Since then, the Derung have had to climb trees in order to harvest honey.

Later, when the couple paid a visit to Meng Peng, he gave them another bamboo tube and asked them not to open it until they were home. Again, One-eyed Fairy couldn't help opening it. Instantly, she was pregnant. The deity had meant for Tan Gapeng to conceive, but since then, women have taken the labor upon themselves.

When they visited the deity a third time, he scolded them for not listening to him and refused to give them anything. Eventually he gave in, as his one-eyed daughter kept pestering him. He told them categorically not to look back despite possible loud noises behind them.

The couple said good-bye and set out. On the way, they heard a great commotion approaching nearer and nearer from behind. They couldn't resist the temptation and turned their heads. At this, the horde of animals that were intended to follow them home to be domesticated were startled and began scurrying in all directions. With tremendous effort, they managed to capture some of them. One-eyed Fairy got chickens, hogs, and goats, while Tan Gapeng caught cattle and horses. The rest of the animals dispersed into the forest and have run wild since.

Before long, the couple had a baby boy. Unfortunately, he died of illness soon after his tenth birthday. Tan Gapeng went to the deity for help and got a potion of resuscitation. Before the boy came to life, a devil paid the couple a visit in the guise of the deity's messenger, telling them that the deity wanted them to bury the boy because he would never be alive again. Before they did so, Tan Gapeng and his One-eyed Fairy wife slaughtered some of the chickens and hogs as sacrifices. Because of the devil's treachery, humans have since had to face inevitable death, and when they succumb, the family and relatives must kill chickens and hogs as part of the funeral ritual.

Courtesy of Dai Yuru and Yunnan Fine Arts Publishing House

Left to right: 1. Miao women with silver ornaments. 2. Yi girl. 3. Ani girls strolling in a Kunming street. 4. Man from Kemu, an unrecognized ethnic group.

Group of Yi boys (left) and couple of Hani girls in Yunnan.

Second from left: Jingpo girl who retold story about waistbands she was wearing.

***Thangka* or *tangka*, painted or embroidered Tibetan Buddhist banner.**

Young Naxi woodcarver at work.

Zhao Shilin, library director, Yunnan Nationalities University Library, shows collection of literary classics from the ethnic minorities in Yunnan to Barbara Ford, former president of American Library Association.

Band playing Naxi ancient music, a time-honored performing art on the brink of extinction.

Dai monastery, where Dai boys are sent to study the Dai scripts, denied to girls.

Lisu children learning Mandarin and their ethnic languages concurrently at school.

Life-sized replica of the Uygur landmark in Urumchi, Xinjiang, found in the Beijing Ethnic Museum.

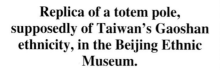

Replica of a totem pole, supposedly of Taiwan's Gaoshan ethnicity, in the Beijing Ethnic Museum.

Left to right: 1. *Ganlan* house (house supported by poles) of the Lahu. 2. Towers and pavilions of the Dong. 3. Dai house. 4. Tibetan house.

Ethnic costumes for sale at a tourist spot in the Ethnic Village in Kunming.

Left to right: fried buffalo rind with Dai flavor, Jingpo frozen fish, Dai shrimp, bamboo rice, Yi qiaobaba (buckwheat cakes), Mongolian hot pot, Miao sour soup, Dai migan (rice noodle), and an ethnic dinner in Xishuangbanna, Yunnan.

Lusheng (reed pipe) performance at celebration in Miao community in Guizhou, China.

Photo by Yang Changbin, Kaili College Library, Guizhou

Top to bottom: 1. Colorful *zhijin* (brocade), heavy fabric interwoven with a rich, raised design, popular among several Chinese ethnic minorities. 2. Tibetan lacquer ware.

Palm tree in Xishuangbanna Botanic Park, Yunnan, which looks like the tale of a peacock, a lucky bird to the Dai living there.

Tourists and Dai locals indulging in a mock Water-splashing Festival ceremony. Dai people believe that water will bring them good luck during their New Year's Day, sometime in April.

Lake in which Princess Peacock and her sisters were allegedly bathing.

Trained elephant apparently winning tug of war against a group of tourists at Xishuangbannan, Yunnan, a sanctuary of the rare Asian elephants.

Lisu farmers working in adverse conditions on the mountainside above the Nu River.

Picturesque, terraced padded fields, characteristic of the Honghe Ethnic Hani Prefecture in Southern Yunnan.

A MOTHER WHO DRIVES THE SUN

This is a myth from the Lisu. Some 634,900 (China, 2002) Lisu people live in the Nujiang Ethnic Lisu Autonomous Prefecture in Yunnan.

*I*n the very beginning, the universe was filled with nothing but chaos. The creator, Ningguanwa, opened up mountains and plains with a huge magic axe. Then he developed nine plots of arable land with nine rivers flowing through them. After that, he created humans with clay. As he placed the little figurines on the ground, they began to sing, dance, and laugh. Soon they grew as tall as he was. Ningguanwa then paired men with women to form families, before setting to work on the creation of animals and birds in the same fashion.

Humans worked by day and had fun at night, dancing and singing around bonfires while beating drums and gongs. Their hullabaloo woke up the sleeping devil Gaozuo Luolei. When he opened his eyes and saw the world transformed completely, he was overwhelmed with jealousy. He wondered who had brought about the changes and swore to get even with him.

When the devil learned that Ningguanwa was behind all this, he went to pick a fight with him at the Solar Mansion on the Solar Mountain of Heaven. He shouted at the top of his voice, "Show your face, Ningguanwa!"

Ningguanwa came out, only to see a ferocious devil in front of him. Though surprised, he tried to be as polite as he could, "My friend, what brought you here? Would you like to come in and have a chat?"

"Why did you create the sky and the earth in the first place? It'd be all right if you created them only, but why on earth did you produce the living creatures, particularly the humans? Their singing and dancing have deprived me of my peace. Don't you know that the universe belongs to me?" Gaozuo Luolei fired a salvo of questions at Ningguanwa in one breath.

"Well, the universe is everybody's," retorted Ningguanwa, suppressing his anger and resentment. "What do you need such a vast space of universe for? Wouldn't you feel lonely without the creatures? What harm will humans do to you when they're having a good time? If you prefer tranquility, then why don't you go somewhere in the universe that can give you that?"

"Give your residence to me," demanded the devil.

"Fine," said Ningguanwa readily.

The answer took the insolent Gaozuo Luolei by surprise. After a pause, he said, "Hmmm, what a generous deity you are! But I've changed my mind. I want the entire universe, and I'll kill off the humans." At this, he drew his sword with a whoosh and, holding it in both hands, began to swirl it in order to release destructive magic power.

"Stop!" shouted Ningguanwa. Wielding his gigantic magic axe, he engaged the devil in a battle that lasted three days and nights, causing gusts of wind that dimmed the heavenly bodies in the sky. Finally, Ningguanwa cut Gaozuo Luolei down. Before he fell, however, the devil thrust his sword into Ningguanwa's chest. The impact threw Ningguanwa onto the ground. In a moment he came to, yanked the sword out and, pressing his hands tight on the wound to prevent it from bleeding, hurried back to heaven.

The mortally wounded devil Gaozuo Luolei struggled down Solar Mountain but fell dead not far from it. Before breathing his last, he used what magic power was left to him to cause Heavenly River to tip. Water gushed out and poured onto the earth, washing away everything in its path.

Only a young man and a young woman of the same tribe survived, because they happened to be herding on a high mountain. When the flood came, they killed four of their cattle and sew their hides into a big, drumlike float. Sealing themselves in it, they drifted on the torrent. They drifted and drifted, and one day the leather drum finally came to a stop. Tearing it open, they found, to their happiness, that the deluge had subsided. After figuring out the direction of their homeland, they made for it, wading through the mud.

One afternoon they spotted an elderly woman looking into the distance in front of a cave, shielding her eyes from the sun with her hand. Tired and hungry, the youngsters went up to her and said, "Granny, can we stay here for the night?"

"Sure, sure," said the spinster, who, in fact, was an ogre. She hadn't tasted human flesh for quite some time, and was only too glad to see the two falling into her trap. Her strange look, however, didn't escape the young woman's keen eyes. She followed the ogre when she went out to fetch water and overheard her singing,

To fetch water, to fetch water,
I'll steam them to make my supper.

Upon hearing this, the young woman hurried back to the young man. When the demon got back, they had already gone. She meant to run after them, but didn't know where they were heading, so she had to give up her pursuit, with a sigh.

The two trekked a few days and nights before reaching a house on a hilltop. They knocked at its door, and there appeared another elderly woman, who claimed to be a mountain goddess. She invited them into her room and settled them down. Then she said she was going out to fetch water. As she had before, the young woman trailed this self-proclaimed goddess, and overheard her chanting,

To fetch water, to fetch water,
I'll cook them a tasty dinner.

The young man and young woman began to trust her and stayed. They soon grew old enough that the mountain goddess began to be concerned with their marriage. Since they were the only humans in the world, where could she find a spouse for each? Finally, she made a hard decision: Even though they were from the same tribe, she had to marry them so that the human race could continue.

The young people were caught in a dilemma: To marry, they would have to go against their tradition. If they didn't do so, humans would die out after they were gone. As they hesitated, the goddess had an idea: Let fate make the decision. She asked the young man and the young woman to stand on two different hilltops facing each other and to roll down at the same time. If they bumped into each other down in the valley, they would have to marry, for it was an indication of heaven's will. This they did, and they ran into each other after they tumbled down the hills. Realizing they were destined to become husband and wife, they performed a simple wedding ceremony, which included bowing to heaven and earth. The goddess served as a witness to the marriage.

Soon the couple had a baby boy and named him Wagang. They and the goddess all loved him very much. When the couple went to work in the fields, the grandma goddess took care of the boy; however, he kept crying and crying until she lost her patience and senses. In a rage, she cut him into eight sections and dumped them in a bamboo forest near the house. When she calmed down, great remorse seized her. She was so ashamed that she didn't have the courage to face Wagang's parents. So she wandered away, going into a self-inflicted exile.

No sooner had the mountain goddess left than the eight pieces of Wagang's body transformed into four young men and four young women, each wearing a pair of glistening earrings. Their looks all resembled that of the little Wagang.

At sunset, Wagang's parents came back home, only to find the mountain goddess and their baby missing. No dinner was ready and the hearth was cold. They weren't sure where the old granny had taken their baby, and they waited nervously. When midnight came, there was still no sign of them. Extremely worried, they began to search for them high and low.

When it dawned, they spotted some young people courting in a bamboo forest nearby. They hurried up to them and asked if they had seen a grandma and a baby boy with her, but their answer was negative. When the mother looked at the youngsters closely, she couldn't help grabbing their hands in her own, claiming they were her missing son, and she was their mother.

Her reaction stunned the young people, who were wondering how this woman of their age could be their mother! They said unanimously, "None of us are called Wagang. We don't even know who our mother is."

The mother was puzzled. Rubbing her eyes to take a closer look, she was even more certain that they were her missing boy.

"How can that be?" One of the young people tried to wake her up from what they perceived as her mental confusion, "He's a wobbling baby, but we're grown-ups. Besides, how can one baby turn into eight adults overnight?"

But the mother, who wept as she held their hands tight, simply turned a deaf ear to them. When the young people asked her to prove it, she was at a loss for words. Then, she kept murmuring, "If only the granny were here. If only the granny were here . . . ."

Then a young man picked up some charcoal from the smoldering bonfire around which they had danced. Handing it to the mother, he asked if she could rinse it white. If so, it would testify to her motherhood. Without delay, the anxious mother took the charcoal and rushed to a stream close by, where she set out to wash it. She rinsed and rinsed until the water became darkened, but the charcoal still remained the same color. The young people left before she knew it. They had gone to a faraway place, where they got married and had their children.

When she turned around and found the youngsters gone, the mother started running after them, so distraught she totally forgot about her husband. She ran and ran but veered in the wrong direction. Eventually she approached the Gate of Solar Mansion on the Solar Mountain of Heaven. The big gate was tightly shut. She sat outside and waited, believing her children were behind the walls. She sat at the gate for so long that her hair began to turn gray.

Ningguanwa was in the Solar Mansion of Heaven recuperating from his wound. He regretted his failure to kill Gaozuo Luolei instantly. Otherwise, the devil wouldn't have been able to destroy the beautiful world he had so carefully cultivated. He had been fully recovered long before and meant to descend to the world to rebuild it. Then he had changed his mind upon noticing the young man and the young woman. He had intended to give them a chance, while watching them every step of the way. When he saw the mother trying to claim that the youngsters were her son, he had almost come to intervene. Then a brilliant idea had dawned upon him. It was a grander plan: He wanted her to drive the sun so that she and her children could see each other on a daily basis. Now that she had stood the test to which he had put her, Ningguawa thought it time to entrust her with the big task. He opened the gate, told her he was the creator of the world, and offered to take her to her children.

As they flew in the sky, she was happy to see that her children had multiplied and each of their families was living a happy life. After they landed, Ningguanwa told the humans that she was truly their mother. Remorseful for not accepting her at first, her children now were squabbling over who would have the honor to take her home and look after her. Ningguanwa quieted them down, telling them he had invited her to drive the sun so that they all could see her every day.

Since then, the mother has been seen driving the sun out in the morning at the crow of roosters and steering it back to Solar Mountain at dusk. The warmth of her motherly love shines persistently on her children and their descendants. It would have been a happy ending but for one thing: Unto this day, no one knows what happened to the husband the mother left behind.

Courtesy of Dai Yuru and Yunnan Fine Arts Publishing House

AH DANG SEEKS THE SEED OF FIRE

This is a folktale of the Hui, one of the ten Muslim ethnic minorities in China. A third of the 9,816,785 (China, 2002) Hui live in Ningxia and Gansu in Northwestern China. Others are spread over almost the entire country. Twenty of its thirty-one provinces and regions each has more than 100,000 Huis. They are descendants of the Han, Uygur, and Mongol who mingled with the Arab merchants who came to China in the seventh century.

Folklore of the Hui bears dual influences of Muslim classics and the traditions of the Han Chinese. The hero Ah Dang in the following story came from the Muslim tradition but lived in a Chinese setting.

*I*n very ancient times, there was no fire in the world, and humans had to eat cold and raw food. One day a volcano erupted, setting fire to mountains and plains alike. Many of the animals were toasted in burning forests and baked on flaming grasslands. After the fire spent itself, humans ventured out, only to find bodies of burned animals scattered here and there. When they picked up some pieces of the carcasses and tasted them, they found them very delicious. For the first time, humans saw the benefit of fire. But they didn't know how to start it since it had gone. How they wished they had kept some of it alive!

Whenever humans gathered together, they would talk about the fire. Some guessed that the seed of it had fallen from the sky while others speculated it had been blown here by wind from somewhere else. As most of them believed in the wind theory, they sent off a young man named Ah Dang to search for the source of fire.

Ah Dang made up his mind to fulfill the task even though he had no idea where to go. He knew, however, if he covered the entire world, he would eventually be able to find it. He set out and traversed seventy-seven mountains, seventy-seven rivers, and seventy-seven forests. He looked on the mountains, in the rivers, and over the plains, but failed to find any seed of fire. He was so fatigued that he began to see things: Almost everything he came across, whether it was a maple leave, a red crag, or a bird feather, would look like the seed of fire. He was disappointed each time. Yet he wouldn't give up searching.

One day, Ah Dang paused to ponder, "I'll get nowhere casting about like this. I must find help." When he saw the sparrows hovering above him, he thought, "Since they travel far and wide, they must know where I can get the seed of fire."

"Sparrow, sparrow, since you fly here and there nonstop in all seasons, have you ever seen the seed of fire?" he asked. "If you do, can you tell me? I'll pay you: gold or silver, whichever you want."

"Yes, we do. But we don't want your gold or silver. If only you humans allow us to build our nests in your homes and don't mind our babies peeing and pooping in them."

"No problem! You can perch on the beams of our homes. Please let me know where I can get the seed of fire."

"On the edge of the sky in the west there's a flaming mountain. But it's so far away that you may never get there in your lifetime."

"Thanks for the advice, but I have to get the fire." With that, he turned and headed toward the west. He trudged on and on for thirty-three days and nights, but he still couldn't see the slightest sign of the flaming mountain. All the same, he was not disheartened. To speed up the search, the clever Ah Dang had another idea: "Why can't I ask the horse for help? Horses travel much faster than humans do." Soon he found one and told it about his mission.

"I can carry you there, but I have a request: I'd like you humans to look after us in the future, giving us fodder and shelter, and prevent tigers from hurting us."

"We'll do it," he said, and mounting the horse, he galloped toward the edge of the earth in the west.

After many days, Ah Dang rode to a big river that separated the earth and sky. A mountain glowed on the other side, radiating its heat across the water. He tested the water, and it was boiling hot. Cooked fish floated in the water—fish of all colors, shapes, and sizes. Ah Dang took one and tasted it, and it was more delicious than the roasted meat he had eaten in the aftermath of the big fire. He began to scoop up fish and piled them up on the bank.

"What are you doing?" asked the horse. "Don't forget what you're here for!"

"No, no. I want to get more of the fish back to my people." Then he paused and asked, "Since the river is simmering, how shall we cross it?"

"See the cave there on the hill by the river?" said the horse. "There's a magic axe of thunder in the cave. But there's also a malicious dragon on guard. If you can beat the beast, the magic axe will be yours. When you point it at the water, it'll solidify so you can walk across it. If you can't subdue the dragon, then you'll become its food."

Ah Dang was not afraid of death, but he was worried that if he failed to conquer the dragon and lost his life, he wouldn't be able to get the seed of fire, and his people would continue eating cold and raw food. He pondered, trying to figure out a way to defeat the dragon. He thought so hard that he saw stars, and yet not a single idea came to him. Then he asked the horse what to do.

"Well, there's no way you can fight the dragon bare-handed. But you can lure it out of the cave and make it run after you. Then keep running in a circle until it curls up and finds it difficult to move. Take the opportunity and run into the cave to get the magic axe of thunder. Once you have the weapon in your hand, the dragon will be at your disposal."

Ah Dang did what the horse told him to, and sure enough, the dragon chased him round and round until it ran itself into a coil, unable to move. He dashed into the cave and grabbed the magic axe. When he came out, the dragon had just untangled itself from the coil. It was about to attack him when it saw the magic axe in his hands. Immediately it threw itself onto the ground and started begging for its life,

"Don't kill me. I'll tell you how you can bring the seed of fire back to your people. Otherwise it would be too hot for you to hold and transport it even after you get it."

"So tell me," demanded Ah Dang.

"On the back of the axe there's a metal cap. Slide it open and you'll see a casket. Only when you place the seed of fire into that casket can you take it back home."

"Hmmm, that's a good tip," said Ah Dang, and he let go the dragon. It thanked him profusely and slunk back to its cave, never again to venture out.

No sooner had Ah Dang pointed the magic axe at the river than its torrent of boiling water came to a stop and turned into a wide slate of ice. The sudden turn of events transfixed him.

"Hurry up, Ah Dang," urged the horse. "Or it will be too late!"

Ah Dang rushed over the ice and came to the foot of the flaming mountain. He picked up two seeds of fire, placed them in the casket on the back of the axe, slid the cover closed, and hurried back. As soon as he stepped onto shore, the ice gave way in a crash.

"What's going on?" asked Ah Dang in amazement.

"When the magic axe has the seed of fire in it, it possesses so much energy that the mere reflection of it will melt the ice instantly."

With the seeds of fire and the cooked fish, Ah Dang rode back home. While the horse galloped, trees on the mountainside bent back, whistling. The horse was so fast that it was almost flying. After three days and nights, Ah Dang was home.

Since then, humans have learned to cook their food with fire. The horse has also become the ancestor of domesticated horses. And sparrows have become humans' frequent guests.

Ah Dang has become a hero of the Hui. In his honor, they still wear a pouch and a huolian *today as ornaments and tools for starting a fire. Made of steel, a* huolian *is shaped like Ah Dang's magic axe. The pouch is said to be its casket, and the flint therein is, of course, the seed of fire. To start a fire, one only needs to strike the flint on the steel edge of the* huolian *to light a cord stowed in the pouch.*

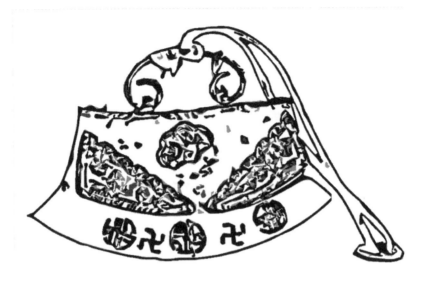

Huolian

THE TOAD GENERAL

This is a legend from the Gin. Numbering 22,500 (China, 2002), they live on the three islands of Wanwei, Wutou, and Shanxin in the Guangxi Ethnic Zhuang Autonomous Region near Vietnam. In fact, their ancestors came from Vietnam five centuries ago. They joined the Han Chinese in fighting in the Sino–French War in 1883–1885, prior to the French colonization of Vietnam. The following story could well be a reference to that conflict.

*T*here once lived on the Three Islands an honest couple who were saddened by their infertility. They would give anything in the world to have a child.

One spring, a temple was built on the Three Islands dedicated to *Zhenhai Dawang* (the King of the Sea). The day of its completion was filled with festivity. That night, the husband and wife dreamt the same dream: A chubby boy wobbled into their welcoming arms, calling them "Papa!" and "Mama!" The couple was rejoicing in the sudden bliss when tolls from a bell in the temple woke them up. Soon the wife had an attack of pain in her belly and immediately went into labor. To the bewilderment of the couple, instead of a baby, she gave birth to something like a papaya fruit. They would have discarded it but for the pleasant fragrance and mesmerizing radiance it gave off. Suddenly, a knocking came from within the fruit-like object, and it cracked. A big toad clambered out of the crevice. As if it already knew the couple, the toad started licking their hands and feet as pet dogs and cats do to their owners.

Day after day, year after year, the couple aged and the toad grew to be an energetic pre-teen. That year, a foreign country invaded China, and the emperor was raising an army at the border to repel the aggressors. The toad saw the bulletin of recruitment distributed on the Three Islands. He jumped back and forth from his father's lap to his shoulders at lunch. Finally, he sat down on the table and opened his big mouth,

"Father, I want to answer the emperor's call. Take me to the army with you." It was the first time he had spoken, which surprised as well as delighted his parents.

"How can you fight when you are so small?" they asked in concert.

"Father and Mother, don't you remember that I came into being in the year when the temple was dedicated to the King of the Sea, or what you call *Zhenhai Dawang*? That was me. I am his incarnation!"

Trusting their toad son, the elderly couple took him to the recruiting station. The officer in charge, however, was not so sure. He asked disparagingly, "Aren't you afraid of being squashed into a meat pie by the enemy horses?"

Irritated, the toad leapt onto the office's shoulder, weighing him down like a thousand-pound burden. Sweating plentifully, the officer couldn't move an inch.

The toad chided, "You good-for-nothing! The country is in peril and you're still amusing yourself. How can you look down upon me? Let me tell you this: If the enemy could crush me into a meat pie, they would probably grind your bones into powder!"

The officer was ashamed of his snobbishness and apologized excessively. Just then report of emergency and a request for reinforcements came from the front. Hearing this, the toad hopped down from the officer's shoulder and said to him, "Don't worry! Go and ask the emperor to have an iron horse made for me. I'll go and fight the invaders."

The emperor immediately ordered the best blacksmiths in the country to manufacture an iron horse and had it shipped to the toad. When he mounted it, the horse collapsed and broke into pieces. Everyone around was flabbergasted. The toad complained to the officer, "Why did you get me a hollow horse? Get me a solid one."

The emperor then had a solid iron horse made. Since it was too heavy to transport, the emperor became worried. When told about the emperor's predicament, the toad said to the officer, "Leave it where it is. So long as it's solid, the emperor may rest assured and expect news of my victory soon."

The toad came to the iron horse. He was very pleased with its craftsmanship. No sooner had he gotten on the horse than it neighed and bucked, to the amazement of everyone around.

The foreign invaders were marching toward the capital when all of a sudden a big iron horse plunged onto the field before the enemy line. Barrage after barrage of enemy fire failed to make a dent in the iron horse. Now it was time for the toad to launch his counterattack. "Fire!" he whispered into the ears of the iron horse. At this, spates of flames came out of its mouth, and the frightened foreign soldiers scurried back, leaving numerous seared bodies behind them.

Instead of admitting defeat, the foreign general came in person and led his army in a counteroffensive against the strange, fiery opponent. He ordered his troops to encircle it and assailed it from all directions. Seeing this, the toad laughed. He patted the iron horse gently and it charged forward and backward, left and right, spitting fire from its eyes, ears, nostrils, and mouth. Unable to ward off such an unconventional onslaught, the enemy troops were utterly routed.

Thrilled by the news of victory, the emperor went out of the court to greet the triumphant toad, only to see a handsome young general on the iron horse instead.

ADVENTURES OF ABA DANI

This is a folktale from the Lhoba, the smallest ethnic group in China, with a population of 2,900 (China, 2002). It is also one of the few ethnic minorities in Tibet.

Once upon a time, there was a deity named Aba Dani. He was an admirable hunter with extraordinary features. He had two additional eyes at the back of his head, capable of seeing through evils. He was married to Dongni Haiyi, the bright and honest daughter of God of Sun. Soon, the happy couple gave birth to twin boys.

One day, Dongni Haiyi talked with her husband Aba Dani about paying a visit to her heavenly father. She asked him to go first to get a couple of back straps. She said they needed them to carry their twins when they traveled to the Solar Palace. Before his departure, she told him to go straight to her father instead of wandering elsewhere.

But Aba Dani wouldn't listen. On his way, he strayed from his course and went to see Gexin Yaming, the sister of a demon named Poge Lunbu. The demon was very happy at Aba Dani's arrival because it provided him with a chance to get rid of the eyes at the back of his head. All demons hated them for their magic power of perception.

The demon's sister Gexin Yaming, however, was surprised to see Aba Dani and worried for his safety. Though a demon herself, she liked him so much that she hated to see him hurt. She wanted to warn him against the danger in store.

Poge Lunbu pretended to be hospitable. Not only did he treat Aba Dani to a fabulous dinner, but he also invited him to hunt with him the next day. In fact, he was planning to kill him.

Knowing what her brother was up to, Gexin Yaming tagged along and wouldn't let Aba Dani out of her sight, much to the dismay of her brother. She asked Aba Dani in a whisper,

"Aba Dani, why are you here? Don't you know my brother is cunning and vicious? You must be careful!"

"I will. Thanks!" said Abu Dani.

"We demons have a favorite game: jumping on a rope hung between two crags far apart," Gexin Yaming told him. "My brother will certainly invite you to dance with them.

But remember this: When they jump twice, you hop once; when they jump three times, you hop only twice." She then gave Aba Dani a slice of ginger and asked him to take it with him.

Sure enough, Gexin Yaming asked Aba Dani to play rope-dancing with them the next morning. In showing off his talent, Aba Dani totally forgot Gexin Yaming's warning. When the demons jumped once, he did twice. When they hopped twice, he did three times . . . . Seeing this, the demon Poge Lunbu was secretly overjoyed, so he encouraged Aba Dani to jump more.

"Go, Aba Dani, you can do even better!"

While Dani was occupied in dancing, the devil cut the rope without his knowing it, so that he fell crashing into the valley. The impact bumped off the two eyes on the back of his head. One of his legs was also broken and hurt.

Seizing the opportunity, Poge Lunbu found the fallen eyes scattered in the bushes and picked them up secretly. He knew that without his magic eyes, Aba Dani was now powerless. Aba Dani's injured leg hurt terribly. To stop the bleeding, he struck a flint to burn the cut and rubbed the gingerroot on it. Poge Lunbu had planned to suck his blood, but when he smelt the gingerroot, he balked; the pungent plant would do him great harm. He snuck away with Aba Dani's eyes.

Aba Dani called upon all kinds of animals to help look for his lost eyes, but none could tell him clearly whether they had found them. He then asked a rooster for help. The bird told him that Poge Lunbu had taken them. Aba Dani then asked Gexin Yaming to talk to her brother and get them back for him. Blaming his sister for her act of betrayal, Poge Lunbu categorically rejected her plea. He said he wasn't fearful of Aba Dani any more and would do whatever he pleased. And so he did: He set free all the demons that Aba Dani had imprisoned and sent them back to the earth.

Now Aba Dani could only painfully watch humans suffer without being able to help them. The best he could do was slaughter some cattle and offer them to the *maiba* (exorciser), wishing that he could rid the earth of the demons. This is the beginning of the traditions of sacrificing and exorcising among humans.

HUMANS AND A GOURD

This is a myth from the De'ang, whose 17,900 (China, 2002) people live primarily in Yunnan.

Gourds play a big role in the Chinese culture in general—not only among ethnic minorities such as the Dai, Hani, Lahu, Li, Miao, Sui, Tibetan, Tujia, Va, Yi, and De'ang, but also among the Han Chinese, as is evident in the stories "Meng Jiang Wails at the Great Wall," "Eight Immortals Crossing the Sea," and "Painted Skin," all retold in The Magic Lotus Lantern and Other Tales from the Han Chinese *(Libraries Unlimited, 2006), another book in the World Folklore Series.*

A long, long time ago, a big flood inundated the earth, wiping out nearly all living creatures upon it. Only a few humans and animals were rescued, by a deity named Kapafa. He placed them in a gourd, sealed it, and let it float on the waters.

When the flood subsided, Kapafa decided to let the humans and animals out. But to do so, he needed to hack the gourd open. Before his sword fell on one side of it, the ox inside cried out, "Hold! I am here!"

Then Kapafa tried to cut the gourd at a different spot, but a dog shouted, "Stop! Don't hurt me!"

Kapafa was at a loss what to do. Then he heard a rabbit shouting from another position within the big fruit, "Here, drop your blade over here!"

But before the sword came down, the rabbit dodged it and gave the crab a push at the same time. The head of the crab was thus cut off, and it has since walked sideways without it.

Being the mother of all waters, the crab raised a flood wherever it crawled. In consequence, the creatures that had survived the initial deluge were decimated. Only a few animals and one man were left. Eventually, the man wanted to have a spouse.

A fairy from heaven began to visit him daily. She cooked for him and helped with his family chores. Nevertheless, every time she finished, she would return to heaven, to the man's great disappointment.

Later, the deity Kapafa told the man to make a waistband and hitch the fairy with it when she appeared the next time. "If you succeed," he added, "she'll lose her ability to fly."

The man acted accordingly. He even made a necklace and a bracelet. When the fairy came to cook for him again, he put the band, the necklace, and the bracelet on her, and sure enough, she was not able to get away. The two eventually got married, had a lot of children, and lived happily.

But good life didn't last long. One day, a large fire broke out on the mountains, followed by a heavy rain. The fire and the flood destroyed almost everything, including humans and animals. Kapafa came to their rescue once again. He put what was left of them in a gourd he had brought with him.

Before long, a gigantic spider descended from heaven, spinning a web large enough to cover the inundated earth. The dust it caught in due course turned into plains and mountains. The seared dirt gave off an especially pleasant aroma, which became so strong that it attracted some deities from heaven. They snuck onto earth to chomp on it. However, by doing so, they became mortal, never able to ascend to heaven. In the meantime, the deity Kapafa opened the gourd and let out the humans and animals.

Eventually, humans were tired of eating the fragrant dirt. They wanted grains instead. But no one knew where to get them. A devil from the underworld overheard their conversation and took them to Kapafa in heaven. The deity told them to turn to rats for seeds of grain. The devil then took humans to see King of Rats, who gave them some seeds, each as big as a football.

The devil took a seed and scurried away, disregarding the humans. Not knowing where to go, they told King of Rats, "The devil brought us here, but now he's gone. We really don't know how to get back."

The king asked two small rats to show them the way to the cow, which led them to the horse, which in turn entrusted them to the care of the python. The python then sent them to the elephant, which finally carried them to where they had come from.

Humans sowed the big seeds and had a bumper harvest the next season. Strangely, the seeds shrank with each generation, finally stopping when they became as small as they currently are.

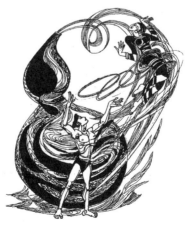

Gourd worshiping is prevalent among many of the Chinese ethnic minorities. Courtesy of Dai Yuru and Yunnan Fine Arts Publishing House

Tales of Love and Romance

Love is the eternal theme of human history, and it permeates the Chinese minority ethnic tales as it does the folklore of all civilizations. Courage and perseverance are always instrumental in getting one's true love. "Love Between a Goddess and a Mortal Hunter," from the Qiang, stood up to repeated tests of a difficult father-in-law. In "A Cloud of Love from a Princess," the cloud carries her undying spirit. The Dai's "Princess Peacock" and her prince husband foiled a treacherous plot. "Two Young Men," from the Jino, shows that where there's love, there's jealousy. The unwavering seventh sister dogs her murderous sister until she recovers her true love in "Seventh Sister and Her Snake Husband." "Princess Wencheng" overcame her cultural shock to unite with her love in faraway Tibet. "Tale of the Xing'an Mountains," from the Ewenki, is another tale about jealousy. The affection of "A Mountain Girl and a Giant Hunter," from the Oroqen, triumphed over a monster's wickedness.

LOVE BETWEEN A GODDESS
AND A MORTAL HUNTER

This is a folktale from the Qiang, a remnant of the ancient Qiang who inhabited a large part of today's Western China. Currently, most of the 306,100 (China, 2002) Qiang people live in the upper reaches of the Min River in Western Sichuan.

God of Heaven Mu Bita had three sons and three daughters. All were married but the youngest son and daughter, whom their father asked to herd on the Wenshan Mountain. The youngest daughter was called Mu Jiezhu. She was not only prettier than her sisters but also an excellent singer. Each time she sang, birds would forget to return to their nests, and her sheep would dance around her.

One day, a young man called Dou Anzhu came to the prairie and was mesmerized by Mu Jiezhu's beautiful song. Mu Jiezhu was also captivated by his handsomeness, and they fell in love at first sight. They started meeting each other every day until the twenty-ninth of the ninth month, a traditional day for the Qiang people to fulfill their promise to God of Heaven. That day, Mu Jiezhu was no longer as cheerful as she had been before. As Dou Anzhu questioned her closely, she told him tearfully who she really was, and that she had to return to heaven. That meant she might never be able to come back to him.

Dou Anzhu was struck speechless. He knew that Mu Bita, the supreme deity in heaven, would by no means allow his daughter to marry a mortal like him. But soon he came to himself, vowing to be with her wherever she went. Mu Jiezhu also pledged to persuade her father to endorse their marriage. She mingled him with the flock of sheep she was herding and brought him to heaven. There, she hid him in a sheep pen and asked him to wait till the next morning.

When day broke, Mu Bita went to court and began to receive his subordinate deities, his children included. Suddenly he caught the smell of a human and asked if any of them was concealing one nearby. At this, Mu Jiezhu brought Dou Anzhu into his presence out of hiding. The sight of a mortal enraged him. He snarled at his daughter,

"Why did you break the rules and laws I set in heaven?"

In an attempt to take the blame for Mu Jiezhu, Dou Anzhu bowed and said calmly, "Your Majesty, God of Heaven, I followed your daughter to heaven because I love her. Please marry her to me."

"What? Marry my daughter to a mortal like you?" Mu Bita fumed, but he quickly calmed down. After all, the polite young man looked handsome and pleasantly strong. He unconsciously lowered his voice. "You must think you're extraordinary, or you wouldn't have the nerve to ask me for her hand. Well, let's see how outstanding you are."

With that, he ordered Dou Anzhu to catch nine stones and nine logs he was to roll over a mountain. Dou Anzhu complied. When everyone left, Mu Jiezhu pulled him aside and asked if he could do what her father had asked him. Dou Anzhu said,

"I'll do whatever it takes to get us married. You know how much I love you."

"You're really silly!" Mu Jiezhu reproached him tenderly. "One must use his brain in addition to his courage." She then told him what to do.

The next morning, Dou Anzhu arrived at the foot of the mountain. He hid himself under a trough shielded by long icicles hanging down from the protruding rock above him. When God of Heaven rolled stones and logs down the crag, he dodged all of them and caught the last log that happened to slide downhill.

Mu Bita wouldn't admit defeat. He asked Dou Anzhu to cut down the trees on nine large stretches of land in a day. It would have been impossible but for Mu Jiezhu's help. She told him to cut a tree from each of the four corners of a wood. Then, she said to him, "Find a rock near you and hide behind it. Disregard any sound that will follow."

The next day, Dou Anzhu did what his fiancée had told him. Sure enough, while taking cover behind a rock, he heard thunderous rumblings in the fields. When things quieted down, he came out of hiding, only to find the trees lying in front of him. It turned out that the gods of the surrounding mountains had helped him at the invitation of Mu Jiezhu.

Mu Bita was surprised at Dou Anzhu's efficiency but still refused to give his consent to his marriage with Mu Jiezhu. He demanded that he burn the trees into ashes. This time, Dou Anzhu didn't bother to consult Mu Jiezhu. He thought he had been good at it when on earth. But he was unaware that fire in heaven was completely different in nature. No sooner had he started the blaze than its flames flared up to engulf him. Fortunately, Mu Jiezhu had anticipated the danger and called in Dragon King, who was one of her brothers-in-law. The dragon snuffed out the fire with a downpour. Although he survived, Dou Anzhu had been badly scalded. Mu Jiezhu told him to descend to earth, place some heated stones in a pot of water, and let the steam heal his injuries.

When he returned to Mu Jiezhu in heaven fully recovered, Mu Bita was stunned. Determined not to relent, he ordered him to sow oil seeds evenly in the nine stretches of reclaimed land. Dou Anzhu said yes, although he was angry at his willfulness. Mu Jiezhu was fearful because she was at her wit's end. Just then the eight giants, who served as Mu Bita's armed escorts, offered to help them. They were unhappy at the deity's determination to create unnecessary difficulties for the couple. The next day, they rallied numerous beasts and birds to scatter the seeds evenly in the fields.

When Dou Anzhu and Mu Jiezhu again asked Mu Bita to allow them to marry, he assented to their request without demur, much to their surprise. Soon they found they were celebrating too soon. The crafty heavenly god attached a condition to his consent. He said to Dou Anzhu,

"Since I've nothing to give you as dowry, the oil seeds to be harvested in the fields will all be yours. But you must collect every seed, no more and no less. Or you won't even have time to regret."

When the sullen couple left, Mu Bita burst into laughter, "Hah, hah, hah! Now I'll see how the rascal can gather all the seeds scattered in the fields. Miss a single one and his head will be chopped off. Ha, ha, ha . . . ."

Mu Jiezhu and Dou Anzhu didn't despair. They turned to the gods of the mountains for help. The gods in turn called in millions of birds to help them pick up the seeds.

Seeing the oil seeds collected so quickly, God of Heaven was first baffled, but after the last seed was counted, he burst into a peal of blustering laughter, "Ha, ha! Guards! Take the man out and execute him!"

"Why?" the couple and the eight giants were all astounded.

"As I had decreed, one single seed uncollected would be the end of this man's life. See how many are missing. He must suffer the consequence of cheating."

"Please wait," the eight giants entreated, "It's all natural if some birds stole the seeds. Why can't you let him go and look for them? If he fails, you can still punish him."

"Fine," said Mu Bita. Turning to Dou Anzhu, he demanded, "You've got half a day to retrieve the missing seeds."

The undaunted Dou Anzhu set out, carrying his bow and arrows. He came across a long-tailed pheasant first. When he asked if it had eaten the seeds, the bird said it had just alighted from the mountaintop and hadn't had the time to do so. Then a few red-beaked crows he encountered were equally unhelpful. At last, he saw a flock of doves and put the same question to them. Some of them admitted that they had eaten the seeds. The kind-hearted Dou Anzhu didn't shoot them as he had meant to. Instead, he pleaded, "God of Heaven wants all the seeds back. What can I do?"

"You won't be disappointed," said those who had eaten the seeds. With that, they darted toward the crag, bumped their heads into it, and fell to the ground dead.

"Go ahead," said the leader of the doves, "open their craws and retrieve your seeds."

With great sorrow, Dou Anzhu did what he was asked.

When he brought back the seeds, God of Heaven Mu Bita could not refuse to marry his daughter to this courageous young man in a wedding with great pomp and ceremony. And before they left for the earth, he gave the newlyweds all kinds of seeds and animals. He asked them not to look back as they descended from heaven. But soon they forgot the warning and gave in to their curiosity. When they turned their heads, the animals following them were scared away. Meant to be human's domesticated animals, they have now become wild beasts.

Back on earth, Dou Anzhu and Mu Jiezhu sowed the seeds, which soon grew into various crops and trees. With wood, they built many houses. They did all this in the hope that their descendants would live happily thereafter.

A CLOUD OF LOVE FROM A PRINCESS

This is a folktale from Bai, an ethnic minority of 1,858,100 people (China, 2002) living mostly in the Dali region of Yunnan.

A natural phenomenon peculiar to Dali has intrigued the Bai people for centuries. Early every winter, a white cloud will appear above the Yuju Peak of Mt. Cangshan, and at its wake gusts of wind will spring up, so strong that they kick up wave after wave in Lake Erhai and reveal a large stone on a submerged sand dune. Before meteorologists could solve the mystery, the Bais had already found the answer in the story retold below.

*O*ver a thousand years ago in the State of Nanzhao, there was a beautiful and kind-hearted princess. She was still single at the age of nineteen, while all her peers had already become mothers. Hundreds of princes came to Nanzhao each year to propose marriage to her, but she turned them away because she didn't like them. At a *raosanling* (Festival of Three Spirits) party, however, she met a young hunter and fell in love with him. He was handsome and strong. Orphaned at a young age, he had been living in a cave on the Yuju Peak of Mt. Cangshan.

After the encounter, the princess lost her appetite and sleep. The hunter's image was so deeply etched in her mind that it would never leave. When her father told her he had betrothed her to a favorite general of his, she was seized with sorrow. She wept the entire evening. Early the next morning, she pushed a window open and gazed at Mt. Cangshan in the distance, where the hunter lived. Grief overwhelmed her again. Just then, a magpie landed on a tree outside the window and caught the princess's attention.

"Little Magpie! Little Magpie! Do you know why my heart is aching?" She found a little comfort in talking to the bird.

"Yes, I do," the bird spoke, to the astonishment of the princess, for she had never expected it to do so.

"Could you please fly to the Yuju Peak and ask the hunter to come to my rescue?" she pleaded as she collected herself.

The magpie nodded, took off, and darted toward the Yuju Peak. It told the hunter about the princess's affection for him. The hunter had also been thinking of the princess since they last met. When he got the message from the magpie, he rushed down the mountain with his bow and arrows. On the way, he came across a white-haired old man limping along, carrying a basket on his back.

"Grandpa, where are you going? What happened to your leg?"

"I've been looking for medicinal herbs in the mountain and fell. With my injured leg, I can never get back home before evening."

"Let me carry you on my back."

The old man didn't decline. Seeing that the hunter was in a great hurry, he asked, "Son, what makes you so hasty?"

"I'm on my way to rescue the princess."

"How can you, when the wall of the palace is so high, and the weapons of its guards are so sharp?"

"What can I do then?" the hunter was confounded.

"Well," after a pause, the old man began, "On the cliff, there's the Phoenix's Eye Cave. A peach tree grows outside its other opening. A bite of its fruit will give you enough power to overcome the obstacles. But there's a catch: The cliff is so steep and treacherous that nobody has ever reached the cave yet."

"Nothing can stop me. I'm determined to rescue the princess!" As he spoke, the hunter suddenly felt no weight on his back. The old man had disappeared. The hunter realized that he was Mountain God and had come to help him. He thanked him by bowing toward the peak of Mt. Cangshan.

The hunter managed to climb into the Phoenix's Eye Cave and approached the opening at the other side. He looked down the steep wall of the cliff and found the peach tree growing from it. He clambered down, knowing that a single misstep would plunge him to his death. Finally he reached the tree, picked a peach, and ate it. Immediately he felt he had lost gravity. With a kick against the crag, he soared into the air.

When evening fell, he flew over the wall into the princess's chamber in the palace and carried her to his cave dwelling in the Yuju Peak. There they became husband and wife. They lived a simple but happy life, hunting and farming together during the day and singing and dancing at night. The assorted birds that hovered around and the various flowers that grew at the opening of their cave became their best friends. Often the birds sang and the flowers danced as the joyful couple entertained themselves.

King of Nanzhao, however, wasn't in such a good mood at all. He dispatched his men to seek his missing daughter high and low. He also sent for an abbot from a nearby monastery. The abbot was very cunning and had tremendous magic power. He told the king his magic mirror had revealed the whereabouts of his daughter. She was with a poor hunter in a cave on the Yuju Peak. The king was very angry at his daughter's elopement because this act would reflect negatively upon his royal family. He ordered his general and soldiers to go catch the rebellious couple. The abbot stopped him, saying, "Your soldiers can't do anything about them because the hunter can fly. If you can't catch them, you'll become a laughingstock of your people." Before the king could ask him what to do, the abbot assured him, "I know what I can do."

One day a crow arrived at the opening of the cave dwelling where the hunter and the princess lived. It told them that it was a messenger from the abbot, who asked the princess to return to his father. "If not," it cawed, "the abbot said he would cover the entire mountain with ice and snow!"

"Go away!" the princess said. "Now that I'm the hunter's wife, I'll stay with him dead or alive."

Sure enough, the next morning the princess and the hunter found the opening of their cave blocked by snow three feet deep. After they dug out, they were met with a blizzard. Cold wind forced them back into the cave. The princess, accustomed to a cozy lifestyle in the palace, was particularly vulnerable to the severe weather. She was trembling all over. The hunter couldn't bear seeing his dear wife suffering like that.

"I'll go to the monastery to steal the abbot's magic gown that keeps a person warm in winter and cool in summer."

"But the abbot has a great deal of magic power. To go to his monastery is to invite trouble or even death."

"I've killed so many beasts in my life that the abbot is nothing. Don't you worry, my dear! I'll be right back." The hunter kissed the princess good-bye and took off.

He landed at the monastery, took the gown, and, stowing it under his belt, soared into the sky. He wasn't aware that every move was under the secret observation of the abbot. He waited until the hunter flew over Lake Erhai. Then he hurled a cattail hassock, a cushion used for kneeling during prayers, at the hunter in the air while chanting an incantation to add magic force to its velocity. The hassock hit the flying hunter at the waist and knocked him off balance. The moment he fell into the lake, he turned into a stone mule.

The princess was standing at the opening of the cave in the wind, waiting for her husband. She waited from morning till night and from night till the next morning. Still there was no sign of him. Shortly the crow showed up, telling her of her husband's death and his transformation into a stone. The sad news, coupled with the cold weather, dealt a fatal blow to the princess. She fell ill and soon succumbed to it. With her death, her spirit went into the air and rose into the sky, where it became a white cloud, which often emerged from behind Mt. Cangshan in search of her husband in the waters below. It would kick up gusts of wind until they became so strong that they raged above the lake and tore open its surface, revealing the stone mule at the bottom. The Bai people have since called this natural phenomenon *wangfuyun*, or "a cloud seeking her husband."

Courtesy of Larry Caillouet, WKU

Mt. Cangshan and Lake Erhai

PRINCESS PEACOCK

This is a folktale from the Dai. Most of its 1,159,000 (China, 2002) people inhabit the beautiful Xishuangbanna region in Yunnan. Unlike the Han Chinese, who regard the imaginary bird the phoenix as the Queen of Birds, the Dai give this honor to the peacock, which they consider a symbol of kindness, harmony, and good luck. The peacock dance is very popular among the Dai people. So is the following story. And the story could have borrowed from Hindu mythology, because it shares many of its motifs. Princess Peacock, for example, could have been the counterpart of the Hindu celestial being called Manohara.*

*T*here was once in the beautiful Xishuangbanna region the Kingdom of Mengbanzha, a thousand miles away from the Kingdom of Peacocks. In the Kingdom of Mengbanzha there lived a handsome young prince named Zhao Shutun. Courageous and intelligent, he was the best hunter in the kingdom. All the young women dreamed of becoming his wife, but he rejected one proposal after another. His royal father, Zhao Menghai, was worried, but the prince would often comfort him by saying, "I'll find my love when she comes."

One day, a friend of the prince and fellow hunter told him that the seven daughters of the King of Peacocks would come to bathe in Lake Lansina the next morning.

"None of the girls is married," he said. "Nanmu Luona is the youngest and prettiest."

"Isn't the Kingdom of Peacocks far away?" asked the curious prince.

"They'll fly over," replied his friend. "They each have a beautiful feather mantle with powerful wings . . . ." He stopped short, his eyes blinking, as if he had a secret to share.

"Spill it. Don't play games with me," Prince Zhao Shutun urged good-humoredly.

"If I were you, I would pay them a visit while they are bathing tomorrow."

"What? No, no! I hate peeping Toms."

"Who'd like you to be one? Let me finish," his friend continued. "Before they are done with their bath, you take away the feather mantle of Nanmu Luona, I mean, the youngest princess. Without it, she won't be able to fly, and then . . . ."

"Then what?"

"You silly! Then you can ask her to marry you."

Prince Zhao Shutun blushed. Early next morning, he went to Lake Lansina, hid himself in a bush, and waited for the peacock princesses to arrive. He waited and waited, not daring to move, when all of a sudden he saw a cluster of colorful clouds coming his way from the distance. Before long, seven graceful peacocks appeared behind the clouds. At first they looked like little birds. Then they loomed larger and larger, until they landed on the bank of the lake. As soon as they touched down, they immediately turned into seven beautiful young women, each in an ornate costume of a different color. The girls danced elegantly before they undressed and waded into the water. The one who went last struck the prince as so irresistibly gorgeous that he could barely remain hiding behind the bush. She must be Princess Nanmu Luona! Prince Zhao Shutun secretly rejoiced at finding his love finally. "Yes, this is the one I've been longing for!"

While the princesses playfully bathed in the lake, the prince snuck out and tiptoed to the heap of winged mantles. He found Nanmu Luona's, took it, and darted to where he had concealed himself. His movement, swift and stealthy as it was, alerted the peacock princesses. Despite their embarrassment, they rushed to the bank, slipped into their clothes, put on their winged mantles, and soared into the sky, without the slightest idea that they had left their youngest sister Nanmu Luona behind. When she found her sisters gone and her mantle missing, she almost panicked. She had just come to her senses when a handsome young man appeared before her, her mantle in his hands. His grace and smile dissolved her fear and shame right away. Even after she put on her magic mantle, she decided not to leave, for she had fallen in love with the prince.

King Zhao Menghai was thrilled that his son had finally fallen in love. His people liked Nanmu Luona, whom they nicknamed Princess Peacock. Everyone was happy except the Prime Minister. He had been trying to betroth his daughter to the prince and hoped that the connection with the royal family would make him more powerful and influential in the kingdom. He had long coveted the king's throne. The prince's marriage with Princess Peacock dashed his hopes. In despair, he made a secret deal with a neighboring king, who had been thinking of invading the Kingdom of Mengbanzha for some time. The minister stealthily asked the enemy to attack and promised to help them as a planted agent.

When the war began, Prince Zhao Shutun led his troops to the battle ground. They fought courageously and won one victory after another. He sent messengers to report the good tidings to his father, but each was intercepted by men sent by the treacherous Prime Minister. Then he spread rumors that the prince had suffered repeated defeats. The kingdom was in turmoil. Not knowing what to do, King Zhao Menghai asked the Prime Minister for advice. Seizing his opportunity, he blamed Princess Peacock for the kingdom's perceived misfortune, accusing her of practicing witchcraft. Then he suggested, "The only way to avert disaster is to put her to death." He added, "If we let her live, our kingdom is doomed." At this, the naive King ordered that Princess Peacock be burned.

On the execution ground, Princess Peacock felt tremendously grieved, not because she feared death, but because she would never be able to see her beloved husband, who was now fighting at the front. Holding back her tears, she turned to her gullible royal father-in-law and made a request: She wanted to perform a dance as a prayer for the safe return of Prince Zhao Shutun. The king consented. Putting on her winged mantle, Princess Peacock started dancing. As she did so, she gradually transformed into a peacock. Before the king and his people realized what had happened, she took off, darted into the air, and made for the Kingdom of Peacocks.

A few days later, Prince Zhao Shutun returned in triumph. But he found his beloved wife missing. When he learned about her departure, he decided to trace her to the Kingdom of Peacocks. The day he left, his friend gave him three gold arrows.

"Take them," he said. "They may be of help on your quest."

Thousands of miles and countless difficulties lay ahead for Prince Zhao Shutun. But he was not deterred at all; his love for Princess Peacock gave him courage and determination. When he reached a pass between two mountains, a huge boulder blocked his way. Using one of the gold arrows his friend had given him, he shot at it, and it immediately fell apart.

Prince Zhao Shutun finally arrived in the Kingdom of Peacocks. The king was still angry about his daughter's mistreatment by her foolish father-in-law. Therefore, he put Prince Zhao Shutun to a test. He lined his seven daughters up behind a curtain, each holding a burning candle on her head. Then he asked the prince to single out his wife by shooting out the flame of her candle.

Prince Zhao Shutun knew his wife so well that he instantly figured out where she stood. With calm and confidence, he produced his second gold arrow, held his breath, and took aim at the candle on her head. The arrow went whooshing toward its flame and snuffed it out in a puff.

The two loved ones finally reunited. Holding each other tightly, they vowed never to separate again. Touched by Prince Zhao Shutun's devotion to his daughter and convinced of his ability to keep her out of harm's way, the King of Peacocks let the couple return to the Kingdom of Mengbanzha.

Back in the kingdom, Prince Zhao Shutun did a thorough investigation. When he discovered that the Prime Minister was behind the persecution of his wife, he decided to punish him. The Prime Minister was, in fact, a devil in disguise. Before the prince came to arrest him, he changed into a vulture and dashed into the sky in an attempt to flee. With the last of the three gold arrows, Prince Zhao Shutun shot and killed him.

Since then, peace has reigned in Xishuangbanna, and Princess Peacock has become a symbol of harmony and happiness to the Dai people.

Courtesy of Dai Yuru and Yunnan Fine Arts Publishing House

---

*For detailed information about Hindu mythology, see *The Story of Prince Sudhana and Manohara*, by Mark Long and Fitra Jaya Burnama (2002). Available at http://www.borobudur.tv/avadana_05.htm (accessed May 5, 2008).

TWO YOUNG MEN

This is a folktale from the Jino. The 20,889 (China, 2002) Jino people all live in the Xishuangbanna region of Yunnan Province. According to a Jino legend, their creator, Yaobai, had originally designed scripts for them and wrote them on a cowhide. But the early Jino accidentally ate the hide and, of course, the words with it. Without a writing system, fairy tales, legends, and folktales have been passed down orally ever since.

A long time ago, two young men fell in love with the same young woman, named Mihuo. One of them was Yuebache, who was from a rich family. Though well fed and clad, he did nothing useful, but idled away his life in pleasure-seeking. The other was Youhuo, who was from a poor family. He toiled in the fields and hunted in the forests from morning till night every day.

Mihuo loved Youhuo only, which made the rich Yuebache very jealous. He challenged Youhuo to a contest so that he could put him to shame and prove himself worthy of the young woman.

"Let's each set a stool where we often meet and see whose Mihuo will sit on," he said.

He placed a gold stool and waited, but Youhuo could only afford a wooden one. When Mihuo came, however, she paid no attention whatsoever to Yuebache's glistening stool of gold. Instead, she went straight for Youhuo and sat on his wooden stool.

Embarrassed, the rich Yuebache said to the poor Youhuo, "Let's offer her some betel nuts and see whose she'd like to chew."

Yuebache placed his betel nuts in a gold casket, but Youhuo could only wrap his in a palm leaf. Mihuo ignored Yuebache but opened Youhuo's palm leaf and chewed his betel nuts as if they were the best she had ever tasted.

Still, Yuebache wouldn't accept his defeat. He challenged Youhuo to a game of cock-fighting. Youhuo was perplexed because he was so poor that he didn't even own a feather of a gamecock, which would cost a fortune. Mihuo loaned him a rooster with a beautiful red brass color.

Yuebache brought out his favorite gamecock with its legs fitted with gold spurs. Metal spurs are customarily used as a spectacle in cockfighting. However, to flaunt his riches,

Yuebache used too much of the precious metal. As a result, it weighed the poor rooster down so much that it could hardly dodge its opponent's attack. In the end, it not only lost the contest, but also the feathers on its head and neck.

While his gamecock gave up the fight, its owner would not. As his anger knew no bounds, Yuebache decided to get rid of his competitor once and for all. He began to befriend the innocent Youhuo and invited him to be his business partner. One day Yuebache said to him, "I'm leaving in advance to make our business arrangements. I want you to come at a later time."

"How am I going to find you, then?"

"Well, I'll mark my trail with rooster feathers. Follow the trail and you'll be able to locate me."

The feathers led Youhuo to the dreaded Village of Witches, as the wicked Yuebache had planned. He wanted the witches to tear Youhuo to pieces. Hiding in a safe place and watching Youhuo enter the village, Yuebache felt he had finally avenged his humiliation. Losing no time, he rushed back to Mihuo, told her of her love's misfortune, and pressed her to marry him. Mihuo had been thinking of Youhuo since his departure. The sad news of his death plunged her into deep sorrow, but she had no intention whatsoever of changing her heart.

The pigheaded Yuebache, however, bombarded Mihuo daily with threats alternating with entreaties, and eventually Mihuo had no alternative but to cave in.

During their wedding, a delightful tune from a flute drifted to them from a distance. Mihuo immediately recognized it. Her beloved Youhuo had always played it. She rushed in the direction of the melody, casting off her wedding ornaments as she ran. She traced the tune to a big tree on the hilltop, and there she saw the poor Youhuo she had missed so much!

Youhuo recounted his adventures. "After I wandered into the Village of Witches, the first witch I ran into was none other than my sister! She told me that there were no witches in that village at all. They were in fact good people as we are." Taking a deep breath, Youhuo continued, "My sister said they were women from different villages. Because they refused to submit to evil men's desire for sexual favors, they framed them as witches and banned them from their communities."

"But how did they come together then?" Mihuo asked.

"I asked my sister the same question. And her answer was 'We bumped into one another and established this community in the forest for mutual comfort and support.' "

"That's understandable."

"Though we were happy to see each other, my sister wouldn't let me stay with her, saying it would be too inconvenient for me to mingle with a group of women. She gave me the little silver she had scraped together and sent me off."

"If I were you, I wouldn't have accepted her money."

"Well, she insisted," Youhuo murmured, blushing.

"OK, why didn't you come straight to me?"

"As I was nearing home, a villager chopping wood on the hill told me about your forced marriage and the wedding. I played the flute, hoping that I could stop it. And sure enough, you recognized it and came to me."

Youhuo and Mihuo were holding each other tight in their arms when Yuebache, having tracked them down, planted himself between them, pushing them apart. He ordered Mihuo to go back to the wedding with him.

"No," Mihuo said, pointing at Youhuo. "This is the man I truly love!"

Youhuo would have forgiven Yuebacha for his previous act of treachery. But when he saw how he treated Mihuo, he couldn't suppress his anger any more. His hand pressing on his waist knife, Youhuo said, "Leave us alone, or I'll . . .!"

Terrified, Yuebache took a few steps back. Unfortunately, he was standing on the edge of a cliff and there was no more room behind him. He crashed into the valley.

Youhuo and Mihuo finally got married. They lived happily thereafter.

Courtesy of Dai Yuru and Yunnan Fine Arts Publishing House

SEVENTH SISTER AND HER SNAKE HUSBAND

This is a tale from the Mulao people. The 207,352 (China, 2002) Mulao live chiefly in the Luocheng Ethnic Mulao Autonomous County in Guangxi.

Parts of the following tale resembe certain motifs in the "Malan Flower" story retold in The Magic Lotus Lantern and Other Tales from the Han Chinese *(Libraries Unlimited, 2006). Compare this story with "Xu Xuan and His White-snake Wife" in that book.*

Chinese have a half human and half snake ancestry and claim to be descendants of dragons. The Han Chinese and some ethnic minorities seem to treat snakes as variant forms of dragons, as is evident in the following story.

*L*ong, long ago, an old couple had seven daughters. The eldest and the youngest looked very much alike, but their personalities and characters were as different as day and night. The eldest sister was greedy and lazy. The youngest, however, was honest and hardworking. Besides, she was also very dutiful to her parents.

One day the old couple wanted to build a new house. They needed a big tree that could be made into the crossbeam. The tree at the back of their house caught their attention. The old man tried to cut it down. Even though he worked from morning till night, he still got nowhere. He wished that he had a son to help him.

"You're daydreaming," his wife said. "But you did give me an idea. How about getting help from someone?"

"From whom?"

His wife had no answer because, living in the depth of the forest on a mountain, not a single soul could be found in a ten-mile radius. Both sank into silence. Finally, the old man blurted out, "I'll marry one of our daughters to anyone who could cut the tree down for us."

As an old adage goes, "Walls have ears." Trees and rocks, too! The old man's exclamation was overheard by a python. He took the old man's "promise" at face value. Before the old man could finish a pipeful of his tobacco, the python had already chopped the tree down. He then went to the old man and asked him to honor his word. The old man regretted being a big mouth but didn't have the nerve to say no to the giant serpentine suitor. In a quandary, he slumped into depression. Without saying a word to the python, he slipped into his room. Confining himself to bed, he refused to get up, not even for meals. But the python wouldn't give up. He followed the old man into his room and coiled up beneath his bed.

When evening came, the eldest daughter came and asked her father to get up and eat dinner.

"I won't, unless one of you marries this snake."

Only then did the eldest daughter notice it curled up under the bed. She was so scared that she fled, screaming, "No, no, I'll never marry a snake!"

The second daughter came in and was equally frightened. She scurried away, shrieking, "I won't! I won't! I'm afraid! I'm afraid!"

The other daughters came one by one, and each refused to take a python as her husband.

Finally, his seventh daughter came. Her sisters' hysterical screeching had prepared her for what was in store in her father's room. As she entered it, the first thing she did was take a glance at the python. To her astonishment, she saw nothing but a handsome young man lying there. When her father reiterated his request, she gave her consent readily, "Father, please get up and have your dinner. I will marry the snake, and I believe that he will provide for you in the future."

The next morning, the seventh daughter said farewell to her parents and, before setting out with the python, asked her sisters to take good care of them. The couple climbed over the mountain and, at its foot, came to a vast expanse of heaving water. It was the sea. The python gave the seventh daughter a stick of incense. He then asked her to hold it in her hands, get on his back, and close her eyes without opening them until she felt the incense begin to burn her fingers.

As soon as she mounted the python and closed her eyes, she immediately felt a jerking movement. Then all she could hear was the wind swishing by and the water swooshing beneath her. Very soon, she felt a twinge of pain in the tips of her fingers. She opened her eyes, only to find that the sea had disappeared. So had the big python! In its stead, there stood in front of her the same smiling, handsome young man she had spotted in her father's bedroom. The young man told her that he was in fact the son of Dragon King.

News of the Seventh Sister's "change of luck" soon reached her sisters at home. All were happy for her except the eldest. She deeply regretted not marrying the Dragon Prince herself. Her jealousy immediately gave way to hatred, which led to a sinister plot.

On her father's birthday, the Seventh Sister and her Dragon Prince husband came to join in the family celebration. They brought with them many gifts.

That day, the eldest sister appeared unusually diligent. She volunteered to do things she had never done before. When evening came, she offered to wash the vegetables used to fix the family dinner. She invited the Seventh Sister to go with her to the well yards away from their house. When they arrived, she asked her sister to look into the water and said, "Don't you see how beautiful you look in your clothes?" She then asked if she could try them on. The trusting Seventh Sister took them off without the slightest suspicion. No sooner had the eldest sister put the Seventh Sister's clothes on than she pushed her into the well.

The next day, the eldest sister posed as the Seventh Sister in her clothes and returned home with the unknowing Dragon Prince. Despite her resemblance to the Seventh Sister, her clumsiness nearly betrayed her. When asked for vinegar, she handed the Dragon Prince a pot of bacon; when asked for salt, she gave him a jar of cooking oil.

"You placed the jars and pots of ingredients in the cupboard yourself. How come you don't know where to find them any more?" asked the perplexed Dragon Prince.

"Well, I must have drunk too much at my father's birthday party, and the hangover is getting to me."

Taking a closer look, he found some speckles on her face that didn't exist on that of the Seventh Sister, and asked her, "Where did you get those spots on your face? You didn't have them before!"

"Er, don't you remember that I cooked at my parents' house? While I was reducing fat to lard, some of it splashed onto my face and left burn marks on it." The eldest sister thus wheedled the naive Dragon Prince into believing her.

The drowned Seventh Sister's spirit transformed into a bird and found her husband's home. Alighting on a tree outside, she twittered,

> *Coo, coo; coo, coo!*
> *My husband from me you took.*
> *Coo, coo; coo, coo!*
> *See how shameful you look!*

Every morning, before the eldest sister went out to mow in the fields with the Dragon Prince, the little bird landed on her shoulder pole and chirped,

> *A mowing spouse, a mowing spouse,*
> *Is my husband in your house?*

One day when the Dragon Prince came out of his house behind the eldest sister, the little bird dashed into it, refusing to leave.

When the eldest sister worked at her loom in the evening, the bird landed on it and began to sing,

> *Tsiek, tsiek! Others weave three yards a day,*
> *Tsiek, tsiek! Big Sister can't even finish a foot.*

With this, the bird clawed the warp on the loom and messed it up. The eldest sister could no longer put up with the annoying bird. She caught it and threw it into a boiling pot. By midnight, the bird remained uncooked. What's more, it was still chanting in defiance,

Bubbling, bubbling, and bubbling!
Cold-hearted sister is killing her sibling.
Bubbling, bubbling, and bubbling!
I can survive three years of boiling.

Frustrated, the eldest sister cast the pot with the bird in it into the vegetable plot in the backyard. A few days later, a verdant bamboo shot out of the soil. Every morning, when the eldest sister passed by, it would extend its branch, catch a few locks from her hair, and make a mess of her hairdo. The infuriated eldest sister asked the Dragon Prince to cut down the bamboo.

He was about to let his chopper fall on its root when the bamboo began to cry out, "Leave my feet alone!"

Then the prince aimed higher. Again, it shouted, "Don't hurt my waist!"

Finally, the prince aimed at its top, but it shrieked, "Don't you chop my head off!"

The confounded Dragon Prince dug the bamboo out of the ground and carried it into the house. But after he and the eldest sister went out to work each morning, the bamboo would turn into a young woman and cleaned their house, cooked their meal, and wove their cloth. When the Dragon Prince returned and saw things in the house different, he was very curious. He wanted to know what was going on. One day he and the eldest sister went out again, but this time he found an excuse and snuck back home early. He peeped into the room through a crack between the door and its frame. To his surprise, he saw a young woman doing his family chores. Gently he opened the door, stole up behind the young woman, and held her in his arms for fear that she might run away.

"Who are you?" he asked.

"Ouch, you hurt me! I am your wife, the Seventh Sister!" Tears in her eyes, she recounted the murder committed by her eldest sister. Then she added, "Although I am still alive, I've lost all my bones. Boil the chopsticks and the wooden ladle to make a soup. After I drink it, my bones will grow back, and I'll become my former self."

At this, Dragon Prince, with mixed feelings of joy and sorrow, made her the soup. Sure enough, a single sip made the Seventh Sister as alive and energetic as before. The couple reunited and loved each other all the more.

In the evening, the eldest sister returned, only to see her youngest sister alive again. She knew the Dragon Prince had learned of her murderous act. Unable to face him and her sister, she plunged into the big water jar outside the house and drowned herself.

PRINCESS WENCHENG

This tale is popular among Tibetans as well as the Han Chinese. About 1,300 years ago, Princess Wencheng of the Tang dynasty (618–907) left for the Tubo Kingdom, which is now Tibet. She was to join Songtsan Gambo, King of Tubo, to whom her royal father had just married her. This interethnic marriage was meant to strengthen the ties between the Tang dynasty and the Tubo Kingdom. Because the historical record is sketchy, the event has become legendary. Historic relics are nevertheless visible on the trail of the alleged wedding trip. Statues of the royal couple are still worshiped in the Potala Palace in Lhasa today.

*I*n the seventh century, Tang became a powerful and prosperous nation under the reigns of Li Yuan (Emperor Gaozong) and his son Li Shimin (Emperor Taizong). Its influence could be felt far and wide.

During Li Shimin's time, a power struggle took place in Tubo, a territory lying southwest of the Tang Empire. Political opponents murdered its thirty-first *zanpu*, or king. Songtsan Gambo succeeded to the throne. Although only thirteen, he was already a shrewd statesman. Soon he built Tubo back up into a unified kingdom and established the capital at what is now Lhasa. Songtsan Gambo has since become a national hero of the Tibetans.

One of his strategies to build Tubo into a powerful kingdom was to introduce foreign cultures into it. To do so, he formed marital relationships with neighboring countries. After marrying a princess from Nepal, he turned his attention to Tang. A hero himself, he admired its Emperor Taizong. He and his kingdom, he figured, could benefit tremendously from marriage with the emperor's daughter.

Songtsan Gambo sent a messenger to Chang'an, capital of Tang. He was to find out if Emperor Taizong would give one of his daughters to him in marriage. The Tang emperor was only too glad to do so. Having a son-in-law at the helm of a remote kingdom would make it not only a peaceful neighbor but also a tributary (a nation that pays tribute to another to show submission). He immediately asked one of his closest ministers to see Songtsan Gambo on his behalf.

The minister went with Songtsan Gambo's messenger, bringing with him a great number of royal gifts. Each item exemplified the Tang Empire's economic and cultural achievements. Songtsan Gambo, impressed, was all the more determined to marry a Tang princess. He sent Prime Minister Lu Tongtsan to Chang'an to deliver his proposal.

One day during the winter, Lu Tongtsan and his attendants arrived in Chang'an. Emperor Taizong received them in his palace. There, Lu Tongtsan presented Songtsan Gambo's letter of proposal. The emperor, however, didn't give his consent right away. Instead, he put Lu Tongtsan and his men up in his royal hotel, where envoys from other countries were also staying. They were in Tang for exactly the same reason. To betroth his daughter to Songtsan Gambo without offending the other envoys' monarchs, the emperor planned contests among them. To make them look fair, he demanded that several rounds be held. He proclaimed that he would marry Princess Wencheng, one of his daughters, to any monarch whose envoy could win the contests.

In the first round, each of the contestants was given a pearl with a hole in it that had nine zigzag curves in it. They were asked to pass a thread through the hole. None knew what to do except the smart Lu Tongtsan. Dabbing a little honey on one opening, he tied a thread to the waist of an ant and sent it into the hole from the other side. He then blew into it gently. Urged by the breath behind and lured by the honey ahead, the ant dragged the thread through the tiny, crooked hole with ease.

The emperor then asked the contestants to match a hundred mares with another hundred colts so each would find her own baby. Again, everyone was at a loss except Lu Tongtsan. He had separated the babies from their mothers and denied them water. The following day, when he let out the horses, each of the thirsty colts rushed to its mother for milk.

The third contest involved a hundred logs with equal diameters on both ends. The contestants were to tell which end of the logs had been the root and which end the top. Again, Lu Tongtsan solved the puzzle easily. He had all the logs pushed into a pond. As the root end was heavier than the top, the logs all stood with their root ends in the water.

The last contest seemed to be the most difficult. The emperor made the contestants single out Princess Wencheng from among 300 maids of honor dressed in the same fashion. From the princess's nanny, Lu Tongtsan had learned of a barely visible mole between her eyes. When the contest began, Lu Tongtsan looked closely at the young ladies in the lineup. To everyone's surprise, he singled out Princess Wencheng without difficulty.

Even though Emperor Taizong had anticipated Lu Tongtsan would be the winner, he was still amazed at his superior intelligence. With pleasure, he not only agreed to marry his daughter to Songtsan Gambo, but also awarded Lu Tongtsan a title of honor.

Before her departure, Princess Wencheng told her father her worries about relocating to a remote land of a very different culture. Her royal father quoted, " 'My heart goes with the rain that nurtures new crops, /My hands fall on the ploughs that open up new grounds.' " Then he asked, "Isn't that what you said to me last spring when you watched the farmers working?"

Princess Wencheng nodded but asked, "What does that have to do with my marriage?"

"Well, it's exactly this aspiration of yours that helped me decide to let you go." The emperor paused briefly and then continued, "I expect you to build a bridge between the two cultures and bring our advanced farming technology to the Tubo people. A Tubo with better fed people could live more peacefully with us."

Hearing this, Princess Wencheng gained confidence. Before her departure, she gave herself an orientation, learning from Lu Tongtsan about Songtsan Gambo, his people, and his land.

Emperor Taizong gave his daughter a huge dowry. Apart from a few articles for her personal use, most of the dowry was intended to promote Tubo's economic and cultural development, including seeds of vegetables hardy enough to weather its cold and dry conditions. Among the gifts were books on medicine, arts, and crafts. A devout Buddhist, the princess brought a statue of Buddha with her. A large number of the people in her company were artisans and craftsmen with skills and know-how in advanced techniques and technologies. For their safety, Emperor Taizong sent a small army to escort them.

The group left Chang'an to travel to Lhasa through Qinghai. To Princess Wencheng, it was an eye-opening journey. She could have never imagined the things she saw and heard if she had still been in her father's palace. At the town of Shan, about 4,000 feet above sea level and a thousand miles from Tubo, she paused. Looking back at the vast land reaching east, she said good-bye to her father for the last time. From now on, everything would be unknown and uncertain. Yet she was ready for the new life and for the person she had never met but who would be her husband.

On the plateau of Tubo, people turned out to welcome the Tang princess. They offered her their horses, yaks, food, and water, as well as boats where there were rivers. They saw to it that she had a smooth trip.

A few months later, Princess Wencheng arrived at Baihai, a town miles away from Lhasa. Songtsan Gambo was already expecting her there. He had traveled all the way from the capital to meet her. In order to create an atmosphere of familiarity, he wore a Han costume. The princess's dread evaporated at the sight of the handsome young king. To minimize Princess Wencheng's cultural shock, Songtsan Gambo ordered a palace to be constructed for her in the style of the Han Chinese. He also had the Ramoche Monastery built for the Buddha statue Princess Wencheng had brought with her. The princess herself also requested that the Jokhang Monastery be built. In front of it, she and Songtsan Gambo planted some willow trees, known today as *tangliu* (the Tang willows).

Today, visitors can still see Princess Wencheng's Buddhist statue enshrined in the Jokhang Monastery. Along with it are the statues of the princess and her Tibetan husband. Tibetans love them so much that they still keep intact the chamber in the Potala Palace where they spent their earlier married lives.

Courtesy of Dai Yuru and Yunnan Fine Arts Publishing House

TALE OF THE XING'AN MOUNTAINS

This is a tale from the Ewenki. The 30,500 (China, 2002) Ewenki people live in the Inner Mongolia Autonomous Region and the province of Heilongjiang in Northeastern China, where the Xing'an Mountains lie.

*I*n the beautiful Xing'an Mountains there lived a young man named Wuhenai. He was as strong as a tiger and could eat a whole deer for a meal. Armed with a bow embedded with sapphires, he was dressed in a silvery armor and rode on a crimson horse equipped with a gilded saddle. His archery was matchless among the Ewenki people.

One day he was hunting near a river when he overheard the whispered conversation of a couple.

"Tell me if there's a female brighter and prettier than I am in the world."

"You are bright and pretty, alright, but you can't match Kala, the younger daughter of King Xiwo. He lives where the sun sets." The male paused a little and asked, "Tell me if there's any male who is smarter and more handsome than I am."

"You may be very smart and handsome, but you aren't comparable to Wuhenai."

When Wuhenai walked around a big rock, he found a pair of deer chattering. Before he could greet them, they had scurried off, startled by his unexpected appearance. He remembered nothing of what they had said except for the bright and pretty younger daughter of King Xiwo, who lived where the sun sets. Riding his crimson horse, he set out in the same direction, full of hope that he would eventually be able to see the prettiest girl in the world. When he took a break, he played his *kouxian*, a small bamboo musical instrument played with the mouth. The beautiful tune attracted hundreds of birds, who danced in circles around him. He then asked them what the younger daughter of King Xiwo looked like. Their answer was, "She's like the best of all flowers. Her face resembles an apple; her eyes, the moon; and her voice, a jingle bell."

Upon hearing that, Wuhenai goaded his crimson horse to run at full speed. He crossed over numerous mountains and rivers while playing his *kouxian*. He also prayed to the gods of mountains as he passed them. Finally, the sound of the *kouxian* dispersed clouds and mists, revealing the splendid palace of King Xiwo. Seeing it, he played even harder, so that the sound reached the king in the palace. The king ordered that Wuhenai be brought into his presence.

King Xiwo liked Wuhenai immediately because he was not only handsome but also capable of playing the wonderful little bamboo instrument. He wanted to reward him, promising to satisfy any of his demands.

"Your younger daughter Kala is the prettiest of all in the world, so I'd like her to be my wife. Would you marry her to me?"

"Sure, I will," the king said readily, and had a wedding planned for them.

According to Ewenki customs, unmarried young women were barred from direct contact with males before the ceremony. All this time, Kala had been in her maiden chamber with her friendly companions, a white and a black rabbit. Aware that someone had come to propose marriage to her, she felt secretly happy, and sent the rabbits to inspect the suitor on her behalf.

However, her elder sister, who lived in a nearby chamber, intercepted the animals. Although plain-looking in appearance and vicious at heart, she wanted to have the handsome Wuhenai as her husband. She grabbed the rabbits and threatened to kill them if they told their mistress the truth about Wuhenai. So when the rabbits came back to Kala, they had to lie to her that Wuhenai was an eighty-year-old man with a beard long enough to reach his waist. Then the elder daughter came over herself, urging Kala to flee from such an unequal match. And so she did.

When the wedding day came, Kala was nowhere to be found. King Xiwo became very embarrassed. Seizing the chance, his elder daughter asked to take her sister's place. The king had no alternative but to let her. Traditionally, a bride has to wear a scarf over her head to cover her face as part of the ritual. The bridegroom is not to lift it until they are in their bridal chamber. Only then does the bridegroom know what the bride looks like. That was exactly what happened to poor Wuhenai. He had to accept the king's homely elder daughter as his wife.

On their way back to Wuhenai's homeland, the newlyweds happened to pass by the forest where Kala had taken refuge. When she saw what a handsome young man Wuhenai was, she realized her elder sister had duped her.

Back in his homeland, Wuhenai's friends and neighbors all laughed at him for taking such an unattractive woman for his spouse. Their ridicule turned him into a quiet man, so much so that he stopped playing his favorite *kouxian*.

A month later, the couple paid King Xiwo a visit. On their way, they stopped at a spinster's home. A young woman there tried to avoid making eye contact with Wuhenai. She was none other than Kala, who had been adopted by the old woman. Mesmerized by her beauty, Wuhenai couldn't take his eyes off her. Embarrassed, she ran out, and Wuhenai followed closely. Seeing this, the elder daughter, who had recognized her sister at the onset, was so ashamed that she jumped into a well outside the house and drowned herself.

Wuhenai ran after Kala until they reached the Heilongjiang River. Once there, Kala told him the whole story. Holding her tight in his arms, he could hear both their hearts thumping as loud as the current of the river.

A MOUNTAIN GIRL AND A GIANT HUNTER

This is a folktale from the Oroqen. The 8,200 Oroqen (China, 2002) had lived by hunting in the Great and Small Xing'an Ranges in Northeastern China until the 1990s, when they changed their lifestyle to farming. They used to live in a primitive communal society, in what is mentioned in the story as xianrenzhu. *A cone-shaped tent of wooden pole structure covered with animal hides and birch bark, it looks very much like the Native American tipi.*

*A*long time ago, in a forest-clad mountain, there was a beautiful young woman named Ayijilun. Having lost her mother at an early age, she was raised by her father. A veteran hunter, he trained her to be as skilled as he was. Without any siblings, Ayijilun made friends with her family horse and dog at home and the flowers and other plants outside. As she grew into a young woman, she came into contact with a handsome young hunter named Lunjishan. A great archer, he was known for not missing a single target in his life. Eventually, the two fell in love and were engaged, with the blessing of Ayijilun's father.

Ayijilun and her father lived a simple but self-sufficient life. Mother Nature offered them inexhaustible food in the form of wild beasts and fowls. Their peace, however, was abruptly cut short when an old monster came to take control of the mountain. At his command, a wild boar patrolled the vast extent of the forest to prevent hunters from "trespassing." And an owl flew back and forth to alert him to "intruders." The monster was also a womanizer.

One day, Lunjishan was visiting Ayijilun in her tipi-like *xianrenzhu*, when two goblins dispatched by the old monster burst into it to abduct Ayijilun. But they proved no match for the valiant Lunjishan, who turned them away easily.

The old monster wouldn't give up and sent more goblins to kidnap Ayijilun. One evening, as she and her father were fast asleep in their *xianrenzhu*, the goblins stole up to it. The family dog detected their movements and barked. The goblins withdrew and hid themselves behind a tree, where they mimicked the howling of a wolf. As the dog came toward them, they threw it a poisoned pie, which it ate and then died. After that, they slipped back to the *xianrenzhu* and blew a cloud of magic powder into it through a crack in its wall of hide. The magic powder put Ayijilun and her father into a coma. The goblins then tied Ayijilun up and carried her away.

After a long time, Ayijilun awoke to find a ferocious monster towering over her, a sharp horn sticking out of his head and a pair of buckteeth protruding from his mouth. The scornful Ayijilun denounced her abductor with the sharpest words she could find. The monster seemed unaffected. Gloating over the poor girl's helplessness, he chuckled, "My residence is so fortified that it's impenetrable. Don't expect your fiancé to come to your rescue."

Ayijilun could do nothing but cry while condemning the monster repeatedly.

The next morning, when Ayijilun's father came to, he found his daughter missing and their beloved dog lifeless. The unbearable grief knocked him out again. Before long, Lunjishan came for a visit as usual. He helped the old man regain consciousness and put him to bed. Just as he was wondering what had happened, the family horse told him everything. He was about to set off to rescue Ayijilun when an elderly birch tree called out,

"Lunjishan, Lunjishan! The old hunter and his daughter have been treating me like one of their own. Take this leaf of mine since I've got nothing else to repay their kindness. You may find it useful." With that, a leaf dropped from a branch and floated to the ground.

Lunjishan had just picked it up and stowed it in his pocket when a flower shouted, "My name is White-edged Morning Glory." Extending a long, curly tendril, it said, "They've never allowed their horse to tramp on me. That's why I can live here carefree and bloom happily each summer. I have only this tendril as a token of thanks. Take it; you may find it useful."

Lunjishan nipped off a segment of the tendril, placed it carefully in his pocket, and mounted Ayijilun's family horse. Sword in hand and bow and arrows on his back, he was ready to set out. Just then a big mass of cloud appeared in front of him. Before he realized it, the cloud had lifted him and the horse into the air and carried them off with a whish. Soon Lunjishan found himself above the mountaintop where the monster lived.

He dismounted the horse and was landing halfway on the cloud when he felt a stir in his pocket. It was the leaf that the old tree had given him. He took it out, and before he had a chance to look at it, he had shrunk to a little worm and perched on it. The leaf then curled up, drifted off the cloud, and, carrying him in his reduced form, alighted on a tree in the courtyard of the monster's residence. From the tree, Lunjishan could hear Ayijilun crying and rebuking the monster while it leered wickedly. As if it could read his mind, the coiled leaf glided to the ground and rolled to the doorstep of the monster's den. But the door was so closely shut that even dust couldn't get in. The leaf rocked back and forth as if at a loss what to do. Just then, a goblin came to see the monster. Before he closed the door behind him, the leaf attached itself to the goblin's pants and was carried into the cave.

"Your Highness, the wedding is ready, and all the guests have arrived. They're expecting you to show up," said the goblin.

"Let them be patient. We're coming," said the old monster.

After the goblin left, the monster took out a richly bejeweled costume and asked Ayijilun to put it on. Sobbing heavily, she refused. The monster became so angry that he started to force the costume onto her. Seeing this, Lunjishan wanted to act immediately. The understanding leaf suddenly sprang open so that his rider resumed his original form. Seeing Lunjishan, Ayijilun was greatly surprised, but her shock soon gave way to happiness. The monster, however, was all the more furious. He wanted to summon his goblins for help. When he opened his mouth, the leaf sprang up, dashed into it, and wedged itself in his throat, leaving him unable to speak. The only thing he could do was try to cough the leaf out. Just then, Lunjishan felt the tendril tugging at the lining of his pocket. No sooner had he taken it out than it turned into a thick rope, threw itself around the struggling monster, and tied him into a wriggling bundle. Just then the monster's lieutenant stumbled into the cave. The monster winked hard at him so that he would help. Before the goblin took the hint, however, Lunjishan had cut him down with his sword and, with another slash, killed his master.

When the couple came out of the cave, the cloud that had transported Lunjishan was still hanging low, with their horse on it. Mounting it together, the two were carried back home. There they were overjoyed to find the dog resuscitated and the father recovered. Their wedding day has become the happiest day of the Oroqen.

Tales of Creation and Ethnic Origins

Humans have been questioning where they came from either as individuals or as groups since their first appearance on the earth. Before anthropology and theology came to the rescue, Chinese ethnic minorities had come up with answers using their imaginations. "Gumiya—Creator of the Universe" brought the Blang into the world. "The White Swan Fairy" saved a soldier and thence the Kazak ethnicity. The pregnancy of "Forty Girls" was tragic but gave birth to the Kirgiz. Many other gods were behind "The Origin of the Naxi People." Seven ethnic groups came from "Seven Brothers" with the same parents. "Miluotuo—A Goddess Who Creates the World" created the Yao. "The Origin of the Gelao Ethnicity" came about because of a young couple's marriage in defiance of social conventions. "The Surviving Nu Ancestry" were left after humankind's annihilation by a flood on a biblical scale.

GUMIYA—CREATOR OF THE UNIVERSE

This is a myth from the Blang. The majority of the 91,900 Blang (China, 2002) live in Yunnan. The primary form of their oral literature is mythology, of which the following is the most famous.

*I*n the beginning, there was neither sky nor earth, not to mention plants and humans. Only clusters of black clouds floated hither and thither. A god named Gumiya and his twelve children were determined to create the universe. As they set to work to find building materials, they caught sight of a giant rhinoceros roaming aimlessly with the clouds. They captured and slaughtered it. Using different parts of its body, they set about generating the elements of the universe. They turned its hide into the sky; its eyes into a pair of stars; its flesh into soil; its bones into rocks; its blood into water; and its horn into various plants. Finally, Gumiya kneaded the rhinoceros's brain into humans after his own image, and its bone marrow into birds, beasts, insects, and fish.

After accomplishing these feats, Gumiya still had two things to worry about: Hanging in the air without any support, the sky could tilt at any time; and resting on nothing beneath it, the earth could overturn without notice. Before long, the wise Gumiya came up with a solution. He shaped the rhinoceros's legs into four colossal pillars and put them at the four corners of the world to hold up the sky. Gumiya then seized an enormous turtle and made him carry the earth on his back, quite against his will. Every time the turtle made an attempt to flee, the earth would quake. To prevent the turtle from moving, Gumiya asked his loyal subordinate, the golden rooster, to watch over him. Whenever the turtle showed signs of moving, the rooster would peck at his eyes. Nevertheless, earthquakes were inevitable because the golden rooster sometimes became so tired that he dozed off. When that happened, people would scatter rice to wake up the slumbering bird.

Everything was now in order: The sky and the earth were steadied, the clouds were beautified with colorful powders, the pair of stars was twinkling, humans were working happily, birds were flying freely, bees were singing joyously, deer were trotting at ease, and fish were swimming merrily in clear waters. Gumiya and his children all felt happy and rewarded.

There were nine solar sisters and ten lunar brothers in a neighboring universe, who were long-time rivals of Gumiya and his children. Jealous of Gumiya's accomplishments, they gathered in the sphere that Gumiya and his children had created to unleash their concerted energy of light in an attempt to destroy everything in it.

Bombarded by heat, the clouds changed colors, stars lost their luster, the earth cracked, vegetation withered, and rocks liquefied. In addition, crabs lost their heads; fish, their tongues; snakes, their limbs; and frogs, their tails. And they remain so even today. Gumiya applied wax to his hat to fend off the heat, but it melted and dripped into his eyes, which hurt him terribly. Vowing to shoot down the suns and moons, he made himself a bow as well as a number of arrows out of different kinds of rattan and hemp. He then made the arrows venomous by dipping them in the water drawn from a pool where a poisonous dragon lived.

Equipped with these lethal weapons, Gumiya embarked on a journey to seek out the vicious lunar brothers and solar sisters. He tramped over mountains steaming like a hot iron and crossed rivers filled with boiling water. At last, he reached the top of the highest peak. There he launched his deadly arrows at the heavenly siblings, who had been celebrating their success. The first arrow hit a sun, and she plummeted, tumbling and rumbling, to the earth. Undeterred, the rest mustered their joint strength and threw blistering heat at Gumiya. Equally undaunted, he kept shooting at them and killed all but a lunar brother and a solar sister. The earth immediately cooled down, and living creatures came back to life again. The blood of the dead moons and suns reddened the foliage of trees, the petals of flowers, and the feet of pheasants.

Extremely terrified by the death of their siblings, the surviving sun and moon took to their heels. The fuming Gumiya, though tired, sprang after them while drawing his bow. Quivering with fatigue, he missed both targets. However, an arrow whistling by the lunar brother sent a chill through his spine, so that the moon has been cold ever since. Eventually the moon brother and the sun sister took refuge in a cave. As a result, the world became dark and cold, knowing no days and nights. At the same time, rivers stopped flowing, and trees quit swaying. People had to hang their lamps on the horns of their buffaloes while working in the fields. And they had to walk with bamboo canes to avoid stumbling.

Gumiya decided to invite the moon brother and the sun sister to come out and provide the world with heat and light. He sent a sparrow to look for their hideout. In a short time, the bird returned with her findings, "Far on the horizon in the east, there is a big cave. That's where the sun and the moon are hiding right now."

Gumiya gathered all the fowls and beasts and asked them if they would like to go invite the sun and the moon to come out. All except two cowardly partridges said yes. One painted its buttocks red and claimed that it was suffering from diarrhea; the other dyed the hair on its head white and pronounced that it was in mourning for a dead relative. Since then, the red end and the white top have become a partridge's infamous signature of weakness. The bird has thus become an object of scorn to the Blang.

The birds and beasts marched toward the big cave in the east in two columns, headed respectively by the vociferous rooster in the air and the burly boar on the ground. The sparrow showed the way and the fireflies illuminated it. Gumiya stayed behind, fearing that his appearance might frighten the sun and the moon so much that they would refuse to come out.

In the meantime, the sun and the moon lived in constant fear—fear of boredom and starvation if they remained in self-inflicted imprisonment and of Gumiya's poisonous arrows if they ventured out to look for food and fun. At their wit's end, they could do nothing but hold each other and lament. They cried and cried. Suddenly they heard a commotion coming from outside their cave. Horrified, they pressed themselves into a corner and held their breath.

The birds and beasts shouted in unison, asking the sun and the moon to show their faces. The more they hollered, however, the more frightened the moon and sun became. The rooster quieted the crowd and began to sing,

> *The moon's smart,*
> *The sun's bright;*
> *Come out you both,*
> *With your heat and light.*

The rooster's sincerity allayed the siblings' fear somewhat. Finally they plucked up enough courage to speak, although very anxiously:

> *We'd rather die in the cave*
> *Than die from Gumiya's bow.*
> *If you really want us to exit,*
> *Get us drink and food, will you?*

The birds and beasts then sang in chorus,

> *To invite you is Gumiya's intent,*
> *Your death he's no longer meant.*
> *Gumi Shafeima, his daughter dear,*
> *She'll feed you from year to year.*

The moon and the sun were still incredulous, even after the birds and beasts talked to them for quite some time. In the end, the rooster made a pledge, "In the future, come out if I crow. Remain where you are if I don't, and you'll be safe and sound."

To show his sincerity, the rooster cut a knot from a tree and split it. He threw half into the cave and put the other half on his head. Since then, roosters have had combs. The practice of keeping half a tree knot as a vow not to go back on one's word in a business deal has also become a Blang tradition. The rooster said if any of his fellows failed to wake up the sun in the morning, that rooster would be condemned. Gumiya's daughter also agreed to feed the sun and the moon. She said she would do so by assuming three different forms each day: a pretty girl in the morning, a healthy woman at noon, and a gray-haired grandma in the evening. She pledged to work diligently and constantly to feed the sun with juice of gold and the moon with juice of silver.

To conclude the negotiation, the birds and beasts, following Gumiya's instructions, asked the sun and the moon to alternate their outings—one by day and the other by night—and meet once at the end of a month. Because the sun was afraid of walking alone in darkness, she was scheduled to come out during the day. Because she was shy, her brother, the moon, gave her a kit full of embroidering needles, with which she could prick the eyes of those who dared to look at her.

When it was time for the sun and the moon to emerge from the cave, they found a huge stone blocking the opening. The birds and the beasts outside tried to remove it, but none could make it budge. The boar came forward, and gathering up all his strength, shoved the stone aside with his powerful snout. The sun and the moon reappeared, bringing day and night to the world again.

Courtesy of Sarah Martin, WKU

THE WHITE-SWAN FAIRY

This is a popular folktale from the Kazak. The 1,250,000 Kazaks in China (China, 2002) live mainly in Xinjiang. Kazak was a tribe that broke away from the Golden Horde, a khanate established by the eldest son of Genghis Khan in the first half of the thirteenth century, during the Mongols' westward expedition. The origin of the term "Kazak" is unclear. Some sources suggest that it means "wanderer" or "digger." Others believe that it stands for "white swan," as in the following story.

*I*n ancient times, a mighty army of cavalry marched westward from their capital, following their great leader. On their way, they came to the boundless Gobi Desert. The urgent military situation of the time demanded that they pass through it as quickly as possible. So day and night, they pushed forward without resting.

It was in the middle of summer, when the scorching sun raged without mercy. What's more, not a single drop of water could be found in the vast sea of sand. Consequently, many cavalrymen and their horses died of thirst. The troop was no longer in an orderly formation, with the distance between each soldier increasing every minute. As time passed, more and more of the soldiers dropped out and lost touch with each another.

One day, a general who was too tired and thirsty to move on collapsed in the sand, dying. He only had enough strength left to move his cracked dry lips as if to ask for help. But despite their respect and sympathy for him, none of his troops had any energy left to stop and attend to him. They had to keep going or they would perish themselves.

Exposed to the baking sun and deprived of water and food, the general was on the brink of death. In a hallucination, he saw a white swan flying toward him from the distance; she soon landed by his side. He vaguely remembered that swans preferred living by the water, so her appearance brought him a gleam of hope for survival. He gathered up all his strength and struggled onto his feet. Strangely, the swan seemed not to be scared or perturbed. Instead of flying away, she waddled along in front of the stumbling general, as if to lead the way. Eventually she led him to a body of water.

The ecstatic general drank to his heart's content and soon recovered his strength and health. When he felt fully revived and looked around, he could no longer find the life-saving swan. In her stead, however, a beautiful young fairy stood in front of him, much to his happy surprise. In fact, the swan had been her disguise.

Eventually the general and the fairy got married. Later they had a baby son, and they named him "Aq Qaz," meaning "white swan." "Aq Qaz" was later misspelled as "Kazak."

When Kazak grew up, he begot three sons, who became the ancestors of the three big Kazak tribes or jüzes (hoard), namely the "higher jüz," "middle jüz," and "junior jüz."

FORTY GIRLS

This is a folktale from the Kirgiz, one of the ten Muslim ethnic groups in China. Its population of 160,800 (China, 2002) live mostly in the Kizilsu Ethnic Kirgiz Autonomous Prefecture in Western Xinjiang. The Kirgiz are from the same ethnic family as the citizens of the Kyrgyz Republic in Central Asia

The beginning of the Kirgiz ethnicity requires more research, but the name of the ethnic group itself offers some clue. The original meaning of the word Kirgiz was "forty girls" or "forty tribes." Hence we have the following story.

*T*here were once in a place called Pushewei'er a brother and a sister, Hanmansu'er and Anali. One day, having nothing to do, they went up a mountain to play. They wandered to a big cave and went into it. To their amazement, they saw a number of young people singing and dancing merrily. Without waiting for an invitation, Hanmansu'er and Anali joined in their frolics.

Unfortunately these playful youngsters were immortals, and it was taboo for worldly people to mingle with them. When a religious leader learned of the violation, he reported it to the king. Furious, the king ordered the brother and the sister to be hanged and their bodies cremated. He also decreed that their ashes be scattered in a river connected to his palace. The river drained into a pond in the royal garden, so the ashes of Hanmansu'er and Anli were transported into it. At the time, forty of the king's concubines were bathing in the pond. While swimming, they heard a female voice crying,

"Anali is wronged! I am innocent!"

Curious, the girls cast about in the water to look for the source of the crying, and in so doing, they were contaminated, so to speak, by the ashes that the current was carrying. All of them became pregnant in no time.

Enraged, the king banished them from his court. Thirty of the girls turned right and went into the mountains. Ten went in the opposite direction and found themselves on the vast plain. Later, they each gave birth to a baby. The descendants of the babies born to the thirty girls living in the mountains became the "right" clan of Kirgiz, and the offspring of the babies born to the ten girls residing on the plain became the "left" clan.

THE ORIGIN OF THE NAXI PEOPLE

This is a genesis myth of the Naxi, an ethnic minority of 308,800 (China, 2002), who live chiefly in Lijiang, Yunnan. The Naxi people have their own spoken and written languages. Many of the Naxi people's history and myths have been recorded by their unique ideographic Dongba script, which uses pictures to represent meanings. This story is from one of the Dongba classics.

*T*he entire universe was once in a state of turbulence. Even trees could talk, and stones could walk. None of the hosts of heaven and features of the earth was in solid shape. They were but obscure outlines. Out of the interaction between the air and sound there emerged a god named Yige Woge. He transformed into a white egg, which in turn changed into a nameless white chicken. He then named himself Enyu Enman. He belonged to the Milidong Zhu tribe.

Before long, another god, named Ige Wona, appeared. He transformed into a black egg which, in turn, gave birth to a black chicken. The nameless bird called himself Fuji Nannan and claimed to be affiliated with the Milishu Zhu clan.

The good-looking white Enyu Enman made a nest out of three clouds in the sky and three bundles of grass on the earth. In the nest, he laid nine pairs of white eggs and hatched them into gods and Buddhist bodhisattvas. The ugly black chicken Fuji Nannan laid the same number of black eggs and hatched them into ghosts and devils.

Nine able-minded gods tried to lift the sky, and seven intelligent goddesses attempted to push down the earth. All failed because the sky and the earth were still intertwined and in chaos. Not until years later did the gods and goddesses think of a way out, that is, to prop up the sky. To do so, they erected a pillar of white shells in the east, a pillar of black pearls in the west, a pillar of gold in the north, and a pillar of tin in the south. They mended the sky with sapphire and weighed the earth down with gold. Finally, they succeeded in separating them. After a short time, gods, Buddhist bodhisattvas, and sages met and built a magic mountain, which stabilized the universe once and for all.

Air and sound again gave birth to three drops of dews, which turned into three oceans. Out of the oceans was born Hennai, who, in turn, brought forth Meinai. Seven generations after Meinai, there emerged the ancestry of humans.

The seventh generation of Meinai was headed by Congren Li'en, who had five brothers and six sisters. Their immoral lives made the celestial gods very angry. Consequently, the sun and the moon lost their luster, and the hills and dales began to moan—a precursor of a crowning calamity.

As Congren Li'en was farming on a mountain, a god released a wild boar to attack him. He killed the beast and was about to cut it up when a half-smiling elderly couple appeared before him. Frightened, Li'en tried to run away. But in his haste, he bumped the old man's silver hat off his head and caused him to scream. He screamed so loud that the sky was shaken. Li'en then knocked the old woman's cane out of her hand, and she uttered a cry. She cried so loud that the earth was upset.

Horrified, Li'en dropped to his knees and asked for forgiveness, but the elderly couple told him that it was too late. They said that a great catastrophe would befall him and his siblings because they sinned too much. Seeing that Congren Li'en was repentant, they showed him the way to salvation.

"Go and kill a white-hoofed male yak and make an enclosed leather vessel out of its hide. Sew it with thin needles and thick thread. Tie the vessel with twelve ropes, three to cypress trees, another three to fir trees, still another three to the sky, and the last three to the earth. Fill the vessel with healthy goats, golden hounds, silver-white roosters, and nine kinds of crop seeds. Two more things that I bet you won't forget yourself: Bring a waist-knife and flint with you. When everything is ready, settle yourself in the vessel and wait."

Congren Li'en returned and told his siblings about the imminent disaster. They, too, went to the elderly couple for advice. They were told to prepare a vessel of pig's hide sewn with thick needles and thin thread.

Three days later, the sky and the earth began to roar. As mountains cracked, beasts of prey were rendered homeless. A flood broke out. Since its waters surged sky high, even otters and fish were choked. Soon the sun and the moon were dimmed, plunging the universe into darkness.

All vanished except Congren Li'en, who was saved by his leather vessel. It carried him and his selected creatures until it docked at a mountain that had just surfaced out of the subsiding flood.

Congren Li'en cut the vessel open with his waist-knife. As he stepped out, he was stunned by what he saw: Not a living soul was visible as far as his eyes could reach. He burst into tears, and so did his animal companions. He left them and wandered alone aimlessly in the barren territory. Then he arrived at the foot of a mountain, where he found an old man with a long, white beard, sighing: "Oh, all humans are gone . . . !"

Excited and joyous, Li'en knelt before the old man and pleaded, "Grandpa, take pity on me. I'm the only man left, and I feel very lonely. I need a companion to work with me by day and chat with me at night. But no other human beings survived in the world. Please tell me what to do!"

The old man, who was a god named Milidong Apu, stopped sighing and, looking up, told Li'en, "At the foot of a high mountain in Meishangen'an there live two fairies; one with vertical eyes and the other, horizontal. The former is pretty and the latter homely. Here's the catch: Marry the fairy with horizontal eyes only."

But Li'en couldn't resist the temptation of the vertical-eyed beauty and took her as his wife. In time, she was pregnant with sextuplets, but Li'en soon discovered the truth of the old man's warning. Instead of human babies, the newborns turned out to be a bear, a boar, a monkey, a pheasant, a snake, and a frog. Li'en hurried to the old man for consultation. The elder chided him for not heeding his warning, but gave him a remedy anyway. This time, Li'en listened. He drove the bear and the boar into the forest, sent the monkey and the pheasant to the mountains, and cast the snake and the frog into the shaded and damp places.

A versatile and wise god, Milidong Apu had made numerous puppets and gave some of them to Li'en. He told him that if he could refrain from looking at them until ninety days later, they would turn into human beings. Then he could take one of them as his spouse. Li'en, however, was too curious to wait that long. As a result, the puppets failed to transform. When he went to Milidong Apu for help, the god was so angry that he cut the puppets into small pieces and disposed of them. The ones he scattered in the mountains became echoes, those he threw into the rivers turned into waves, and the rest, which he tossed into the woods, grew to be wild animals.

Congren Li'en became lonely again, drifting from place to place, bursting into fits of anger and sorrow alternately. Eventually he stumbled into a garden of twilight, whose beauty was beyond description. A plum tree was particularly captivating, with its blossoms facing each other in pairs. His fatigue and sorrow dissipated instantly. He was indulging himself in the wonders of the garden when a gorgeous young woman accosted him, "Hey, you must be a very unique person, traveling all by yourself. Where're you going?"

Congren Li'en was startled. He had never imagined coming across such a beauty in a world he thought was devoid of human beings. He introduced himself and said he was looking for a companion. Before long, they became good friends.

From their conversation, Li'en learned that the girl's name was Chenhong Baobaiming. She was, in fact, the daughter of a heavenly god named Zilao Apu. Her father had betrothed her to the Keluo Kexing family in heaven, against her will. Reluctant as she was, she didn't have the courage to reject her father's decision. Depressed, she landed in the garden to seek some peace of mind. The encounter with a handsome young man like Congren Li'en also proved to be a happy surprise to her. They fell in love, and the goddess invited Congren Li'en to her home. She transformed into a crane and carried Li'en on her back.

Once in heaven, the goddess planned to announce her secret love at the right time. So she hid Li'en in a big bamboo basket behind the door of the family's sheep pen. In the evening, her father, Zilao Apu, returned from sheep herding. When he found that his sheep refused to enter the pen and his shepherd dog barked at it, he knew something was wrong. He began to hone his sword. Seeing this, Chenhong Baobaiming pleaded with her father,

"Father, a bee wouldn't flee if its hive were safe; a slave wouldn't run if his master were kind. What a great young man Li'en is since he was able to survive the collapsing mountains and overwhelming floods we've just witnessed! I brought him home because I love him. Please, Father, don't be angry with me. He can thresh our grain when it's sunny and dig canals for us when it's rainy."

"I have to know who he is!" the father rumbled in a muffled voice.

Before the scheduled time came to meet the goddess's father, Li'en had rushed to the river to bathe and applied ghee ointment to his body so it appeared shiny and smooth. Eyeing him from head to toe, the heavenly father Zilao Apu commented, "You look too pale, son. Evidently your father didn't train you well."

Li'en dropped to his knees and, begging for mercy, told the celestial god that all human beings except him had perished. "I want to live on and want the line of humankind to continue. So please marry your daughter to me," he requested.

"Fine, but you must fell nine forests of trees and bring the logs back to me."

Chenhong Baobaiming taught Li'en how to accomplish the demanding task. The next morning, acting upon her instructions, Li'en placed a big axe in each of the nine forests and chanted,

> *White butterflies, come and work for me;*
> *Black ants, come and work for me;*
> *And I'll work together with you.*

Immediately, all the trees in the nine forests were cut down and then transported to Zilao Apu as logs. Li'en lost no time asking him for the daughter's hand, but the celestial god assigned him another task: to burn the tree stumps and make the land arable.

The goddess again told Li'en what to do. The next morning, he left a torch in each of the forest lands and chanted the same incantation. Sure enough, everything on the ground was immediately burned to ashes.

Once again, Zilao Apu refused to give his consent to the young couple's marriage. Instead, he gave Li'en nine sacks of grain seeds and demanded that he farm the forest lands.

"Don't come back until you harvest the crops," he added.

Several months later, Li'en returned with the crops. Before he had time to open his lips, Zilao Apu alleged that three grains were missing: two in the craw of a turtledove and one in the stomach of an ant.

"Go and retrieve them," he demanded.

The next morning, a turtledove landed on a tree in the courtyard, where the fairy Chenhong Baobaiming was weaving. Li'en tried to shoot the bird with his bow and arrow but was too nervous to take good aim. The worried goddess gently nudged him with her shuttle, which made him let the arrow go. It hit the turtledove right under its neck. In its craw, they found the two grains. Since then, all turtledoves have had a red patch on their chests.

Congren Li'en then turned a stone and found an army of ants, one of which had a bulging belly. He tied a thread that the goddess had given him around the ant's belly and pulled it tight. A grain popped out, and ants have since had very thin waists.

Holding the three grains, Li'en went happily to see the celestial god, saying, "Now that I've done what you asked me, please give me what I want."

Zilao Apu responded, "I know you are a good man, but I still can't let you have my daughter yet. I want you to hunt *bharals* (that is, mountain sheep) with me this evening."

Li'en accepted his invitation, although he was secretly unhappy. The goddess Chenhong Baobaiming, having learned of the planned hunting trip, tipped him off,

"Be careful, Li'en. My father's not going to get any *bharal*. He means to get you." With that, she told him how to head off the danger.

That evening, Zilao Apu took Li'en with him and camped for the night in a small cave halfway up the mountain. He asked Li'en to sleep with his head toward the cave opening while he himself would do the opposite. Remembering his girlfriend's warning, Li'en remained alert, and when he saw the celestial god fast asleep, he quietly crawled out of the makeshift bed of felt they had brought with them. He then placed a large stone in it to pass for his sleeping self. After that, he snuck back to the goddess. Deep in the night, Zilao Apu woke up and kicked the stone out of the cave. When the stone tumbled down the mountain, it happened to hit a *bharal* on its head and killed it. Early in the morning, Li'en retrieved the *bharal*'s carcass and carried it back in anticipation of Zilao Apu's return.

The next evening, Zilao Apu repeated the same trick on a fishing trip. Chenhong Baobaiming alerted Li'en to the possible risk again, and he returned safe and sound as she had expected.

Refusing to relent, the celestial god ordered that Congren Li'en get him three drops of tiger's milk. This time, the frustrated Li'en didn't mention it to the fairy because he thought he had a simple solution. The next day, he came back with some milk. The suspicious Zilao Apu had his horse smell at it and, when he found it unperturbed, said to Li'en, chuckling, "You're too young to fool me yet. This is not tiger's milk at all!"

Li'en had to admit that it was the milk of a wild cat, secretly admiring Zilao Apu's intellect. He promised to bring him real tiger milk the next day. That evening, Chenhong Baobaiming taught him how to milk a tiger.

"Take this magic pill with you. Feed it to the cub to put it to sleep while the tigress is away looking for food," she told him. "Here's a tiger skin. Take it with you, too. Hide the sleeping cub, cover yourself with this skin, and wait. The tigress will be back to feed the cub at breakfast time. Then, when she hops three times, you jump three times with her. When she cries, 'A, ge, mi, ge' three times, repeat with her. The tigress will then think of you as her cub and throw herself on the ground ready to breastfeed you. Then get the three drops of tiger milk and sneak out."

This time, however, the otherwise courageous Congren Li'en was hesitant, fearing that he would never survive the adventure. Chenhong Baobaiming encouraged him, "No pains; no gains. Besides, you have got to trust me. This could be the last of my father's tests. Show me the courage you always do."

Eventually, Congren Li'en brought the tiger milk back. When he found his horse terrified at the smell of the milk, Zilao Apu accepted it as real. He talked about Li'en's proposal with his wife, who tried to persuade him to give in. But he still begrudged the concession. The next day, he asked Li'en about his tribal background. Li'en told him that he was the only human being left.

The celestial god then asked, "Do you have any betrothal gift for my daughter?"

"Well, think of what I've done for you and what adventures I've gone through. Won't those be enough to substitute for the gift?"

At long last, Zilao Apu relented. Congren Li'en and his beloved Chenhong Baobaiming finally became husband and wife.

The newlyweds worked hard every day to prepare for their descent to the world. When it was time to go, Chenhong Baobaiming's loving parents presented the couple with a dowry of nine riding horses, seven horses of burden, nine pairs of farm cattle, seven pairs of yaks, nine silver bowls, seven gold bowls, nine varieties of grain seeds, and seven kinds of domestic animals.

Seeing no cat among the animals, Congren Li'en stole one and concealed it under his coat. When Zilao Apu later found cats on earth, he realized what had happened and became very angry. So he made cats purr during their sleep and their meat inedible by humans. Among the seeds, there was no turnip. Chenhong Baobaiming stole one and hid it under her nail. When Zilao Apu found turnips growing on earth later, he condemned them to becoming non-staple food for humans and fluidifying when boiled hard. These qualities of the vegetable persist to this day.

Congren Li'en and Chenhong Baobaiming began their journey back to the earth. On the third day, there suddenly sprang up a white cloud of wind on their left and a dark cloud of wind on their right. From the clouds poured torrential rain mixed with hailstones as big as walnuts. Soon, all the valleys were flooded, blocking their way to the earth.

It turned out that the Keluo Kexing family had caused the inclement weather as retaliation for Chenhong Baobaiming's rejection of their marital proposal. The goddess then burned incense she had made out of ghee, wheat flour, and cypress leaves and prayed to the Keluo Kexing family. In her prayer, she thanked them for appreciating her and asked them to pardon her for declining their kindness. The family accepted her apology and answered her prayer. The rain and hail stopped immediately, and the flood subsided soon afterward, revealing roads and bridges ahead of them. The couple resumed their journey back to earth.

After climbing over countless mountains and crossing innumerable rivers, Congren Li'en and Chenhong Baobaiming finally reached the famed Lijiang in today's Yunnan Province of China. They erected a monument and a pillar of triumph before setting up a white tent as their home. Herding their domestic animals on the plateau and planting their crops on the plain, they led a happy life of self-sufficiency.

In a short time, Chenhong Baobaiming gave birth to three children. They brought their parents happiness at first but soon a great deal of worry, for by the time they were three years old, they had not yet uttered a word. Congren Li'en and Chenhong Baobaiming sent a magic bird to ask their celestial parents for help. Instead of offering a helping hand, the parents complained that they had been neglected since the young couple had left them. Li'en and his wife held a memorial ceremony to express their thanks to the celestial god Zilao Apu and his wife as well as the Keluo Kexing family. This practice led to the annual tradition of worshiping heaven by the Naxi people.

One morning, the three sons were playing in the turnip plot when a horse broke into it and began to eat the greens. Panic stricken, the children screamed for help, but strangely, each cried in a different language. When they grew up, they became the heads of three ethnic peoples: the eldest of the Tibetans; the second of the Naxi; and the third of the Minjia or Mosuo, who are a branch of the Naxi today. They rode different horses, donned different costumes, and lived in different locations.

Mosuo (left), Naxi (middle), and Tibetan (right) young people

SEVEN BROTHERS

This is a folktale from the Va, whose 396,600 (China, 2002) people primarily live in Yunnan. Their oral literature consists of mythologies, epics, and folktales.

The following is one of several Chinese ethnic stories that highlight the same origin of multiple ethnic groups. To verify the true origin may take more than a folktale, but a tale of this nature does help the reader to understand why Chinese ethnic groups have for the most part been living peacefully together.

*O*nce upon a time, there were seven brothers in the world. Born of the same parents, with dark hair and bright eyes, nobody could tell them apart. They were all kindhearted, but each had a different temperament. The eldest brother was quiet and pensive. The second brother was lively and talented in singing and dancing. The third was an adventurer and good horseman. The fourth liked water and was known for being neat and tidy. The rest of the brothers all liked green mountains, for various reasons. The fifth brother was fond of planting trees on the mountainside; the sixth was keen on shepherding in the open areas at its waist; and the seventh had a propensity for climbing up to the mountaintop where, he claimed, he could see the world.

As days went by, the seven brothers grew up into handsome and intelligent young men. One day their father brought them together and said to them,

"My sons, now that you have grown up, it's high time you saw life in the outside world. Like full-fledged eagles, you can fly now, and to wherever you want. One thing, however, you must remember: No matter where you are, help one another and others. Come back to me in ten years, and each of you bring me the best present you can find."

The seven brothers bid farewell to their parents and set out. On their way, they performed numerous good deeds while encountering many things they had never experienced before. One day they reached a plain, where they saw a young woman weeping as she worked in the fields. When asked why, she complained,

"My crop is being overwhelmed by the weeds that keep growing. I'm afraid I can never get rid of them. Apparently my family will go hungry for the coming season."

The eldest of the brothers said to the others, "Let me stay and help her weed the fields." Losing no time, he set about working for the girl.

Part 3: The Tales

The other brothers said good-bye to them and resumed their journey. When they approached a lake, they spotted a young woman crying on the shore. They went up to her and asked why. She said she felt very lonely because she had just lost her parents. "I'll never be happy in my life," she sobbed.

The sixth brother said to the others, "Let me stay with her and make her happy with my songs and dances." He did so immediately, and the young woman broke into a smile, the first since her parents' deaths.

The rest of the brothers went on their way. As they arrived at a grassy mountainside, they came across a young woman moaning for her lost sheep. She told the brothers that she and her flock had been attacked by a wolf. The third brother volunteered to help the girl. Mounting a horse grazing nearby, he galloped away to hunt the wolf down.

The other brothers moved on, and on the way found a young woman laundering at a riverside, her face covered with tears.

"Why are you so sad?" asked the brothers.

"I live by washing clothes for others. Although it's getting late, I still have a lot to finish. What shall I do?"

At this, the fourth brother decided to stay and assist her.

The rest of the brothers embarked on their journey again and, after a few days, came to a green mountain. They were so happy that they couldn't help singing. Their songs caught the attention of three young women picking tea leaves on the mountainside. They beckoned the brothers,

"Hey, young men, come and help us. Don't you see the tea leaves nearly getting over-ripe? And we have so many that we can't finish picking them in time."

The three brothers stopped to help them. They were working and singing when two of the girls, who had already reached the far end of the plantation, screamed,

"Help! Help! A tiger is here to attack us!"

The sixth and seventh brothers asked the fifth brother to stay and protect the girl beside him while they rushed in the direction where the tiger had been spotted. They were searching for the beast in the bushes when it dashed out of hiding and charged at them. At once, the seventh brother drew his bow and launched an arrow, which went straight into its hip. Giving a growl of pain, the tiger scurried up to the mountaintop. The seventh brother asked the sixth brother and one of the girls to stay. He and the other girl traced the tiger to the summit. There, they looked for the elusive beast day after day.

Ten years passed. Each of the brothers had married the girl he had helped and raised a family with her. The brothers returned to visit their parents at the same time, bringing with them their families as well as the best presents they could think of. The gifts included an ear of golden millet from the eldest brother, an exquisite musical instrument, a *yu-kin*, from the second brother, a soft and sleek blanket from the third, a beautiful costume from the fourth, a basket of tea from the fifth, a fat calf from the sixth, and a brand-new crossbow from the seventh.

"My children," the satisfied and happy father began. "I'm so proud of you! You have all done a good job!"

The seven brothers introduced their children to their grandparents. Stroking his white beard, the grandfather named the children Han, Bai, Yi, Dai, Hani, Lahu, and Va.

Later, the seven brothers and their families went back home. In due course, their children grew up and raised their own families. As they expanded, the seven families became seven ethnic groups. They lived peacefully with one another, never hesitating to extend a helping hand when it was needed. After all, they came from the same ancestor!

MILUOTUO—A GODDESS
WHO CREATES THE WORLD

This is a famous myth from the Yao. The 2,637,400 Yao people (China, 2002) are scattered among 130 counties in the provinces Guangxi, Hunan, Yunnan, Guangdong, Guizhou, and Jiangxi. The Yao people have no written script and speak four mutually unintelligible dialects. Their oral literature abounds with myths, legends, and folktales.

The Festival of Zhuzhu, which means "never forget" in a Yao dialect, falls on the twenty-ninth day of the fifth lunar month. It's a celebration of Miluotuo, the mother of the Yao people, who is said to have started many of the Yao traditions.

*T*ens of thousands of years ago, Miluotuo used her master's rain hat to create the sky. She turned his limbs into four columns to uphold its four corners and placed his trunk in the center to support the zenith, thus completing the task of creating heaven and earth. After that, she set to work to produce rivers, plants, mammals, fowls, and aquatic creatures such as fish and shrimp.

Miluotuo delegated the making of mountains to a god named Gao'en. During a break, he wanted to smoke. But the sparks he used to light his tobacco accidentally set fire to the vegetation on earth. It was scorched so that nothing was left. Seeing the land barren again, Miluotuo felt very sad. She masked the earth with black and white cloths in the hope of making it look better, but it didn't help. She then gave another god, called Yayou, some silver and asked him to buy a lot of tree seeds and plant them. With the help of the wind, the god spread the seeds evenly over the mountains.

When the trees were in their prime, Miluotuo discussed with Gao'en and Yayou what to do with them. They decided to use some of them to build houses. They managed to make beams and columns out of the timber, but found it difficult to shape the timber into planks.

One day Yayou saw a big grasshopper perching on a palm tree and took notice of the sharp, spinelike structures on its hind legs. Out of curiosity, he captured the grasshopper. Although he was especially careful not to hurt his hand on the insect's legs, he overlooked the jagged edges of the palm leaf and caught his hand on its serration. Indifferent to the bleeding, he was curious about how he had been hurt. Suddenly an idea dawned: How about making something in metal with a similar teethlike structure? Then it would be possible to cut into wood as fast as the palm leaf had his hand. And he could easily separate timber into planks! He took the insect and the palm leaf back home and manufactured metal saws accordingly. With plenty of beams, columns, and planks, the gods were able to build many houses.

With the houses completed, Miluotuo set about creating humans. To do so, she tried all kinds of materials, but none worked as she had expected. At first she used clay, but it turned into water jars. Next she tested rice, but it only became wine. Then she experimented with palm leaves, but they all turned into locusts. The pumpkins and sweet potatoes she tried produced nothing but monkeys.

After much trial and error, Miluotuo finally realized that she needed a better place to accomplish the task, so she wanted someone to look for it. She sent a Eurasian badger first, but he only rooted about for earthworms on the hillside. He didn't come back until he had eaten his fill. Miluotuo was so angry that she hit him with a twig, leaving a white mark on his ears.

She then dispatched a wild boar. Like the badger, she stopped halfway down the hillside and indulged herself in digging with her snout for sweet potatoes. The vexed Miluotuo poured a pot of boiling water on her. Wild boars have since had tough and coarse skin, caused by the scalding.

Then Miluotuo sent a bear to look for the ideal place where she could create humans. However, he was distracted by ants and ate them to his heart's content. When he came back, Miluotuo, who was in the middle of dyeing her cloth, emptied the indigo dye on him and colored his body pitch black.

Miluotuo then tried a musk deer, who disappointed her as her predecessors had done. The deer forgot her assignment because she couldn't resist the temptation of the young grass on the hillside. When the deer returned, Miluotuo was in the middle of cooking. Pulling a burning stalk from the hearth, she threw it at the deer. As the stalk hit the deer's belly, it left a blistered mark. That's where the musk deer secretes its musk today.

Fed up with the beasts, Miluotuo thought of the birds. The first that came to her mind was the woodpecker. When he flew into a wood, however, he began to treat himself to the worms in the trees. Seeing this, Miluotuo hit him with her colored strap, and the startled woodpecker took to flight with the strap, resulting in a colorful back.

Miluotuo then dispatched a pheasant, but she could not resist the lure of a delicious tower gourd and helped herself to it. Miluotuo shot the pheasant with a bow and an arrow, which lodged in her tail. Scared and in pain, the bird ran off with the arrow. That's why pheasants still have long tails today.

The third bird Miluotuo sent out was a crow. When he flew over a burning mountain, he stopped to search for small animals roasted in the flames. While circling above the smoky mountain, the soot and fume colored his feathers black. When he came back without accomplishing anything, Miluotuo was so mad that she stuffed a pebble in his throat so that he could never sing beautifully. That is why he caws all the time.

The last bird that Miluotuo sent off was an eagle. Before her departure, she had a good breakfast. She took along enough food for a long journey. Soaring into the sky and hovering in the air, she scanned down below with her eagle eyes, looking for the perfect place for Miluotuo to create humans. She didn't return until she had found it.

Miluotuo followed the eagle to the ideal location, where the climate was as genial as spring, and azaleas of diverse colors bloomed all over the mountains. Miluotuo went into a forest and stopped by a tree because she caught sight of a bee hive in a large hole in its trunk. The bees were bustling back and forth from their hive to the azalea bushes. They were busy gathering pollen to make honey.

Miluotuo cut the tree down and brought it back along with the bee hive. She gave the bees three coaching sessions during the day and another three at night. Then she placed them in a box and waited for their transformation. Nine months later, cries were heard coming out of the hive. She opened it, and it was full of human babies! She couldn't help exclaiming, "I've got it! I've got it!"

However, the babies were crying piteously for food. "What am I going to feed them?" Miluotuo asked herself. Pacing back and forth, she finally figured out what to do. She washed the babies, wrapped them in swaddling, and breastfed them one by one until they grew up.

As grown-ups, they went their own way in groups. Each group built a village on a mountain, where they cultivated the hillside and started farming. Since then, humans have worked as diligently as bees, with men farming in the fields and women weaving at home.

THE ORIGIN OF THE GELAO ETHNICITY

This is a folktale from the Gelao, whose 579,400 people (China, 2002) live mainly in Guizhou. The tale shows traces of borrowing ideas from another culture. For instance, mythological figures like Jade Emperor of Heaven, Weaving Girl, Lao Zi, and Dragon Princess are all common characters found in tales from the Han Chinese.

*T*he Gelao once lived a miserable life on earth. Jade Emperor of Heaven, who couldn't bear seeing them suffer, decided to give them refuge in heaven. He sent a fairy named Weaving Girl to pick them up. The fairy transformed into a gigantic eagle, swooped down to earth, and carried them up to heaven on her broad back.

One day, Jade Emperor had a whim to do a head count of the people on earth and found the Gelao missing. Then he realized he had caused them to live in heaven, so he wanted some of the Gelao to go back to earth to multiply. He picked Ali and Dale, the youngest man and woman of a Gelao tribe. Jade Emperor asked Lao Zi, the creator of Daoism, to give the two youngsters some of his magic pills so that they could enjoy long and healthy lives. Afterward, he ordered Weaving Girl to take them back to the world.

Though young, Ali and Dale worked very hard. They turned the wilderness into tract after tract of fertile land, on which they grew a variety of crops like millet, corn, soy, and cotton.

As time went by, Ali and Dale grew into a young man and a young woman. But they were too shy to talk about marriage. One day, Dale couldn't help suggesting,

"Brother Ali, you're twenty now. It's time you got married." She called Ali "brother" because she liked him. That is what young people from some ethnic minorities customarily do.

"You read my mind, Sister Dale," Ali replied. Apparently, he felt drawn to her as well. "That's exactly what's on my mind lately."

Before Dale had a chance to say anything, Ali continued, "See what an awkward situation we are in: We two are the only Gelaos here on earth. Apparently, the hope for the Gelao ethnicity to continue lies in our raising a family. But we are somewhat related, and it would go against our tradition if we . . . ."

"What you said makes a lot of sense," said Dale.

The two never touched on the topic again. Two years quickly passed. One day, Ali and Dale saw fish swimming in pairs in the river and birds flying by twos in the air.

"If only we were not related," Ali sighed.

"Don't lose hope, Brother Ali!" Dale tried to comfort him. "Jade Emperor will have a plan for us."

Indeed, Jade Emperor of Heaven didn't forget them. When he saw Ali and Dale maturing, he sent the fairy Weaving Girl down to earth to make them husband and wife so that they could carry on their ethnic line.

As the fairy landed in the form of the same eagle that had carried them down to earth, Ali and Dale recognized her. They greeted her, surprised at her reappearance.

"Ali and Dale, you were born to be a couple," said the fairy. "Now that you've grown up, it's time you started a family."

"How can we?" the two said unanimously. "It is against our tradition to marry someone who is related."

"You are related alright, but there are no other Gelao tribes on earth. Besides, Jade Emperor simply doesn't want to see the Gelaos disappear after you."

"But . . . ," the two stuttered, their faces as red as a beet.

"Emperor of Heaven insists that you get married. What say you?"

"If that's his will," said Ali and Dale, "then prove it."

"Well," said the fairy eagle, "you only need to perform three tasks to see if it's so."

"What tasks?" Ali and Dale asked earnestly.

"First, you know millstones have two pieces, and their grooves face each other and are properly aligned. Well, I have placed one piece on the top of the Eastern Hill and the other on the top of the Western Hill. You must try to push them into the valley at the same time. If they come down with the grooves in line, it will testify to the will of Jade Emperor, and you must get married. If not, you can have your own way."

"What's the second task, then?" asked Ali.

"You each are to sling a dustpan, one of you from behind the Southern Mountain, the other from behind the Northern Mountain. See if the dustpans meet in the gorge between them. If they do, you're bound to become husband and wife."

"And the third task?" Dale questioned.

"You're to thread a needle. Dale, you hold a needle on one side of the river. Ali, you carry a thread on the other side and cast it over to Dale. If the thread enters the eye of the needle, you are destined to marry."

The next morning, the fairy eagle placed the millstones, the dustpans, and the needle and thread in their proper places and gave the order to begin the tasks. Ali and Dale climbed up to the hills and each pushed a piece of the millstone down the valley simultaneously. To their great astonishment, the stones met with their grooves aligned perfectly.

To complete the second task, Ali went behind the Southern Mountain, and Dale positioned herself behind the Northern Mountain, each holding a dustpan. Upon the fairy's command to go, they threw the dustpans over the mountains at once. The result was equally dumbfounding: The dustpans conjoined like a clamp.

The miracles surprised Ali and Dale so much that they could barely think straight. Finally, they collected themselves and went to either side of the river, Dale holding the needle and Ali, an end of the thread. As soon as the fairy said "go," Ali flung the thread across the river. Like an arrow leaving a bow, the thread raced over the water toward Dale and rushed through the eye of the needle in her hand.

The jubilant fairy eagle couldn't help exclaiming, "Hah, you did it all! So you have to believe that it's Jade Emperor's will that you marry."

"If that's the case, we will comply. But who's going to oversee our wedding?"

Upon that, the eagle flapped her wings three times and revealed her true nature as the beautiful Weaving Girl. With a palm fan in hand, she said, smiling, "To tell you the truth: Jade Emperor of Heaven has asked me to come and oversee your marriage."

Ali and Dale dropped to their knees to thank the heavenly emperor and the fairy. Then they made a request, "We still need a witness, but there's no one else around here."

"Well, that's easy," said the fairy. With that, she passed her palm fan three times over the river and raised wave after wave. A gorgeous young woman emerged among them. With a smile on her pretty face, she sang,

> *Hark to me ye Ali and Dale dear,*
> *You're bonded by Heaven premier.*
> *Dragon Princess is my name,*
> *Witness your marriage, I'm here.*

She was the third daughter of Dragon King, called up by Jade Emperor of Heaven to witness the marriage of Ali and Dale.

When Dragon Princess came on shore, the wedding began. The couple bowed to heaven, to earth, and to each other. To consummate the union, Weaving Girl and Dragon Princess sang their blessing:

> *By the river your marriage we witness,*
> *Sincerely we wish you eternal happiness.*
> *Farm and weave on earth hand in hand,*
> *You'll build a world better than fairyland.*

After that, the two goddesses said good-bye to the newlyweds. Weaving Girl made for the sky and returned to heaven. Dragon Princess waded into the river and retired to the Dragon Palace. The couple went on with their celebration. While Ali was playing his favorite *paomutong*, a vertical flute made from the paulownia tree, Dale danced to its melodious tune.

The next year, they gave birth to a chubby boy, and from him descended the Gelao, who went on to multiply from generation to generation.

Millstones

THE SURVIVING NU ANCESTRY

This is a folktale from the Nu. With a population of 28,800 (China, 2002), the Nu live primarily in the Ethnic Lisu Autonomous Prefecture in Yunnan. The four distinct branches of Nu each speak a different dialect of the Sino-Tibetan family, but none has a writing system. Myths, legends, and folktales are part of their folklore.

After a deluge annihilated humans, God of Heaven sent a young man and a young woman named Lapu and Yaniu to repopulate the earth. Lapu was strong and skillful at archery. Yaniu was diligent and kindhearted. They lived in a cave, on the game they hunted.

As days went by, Lapu and Yaniu grew into adults. Because they were the only humans living on earth, finding someone else for a spouse was out of the question. Lapu pondered, "If we don't become husband and wife, after we're gone, there won't be humans on earth any more."

Then he said to Yaniu hesitantly, "You and I are old enough to get married; however, we're the only ones on earth. It seems that we have no choice."

"Well, how can we marry ourselves?" questioned the bashful young woman.

"You're right, but have you wondered why God of Heaven sent us here after the big flood destroyed our fellow beings? Don't you think it's his intent that we have children so that the world will see people again?"

"What you say seems right," said Yaniu, "but who will witness our wedding? We can't marry without a witness. That's our tradition!"

Both sank into thinking.

"I've got it!" Yaniu suddenly blurted out.

"Got what?"

"How about shooting the four poles of the loom with your crossbow? If you hit the targets, it will be evidence of god's will that we can get married."

"That's a marvelous idea!" exclaimed Lapu. With that, he drew his bow. "Whoosh, whoosh, whoosh, whoosh" went four arrows. "Clang, clang, clang, clang," all hit the targets. So Lapu and Yaniu became husband and wife.

Several years later, they brought forth seven children. When they grew up, they were all married, one to a snake, one to a bee, one to a fish, one to a tiger, and the rest to various other creatures. Their descendants formed different clans, worshiping their respective ancestors as their totems.

One day a fire broke out on a nearby mountain. Curiosity drew Lapu and Yaniu to it, and there they found baked animal carcasses scattered on the smoldering mountainside. When they picked up some pieces and tasted them, they found them more tasty than raw meat. To eat cooked food, however, there must be fire. But it was difficult to find one in a natural environment.

"We must have something that can start a fire—something that we can call a fire seed," Lapu proposed.

"Where can we find one?"

Lapu was silent because he really didn't know. For days theytried to figure out where to find a fire seed, but the answer was hard to come by. One day, however, an incident gave Lapu an idea: While rubbing bamboo to make arrows, he nearly burned his hands.

"What if I rub bamboo on a stone for a longer time? It will make enough heat to start a fire," he shared his thought with his wife immediately.

"Why not give it a try, then?" the excited Yaniu suggested.

So they set about rubbing bamboo against a rock. They rubbed and rubbed for three days and nights, until the bamboo began to smolder. Losing no time, they started a fire and kept it alive. Since then, humans have had the habit of eating cooked meat.

Many years later, Lapu died. Yaniu cremated her husband, and her children did the same to her when she passed away years later. The Nu have since had the tradition of cremating the dead.

Lapu and Yaniu had spoken the Nu dialect. When their children and grandchildren relocated to where the Lisu people lived, they picked up their language. As a result, the Nu today speak the Lisu dialect.

Courtesy of Dai Yuru and Yunnan Fine Arts Publishing House

Tales of How Things Came to Be

Humans have always been concerned not only with their own origin, but also with the beginning of the things and phenomena surrounding them. The Pumi believe that grain and domestic animals appeared after an eventful "Deluge." The Hani thank "A Monkey Boy Stealing Rice from Heaven" for their improved lives. The Miao attribute the origin of stars and clouds to a "Sky Mended with a Dragon's Teeth." The Tu seemingly have an answer to "Why Are Oxen Preferred to Till Our Land?" The Buyei, Tajik, and Mongol can explain, respectively, "The Origin of the Bronze Drum," "The Origin of the Eagle-bone Flute," and how "The Fiddle with a Horse Head" came into being.

THE DELUGE

This is a folktale from the Pumi. The 33,600 Pumi people (China, 2002) inhabit the Lisu Ethnic Autonomous Prefecture of Yunnan. They speak two mutually intelligible dialects and have a very limited pictographic writing system, used only for religious purposes. The primary form of their oral literature is myth, of which the following is an example.

*O*nce upon a time, there were three brothers, who went to a forest to open up land by turns. One day, the eldest brother was digging with his wooden hoe when a crow perching on a tree nearby opened its mouth and said,

"Caw, Caw! If you give me your lunch, I'll tell you something important."

"Go away, you wicked crow! Don't you try to cheat me of my lunch," the angry eldest brother cursed as he threw a rock at the bird to drive him away.

The next day, when the second brother came to the forest, the crow showed up again. He expelled him the same way the eldest brother had done.

On the third day, the third brother arrived at the forest. When the crow asked him for his lunch, he complied. After he finished eating, the crow told the third brother to flee from a deluge that was to come that afternoon. At this, the third brother rushed home, but on his way, he was stopped by a frog. Politely, he told her that a flood was coming, and he was going back home to tell his brothers about it. Then he asked the frog if she had any tips to help them escape the imminent danger.

In the same civil manner as the crow, the frog said, "Tell your brothers to get a rope each. As for you, besides a rope, you also need to bring along a dog, a cat, a rooster, and a pestle. Let's meet at noon, and I'll take you all to the moon." Then the frog vanished.

When he returned home, the third brother told the others what he had seen and heard, and they set about preparing their escape. Shortly before noon, the frog came, and the three brothers followed her to the moon, riding on the clouds and mists. Then the frog led them to a magic tree and tied them to it with their ropes, the eldest brother at the foot, the second in the middle, and the third at the top. Before she left them, the frog told the third brother, "Throw the dog, the rooster, and the cat into the water when it reaches your heels. They will repel the flood once and for all."

At sunset, in the wake of terrifying rumblings, there came a huge flood. It surged higher and higher until it reached the moon. Soon the water submerged the eldest brother at the bottom of the tree and the second brother in the middle. The tide continued to rise until it touched the heels of the third brother at the top. Remembering the frog's words, he threw the cat and the dog that he had brought with him. As soon as they dropped into the water, it began to subside. He then let go the rooster and the pestle. In an instant, he heard them hit the ground with a couple of thumps, which told him that the water had completely gone.

Tied to the treetop, however, the third brother couldn't move. Fear crept over him that he might die that way. Eighty-one days passed, but he was still alive. He was trying to figure out how to get free when he caught sight of an eagle's nest on a branch of the tree not far from him. With all his might, he broke loose from the bonds and clambered to the nest, where he found an eagle chick and some deer meat. He grabbed a piece of the venison and gobbled it up. When the chick told his mother what had happened, she was not angry at all. In fact, she rejoiced at the survival of humanity. She carried the third brother down to earth and told him to climb his way to the God of Mountain. She warned him against wandering into the devils' den in the Bamboo Valley.

But because he felt too hungry to go up, the third brother tumbled down into the valley. Before he realized it, he had reached a big cave. He peered in, only to see a couple of devils, a male and a female, their heavy eyelids hanging low enough to cover their eyes completely. They were munching rice cakes. The starved third brother tiptoed up to them and stole their cakes. The devils began to blame each other for not sharing the food. Then the female devil lifted up her eyelid with a stick and spotted the third brother chomping on the food. She picked him up, placed him in her big mouth, and gulped him down. Just then the frog appeared, claiming the third brother to be her nephew. She threatened,

"If you don't throw him up alive, I won't grind your grains anymore, and you'll never have cakes to eat!"

At this, the she-devil flew into a rage, "That's fine! I've got 3,000 of your kind in the east and another 800 in the west. Go away! I don't need your service anymore!"

The frog was as good as her word and left for the Dragon Palace. The devils had to invite a magpie to work at the mill, but the poor bird couldn't move the heavy millstones. Then they called a python, but it too failed them. The devils had no alternative but to go to the Dragon Palace to invite the frog to come back.

"I'll go with you as long as you spit out my nephew," the frog said.

"I can do so only if you knock me on the back with a stone," replied the devil.

The frog accordingly did so, and sure enough, the devil coughed up the third brother. The delay, however, had its consequences. The third brother lost parts of his hands and feet, so he had fingers and toes. His big ears were also corroded. The frog had to create a pair of smaller ones with the bits of his flesh the devil had regurgitated.

After his rescue, the third brother resumed his journey to the home of the God of Mountain. Before long, he reached a splendid palace, but when he entered it, he found it vacant. In the lounge, he saw a table spread with plenty of food. As he was helping himself to the food, the God of Mountain returned with his three daughters. Having no time to flee, the third brother crawled underneath a bed. The deity smelled him and dragged him out. Like the magic eagle, he was delighted to see a human still alive. He then asked the third brother if he could use a bow and arrows. When the third brother nodded yes, he asked him to help fight a monster.

"During the battle," the deity told him, "you'll see a number of logs combating one another in a tangle. One of them has a black spot on it, and if you hit it, you'll defeat the monster."

The next day, the third brother followed the God of Mountain to the battleground. Soon he saw the fighting logs and the one with a black spot. The moment he lodged an arrow in it, the monster died, revealing its original form. The God of Mountain was very happy and asked the third brother if there was anything he could do for him. The third brother said he desired nothing but the god's youngest daughter. The God of Mountain granted this request readily and asked him to come to the mountain pass opposite the palace early the next morning.

When the time came, the third brother went to the pass with his bow and arrows. After a short time, there suddenly sprang up a gust of wind. In its wake, a tiger emerged and darted toward the mountain pass, but he let it go. Then a leopard followed, and again he took no action. When a python appeared, he lost no time tapping its tail with his bow, and the serpent immediately reverted to its original form: the third daughter of the God of Mountain.

"My eldest sister can make nine cakes with a single grain of barley, my second sister can make six with it, but I can only make three. How come you picked me for your wife?"

"Well, three cakes are enough: one for you, one for me, and the third for our children."

Eventually the two got married. Saying good-bye to the God of Mountain, they came to the plain, settled down, and opened up a piece of wilderness. But they soon realized that they had neither livestock nor grain. The third daughter decided to go home and ask her father for them. Before she left, she said to her husband, "As soon as you hear thunder and rain, burn incense and pray to heaven." The third brother promised to do as she asked.

Days passed, but the third daughter failed to return. Eventually the third brother forgot her words. When it thundered and rained, he set fire to a heap of wood he had gathered. The smoke drove his wife back into heaven just as she was about to return with the grain seeds and cattle that she had brought with her.

Later the third daughter came back to the third brother. She blamed him for not remembering what she had told him and thereby foiling her plan. She was going to try again. Before her departure, she mixed ashes with water and kneaded the dough into a young woman after her image. She meant for her to take care of her husband during her absence.

A day in heaven equaled ten years on earth. After thirty years had passed, the third brother thought that his wife would never return, so he married the ash girl and had children with her. When the third daughter came back after three days in heaven and saw her husband married again, she decided to go back, never to return. As she took off, taking with her the grain seeds and the animals she had brought from heaven, the third brother launched his arrows and shot down five grains and turnips. He also shot down some fowls and mammals. Soon the fallen seeds grew into crops, and the creatures became poultry and livestock.

A MONKEY BOY STEALING RICE FROM HEAVEN

This is a legend from the Hani. More than 90 percent of the 1,439,700 (China, 2002) Hani people live in Southwestern Yunnan. Predominantly agrarian, the Hani are known for their picturesque terraced rice fields. (See photo section.) The following story tells of a hero whom the Hani believe started their rice cultivating tradition.

A long time ago, a middle-aged widow known as Api lived in a mountainous village called Dasha. The recent loss of her only son made her lonely and wretched. Finding it hard to accept his death, she expected him to return every day. She often mistook the crows and croaks she heard outside as the cry of her baby. When she returned from her work, she would look up at the clouds shrouding the mountaintop and wail, "My baby, where are you? When are you coming back to me?"

One day, Api was sowing buckwheat on the hillside when she heard a child crying. She asked her fellow farmers if they heard it, but no one said yes. A young woman couldn't help teasing her, "Api, your grief over your son must have made you see and hear things."

Despite their disbelief, Api went up to the hill. To her great disappointment, she found no trace of humans at all. Only a little white monkey was there, clinging to a vine hanging down halfway from a cliff. Strangely, when it noticed Api looking its way, it called out,

"Mother, help me! If you save my life, I promise you'll have a son."

"But how?" Api asked. "I can't climb up there."

"Catch me in your *linggua* when I drop into it." *Lingua* is an elaborate garment that covers the entire back of a Hani woman.

Taking the *linggua* off her back, Api gripped two of its four corners in each hand so it formed a bag and waited. With a light thump, the monkey fell into it. When Api held up what she thought to be the animal, she was stunned and thrilled: Instead of the monkey, she had a human baby in her hands! She was bursting with joy. She announced to everyone she saw on her way home, "I have my son back! I have my son back!"

Back home, the first thing Api did was name the baby. Because she was a widow, she called him Mamai, or "Fatherless Child." From that moment on, Api would never leave Mamai alone as long as the blink of an eye. She carried him on her back while she mowed in the bamboo forest on the hillside. She built a makeshift shed to shelter him from the sunshine while she tended her buckwheat crop in a nearby field.

After watching his mother work when he was very young, Mamai had learned all about the hardship of labor and the value of grains. He found that their toil could only produce half a year's food supply. In time of disasters like flood or drought, the yield of buckwheat was even worse. Sometimes they had to survive on yams and wild fruit they scavenged in the mountains.

One day, Mamai pondered during a break, "Buckwheat is not productive enough. I must find the seeds of a new grain that can produce a much better harvest. Then I'll share the seeds with my fellow villagers so none will suffer from shortage of food any more."

He had heard that the God of Heaven had all kinds of high-yield grain seeds. He wished he could ask him for some.

"But how can I?" he asked himself. "He's high above in heaven, and I don't have wings to fly."

As it happened, on Mamai's eighteenth birthday, there appeared a golden horse on the hillside near the village of Dasha. Having a good appetite, he soon wiped out large tracts of buckwheat shoots. Angry villagers tried to drive him away, but he ran as if he could fly. He was a superb jumper as well, hopping from one hill to another with ease. Eventually, Mamai traced the horse to a cave. One early morning, he hid himself above the opening. The golden horse had just emerged from the cave when Mamai jumped onto his back. Startled, the horse ran like mad, trying to buck the stranger off. Mamai held onto the horse as tenaciously as a snake entangles its victim. With neighs of fury, the horse extended his hidden wings and covered 999 hills without a break. At long last he halted, too exhausted to move further.

"I surrender," the horse said, panting heavily. "Tell me what you want, and I'll do my best to satisfy your demand."

"First tell me where you come from," inquired Mamai.

"I used to live in the stable of the God of Heaven. I fled because I was bored."

"Take me to him. I want to ask him for grain seeds."

Reluctantly, the horse carried Mamai to heaven. There, the benign sovereign gave them a warm welcome and pardoned the horse's previous unruliness.

"There are too few grain seeds on earth. A year's labor in a buckwheat field yields only half a year's crop. Please give me some high-yield grain seeds. I want my mother and my fellow villagers to have sufficient food," entreated Mamai in one breath.

"Well, each of my twelve daughters takes care of a different kind of seed," said the God of Heaven, "To see them, you have to show me your worthiness. Can you draw a 1,000-pound iron bow to its full length and shoot down nine vultures?"

"Sure I can," responded Mamai.

The God of Heaven took him to a tall dragon tree where an iron bow of over three feet long was hanging. Beside it was a quiver with nine arrows, matching the number of the birds hovering in the air. Mamai drew the bow almost to 360 degrees and then shot at the vultures. They fell into the forest on the hillside, one after another. Admiring Mamai's strength, the God of Heaven showed him his garden at the back of the palace. There Mamai found twelve earthen pots, each with a different kind of grain growing in it, laden with seeds.

"Now you can choose the seeds from the plant you like," said the heavenly sovereign amiably.

"I like that one," responded Mamai, pointing at a golden plant.

"That's rice."

"I'll try growing rice . . . ."

Before he had finished, the golden rice suddenly turned into a young woman. She was Rice Fairy. The youngest and the prettiest, she was the only one that remained single. It turned out that the God of Heaven had been testing to see whether Mamai qualified to be his son-in-law. While the test had been going on, Rice Fairy had watched in secret and fallen in love with him.

With a smile, she broke the silence, "Since you've chosen me, I have one thing to ask of you."

"What is it?" Mamai questioned.

"My father gave the rice seeds to me as my dowry. So, if you take the rice, you must take me with it."

"I . . . ," Mamai was about to say that he was here to get grain seeds, not a wife, and he had to go back to earth to take care of his mother, when the golden horse cut in with a murmur,

"Say yes and ask her to teach you how to grow rice before the wedding."

Mamai did as his horse friend suggested. Rice Fairy took him to a field of mud. Producing a handful of rice seeds from her pocket, she scattered them into the waterlogged soil. In a moment, green seedlings came out. Then she called in a group of fairies to help her transplant the seedlings to another plot of mud. Soon the seedlings grew up and bore heavy ears of rice.

"Now it's time you marry me," demanded Rice Fairy.

Mamai was going to say no and tell her that his people were waiting for the seeds because they were suffering from starvation due to a drought, when the horse stopped him again, whispering, "Give her your consent first. Then you may get out of here after you put her to sleep."

"What about the rice seeds?" Mamai whispered back.

"I know how to take them back to earth," the horse reassured him.

That evening, the God of Heaven performed a wedding for Rice Fairy and Mamai. During the subsequent feast, Mamai tried to get his bride drunk, without knowing that she had a great capacity for liquor. She fell asleep only after Mamai managed to get her to drink nine jars of the best rice wine from her father's cellar. Putting her to bed, Mamai snuck out and met the horse at the rice field.

"I have swallowed almost all the rice the Rice Fairy grew during the day. When we're back on earth, I'll throw them up."

Mamai was very pleased with the horse's ingenuity. Fearing that Rice Fairy might wake up at any minute, they set out for the earth at once. Before long, Rice Fairy came out of her stupor, only to find Mamai and his horse gone. Immediately she realized where they were going and rushed out to chase them. But they were already too far away. In her anger, she cast her magic sword in their direction. It soon caught up with them, and with a swish, it cut the horse's flapping wings off, sending the poor animal tumbling to the earth with Mamai on his back. The impact killed Mamai and the horse. The rice that the horse had swallowed was thrown into the low-lying fields from his gaping belly.

The grateful and mournful villagers buried Mamai and his loyal golden horse beneath a dragon tree. No sooner had they finished than dark clouds gathered above them. A downpour followed and filled the lowland where the rice was accidentally planted. Soon seedlings emerged and, in due course, golden ears grew out of them. Ever since, the villagers have had bumper crops of rice, which they prefer to buckwheat. Whenever they eat rice, they can't help missing their heroes, Mamai and the golden horse.

SKY MENDED WITH A DRAGON'S TEETH

This is a folktale from the Miao, who, with 8,940,100 people (China, 2002), are the fourth largest of China's ethnic minorities. They are scattered mostly in Guizhou, Yunnan, Hunan, Sichuan, and Guangxi. The Miao people are known for their mythological epics, which sing of love and cultural heroes. The following is based on one of these epics.

A long, long time ago, there lived in a village a couple who were still childless even when their hair turned gray. One day, they were tilling their corn fields while lamenting the lack of a helping hand as usual when, all of a sudden, a huge rock crashed down from a mountaintop and landed near them. There was a mass of cotton in a crack in the rock, and from it came a tender voice.

With great curiosity, the old man pulled the cotton out of the crack and opened it carefully. To their great surprise, they found in it a cooing, chubby boy, paddling his arms and kicking his legs as if to entertain himself. The old man burst out, "A baby! It's a baby!"

The old woman held it up and exclaimed, "Heaven has granted us a boy! We have a son now! We have our own son now!"

With great delight, they took the baby boy home, and with extreme love and care they raised him. He grew up having square shoulders and sinewy limbs and looked much stronger than his peers. The old man predicted, "This boy of ours will definitely be a great hero in the future. So let's name him Sang." The Miao call a strong and courageous man this name. Soon Sang grew to be a big young man as well as an adroit hunter and farmer. The villagers nicknamed him Brother Sang out of love and respect.

At the time, there were two black dragon brothers. The elder one lived in the Northern Sea and the younger in a cave in the Southern Mountain. At the entrance of the cave there was a peach tree. One day, the elder dragon brother came to visit his younger brother. As he approached the cave, he found nine succulent peaches dangling from the bent branches.

The brothers wanted to share the fruit, but found it hard to divide it evenly. The younger black dragon brother argued,

"Since the peaches grow at the entrance of my cave, I should have five."

The other rebutted, "As I am the elder brother, you must eat four."

Their dispute finally led to violence. They fought back and forth from the Southern Mountain to the Northern Sea. Their entangled battle kicked up so much dust and mist that they darkened the world. Fighting blindly, they happened to bump their heads into the vault of heaven, cracking it and, at the same time, fracturing their skulls. The elder dragon brother fell into the Northern Sea and languished at the bottom; the younger one dropped onto the Southern Mountain and wasted away in the cave.

The crack in the sky was right above where Brother Sang and his fellow villagers lived. In summer, rain gushed from it like a waterfall, and in winter, hail dropped from it like stones. As a result, trees fell, houses crumbled, and livestock died in droves. Frightened humans took refuge in caves and feared to venture out. Seeing this, Brother Sang asked his parents,

"Is there any way to mend the sky?"

"I heard that there was a big camphor tree growing horizontally from the crag at the waist of the Lainong Mountain. On the tree was a huge bird's nest, where a green-bearded old man lived," said the father. "Perhaps he can help us. Go and ask him."

"But who will take care of you while I'm gone?"

"Don't worry, son," said his mother. "Go and do what you think is right."

"The cliff is too slippery to climb," said his father, "but the green-bearded old man always gets up early to comb his long beard. When he does so, he will lower it out of the nest. Then you can grab it and climb up."

Brother Sang set out. He trudged day and night, braving wind and snow. After he exhausted the food he had brought with him, he had to eat tree leaves and drink water from the streams. One evening, after overcoming ninety-nine rivers and ninety-nine mountains, he finally reached the Lainong Mountain. As his father had told him, there was indeed a camphor tree growing horizontally from the crag. And on the tree was a huge bird's nest. There was no sign of the green-bearded old man, however.

"He must be still sleeping in the nest," figured Brother Sang. The quietness of this lonely place made the already fatigued Brother Sang very sleepy. He dropped to the ground and soon fell asleep on the grass.

The next morning, when Brother Sang awoke, he heard a song drifting from the bird's nest,

Here in the nest sits me, the green-bearded man,
Yet, so many wonders in the world I have seen,
With a comb I'm tidying up my long, long beard,
Now I'm lowering it as far down the tree as I can.

Sky Mended with a Dragon's Teeth

And sure enough, Brother Sang saw the beard extending from the nest. He sprang up, grabbed it, and began to climb. When he was halfway up, the old man put his head out and spoke to him,

"Son, you'd better stop because it's too high up here. Tell me what you want, and I'll see if I can help."

"The sky above us has cracked and caused great calamities," said Brother Sang. "I'm going to mend it, but I need something to do that with."

"I see," the old man responded. "The Bear King on the Wuliu Mountain has three daughters. See which one will be able to help you. Go and marry her. If the Bear King refuses, stomp the ground three times in these sandals." Thereupon he dropped a pair of green straw sandals.

Brother Sang slid down the old man's beard, slipped into the straw sandals, and rushed to the Wuliu Mountain. When he arrived, he was stunned. The mountain took the shape of a stele, standing so tall that its top reached well into the clouds. When he turned his eyes down, he found the walls of the mountain so slick that even ants wouldn't be able to walk on it.

He remembered the green straw sandals and the green-bearded man's words, so he stomped hard on the ground three times. As he did so, he shouted,

> *Here I am, stomp, stomp, stomp,*
> *Each foot in a green straw sandal;*
> *Old Bear King, to you I speak,*
> *Your daughter I want at my bridal.*

As he stomped, the mountain shook. Then he heard a plea coming from the mountain-top, "Stop!" And in its wake, there came down a long, long green rattan rope. At its tip was a big red flower, in which a young woman dressed in a green costume was riding on a green deer. With a poker face, she said, "I'm the eldest daughter of the Bear King. My name is Sister Green."

"Sister Green, would you help me mend the sky?" asked Brother Sang.

"That's hard work," said she, looking up listlessly. "I like pleasure and fun better than anything."

"Then I don't want you to be my wife. Go back to your father and ask him to send down another of his daughters."

So the girl in green went back to the mountaintop.

Brother Sang waited and waited, but there was no sign of movement. He began to stomp again and again until the mountain trembled. As if accustomed to his heavy treading, the Bear King paid no attention to him. Not knowing what to do, Brother Sang had to return to the green-bearded old man for advice.

The old man gave him a pair of black gloves and told him to push the Bear King's mountain, which he did as he sang,

> *Here I am, push, push, push,*
> *Each hand in a black glove,*
> *Old Bear King, to you I speak,*
> *Your daughter I want to be my love.*

As he pushed, the mountain began to quake. Then he heard a request coming from the mountaintop, "Halt!" And in its wake, there came down a long, long black rattan rope. At its tip was a big red flower, in which a young woman wearing a black dress was straddling a black cow. Expressionlessly she said, "I'm the second daughter of the Bear King. My name is Sister Black."

"Sister Black, would you help me mend the sky?" entreated Brother Sang.

"That's hard labor," said she, turning her face away from him. "I like leisure and merriment better than anything."

"Then I don't want you to be my wife. Go back to your father and ask him to send another of his daughters down."

So the girl in black returned to the summit.

Brother Sang waited and waited, and nothing stirred. He pushed the mountain again and again until it quavered. As if used to his violent ramming, the Bear King no longer responded to him. Once again, Brother Sang had to go back to the green-bearded old man for guidance.

This time, the old man gave him a white hat and told him to bump the Bear King's mountain with his head. Brother Sang did as the green-bearded man had instructed while chanting,

> *Here I am, bump, bump, bump,*
> *A white hat I wear on my head,*
> *Old Bear King, to you I speak,*
> *Give me your third daughter instead.*

As he bumped, the mountain began to rock. Then he heard a demand coming from the mountaintop, "Hold!" And in its wake, there came down a long, long white rattan rope. At its tip was a big red flower, in which a gorgeous young woman wearing a set of white apparel was riding a white sheep.

Beaming and blushing, she said, "I'm the third daughter of the Bear King. My name is Sister White."

"Sister White, would you help me mend the sky?" requested Brother Sang.

"Sure," said she, smiling. "Let's go."

After Brother Sang helped her get off the big flower, she told him how they could accomplish the task:

"We need two things: nails made of a dragon's teeth and a hammer crafted from a dragon's horn."

"Since the black dragons broke the sky in a fight, we can get their teeth and horn as retribution," suggested Brother Sang.

Sister White agreed. Then, she handed a sheepskin pouch and a pair of gold pliers to him. In his white hat, black gloves, and green straw sandals, Brother Sand set off. They had agreed to meet in a cave at the foot of the Wuliu Mountain when he finished.

Brother Sang traveled forty-nine days and nights before arriving at the cave of the Southern Mountain, where the younger black dragon brother was recovering from his head injury. Brother Sang stamped on the ground in his green straw sandals, knocked at the door of the cave with his hands in the black gloves, and banged at the rocks with his head in the white hat. Soon the dragon stuck out its bandaged head. Pointing at the beast, Brother Sang demanded,

"Listen, you rascal, I'm going to mend the sky. It's you that damaged it in a brawl with your brother, so I need your teeth to make some nails. Hurry and open your mouth!"

The dragon kept quiet.

"If you pretend not to hear me, try my fist in the black glove that can topple your mountain. One blow and your skull will be crushed."

The dragon had to open his mouth, revealing his white teeth. Brother Sang then pulled them out one by one, which he carefully placed in the sheepskin pouch. When he was done, he patted the dragon on the head and said to him, "Old pal, go back to your cave and get your wounds healed. Never come out to fight with others."

His cheeks hollow, the dragon recoiled in obedience.

Without resting, Brother Sang headed for the Northern Sea. Carrying the sheepskin pouch and the gold pliers, he traveled forty-nine days and nights. As soon as he arrived, he began to summon the black dragon. At his first stamp in his green straw sandals, waves sprang up and began to beat the shore. Then he pinched them with his hand, which sent them higher than the tallest trees. He bumped them with his head, and the entire sea began to surge, thrusting the waves sky-high. Before long, the dragon's bound-up head emerged from the surface. Pointing at him, Brother Sang commanded,

"Listen, you scoundrel, I'm going to mend the sky. It's you that fractured it in a scuffle with your brother. So I need your horn to make a hammer. Hurry and rest your head on the beach."

The dragon remained still.

"If you refuse to respond, I'll destroy everything in the waters, not to mention your skull."

The dragon had to place his head on the sand. Brother Sang then yanked out one of his horns and stowed it in the sheepskin pouch. When he had finished, he stroked the dragon's head and said to him, "Old black dragon, go back to the bottom of the sea and recover from your injury. Never again pop out to battle anyone."

The poor dragon nodded and slipped back into the sea. Brother Sang then hurried to the Wuliu Mountain to join Sister White, carrying with him the gold pliers and the sheepskin pouch filled with the dragon teeth and horn.

Meanwhile, Sister White had fleeced her sheep and made two mantles out of the wool. Upon seeing Brother Sang, she smiled. "Brother Sang, let's put on the mantles, ride the sheep, and mend the sky right away."

As they mounted the sheep, wings grew out of it miraculously. Soon they approached the section of the sky with the crack. Despite the hail beating down like rocks right in their faces, the couple started the mending project. Sister White took off her white scarf and shook it open in the air, turning it into a broad and long band. With it, she covered the crevice. Then Brother Sang hammered in the nails of the dragon teeth to fasten it to the vault of the sky.

As soon as they had finished, people turned out to celebrate. Brother Sang and Sister White could hear their hurrahs even from high above. Brother Sang's parents were in the jubilant crowd. Looking up, his father said to his mother with great pride, "I told you: Our son is a great hero!"

The celebration lasted into the evening, when a young woman looked up and suddenly discovered something no one had noticed before. "Look," she blurted out. "The white and long stripe up there must be the scarf of Sister White!"

"There," a young man also made a discovery, "the twinkling dots must be the nails of the dragon teeth."

People later named the shiny dots "stars" and the long stripe "Silvery River," which Westerners call the Milky Way.

Brother Sang and Sister White have since stayed in the sky. They are watching over the mended part of it, fearing that it may fail again. People can no longer tell them from the roaming clouds because they are so much like them in their white mantles of wool.

WHY ARE OXEN PREFERRED TO TILL OUR LAND?

This is a folktale from the Tu. The 8,028,100 Tu people (China, 2002) live largely in Qinghai and Gansu. The following tale shows how much importance the ancestors of the Tu attached to cattle, their choice beasts of burden. It also reveals that like some other ethnic minorities, they share the deity Jade Emperor of Heaven with the Han Chinese.

*A*fter Jade Emperor of Heaven created human beings and settled them on earth, he returned to his heavenly palace. Since then, he had never come back to visit them. For that reason, he had no idea how his creatures lived.

One day, he summoned Giant Ox, one of the gods, to his court.

"I left the humans I created on earth, hoping they could make a living by themselves," the emperor said to the ox. "But I really don't know how they have been doing. I want you to take a look for me."

"No problem!"

"Wait!" Giant Ox was about to leave when Jade Emperor stopped him. "Listen carefully. If you find them living miserably, tell them to eat once and wash their hands and faces three times a day."

With Jade Emperor's decree, the ox sped to the earth, riding on the clouds and mists. When he saw humans working in the fields, he yelled to them in a very arrogant manner,

"Hey, listen, you block-headed humans! I'm here to inspect you on behalf of Jade Emperor. He demands that every day, you eat . . . eh . . . three times and wash your hands and faces once. Only by doing so can you be prosperous."

As soon as he had finished, he got on the clouds and returned to heaven to report back to Jade Emperor.

"What did you tell the humans?" asked the heavenly emperor.

"First of all, Your Majesty, I must say that I felt a great honor to have been your envoy to the world . . . ."

"Cut to the chase," demanded the emperor, who hated nonsense.

"Down there, I found the humans doing very well. They had learned the skill of making a good living on the beautiful and bountiful land. I told them that it was your intent that they should eat three times, and wash their hands and faces once a day."

Upon hearing that, Jade Emperor flew into a rage. He sprang up from his throne and gave the stupid Giant Ox a good kick in the mouth, breaking his front teeth. (This is why cattle have no front teeth even today.) As if he hadn't completely vented his anger, the emperor bellowed,

"You fool! I asked you to tell humans one thing, but you told them the other. This is awful! If they eat so many times a day, where can they get enough food?"

Before the poor ox had time to plead for mercy, the seething Jade Emperor continued, "Well, since you told them to eat three meals a day, then you go and help them to produce the food they need!"

While Jade Emperor was indulging himself in this harangue, Giant Ox trembled with fear. He was not certain if his head would still be connected to his body the next minute. Stressed, he rubbed his neck repeatedly. This is why cattle have oxbows below their necks.

The sentence that Jade Emperor of Heaven had meted out came as a great relief, though. So Giant Ox thanked him liberally and promised he would immediately descend to the world to help humans with their farming.

Courtesy of Dai Yuru and Yunnan Fine Arts Publishing House

THE ORIGIN OF THE
BRONZE DRUM

This is a legend from the Buyei, whose 2,971,500 people (China, 2002) for the most part inhabit Guizhou. Others are scattered in Yunnan, Sichuan, and Guangxi.

Bronze drums are cultural relics of ethnic groups such as the Miao, Yao, Dong, Zhuang, Sui, Gelao, Va, and Buyei. The oldest drums unearthed are over 2,700 years old. Artistically embellished, bronze drums have been used as musical instruments as well as sacred objects. Various folktales try to explain how bronze drums originated. The following is one of the tales popular among the Buyei people.

*A*long time ago, there lived by a lake a young man called Gujie. Orphaned when he was a child, he had to work for a vicious landowner by the name of Suhaiba. Though a hard worker, Gujie was unable to earn a decent living. On the morning of New Year's Day, he went to the lake to go fishing, hoping that a good catch would provide him with a delicious meal. But the odds seemed to be against him, for he had been angling the whole day without even catching a little shrimp. Night fell. He was about to give up when a big red carp took the bait.

Back home, Gujie couldn't wait to cook the fish. As he picked it up, however, he hesitated. Wiggling and gaping at him, it seemed to be begging for mercy. The kindhearted Gujie put the fish in a big jar, where he kept his drinking water, which he had drawn and carried over from a well nearby. He was preparing to go to bed on an empty stomach when Suhaiba and his men broke into his rickety hut. Suhaiba came to claim the fish, saying that it belonged to him because the lake was part of his family's property. Gujie told Suhaiba to spare the fish.

"I can let it go if you pay off the debt you owe me," said Suhaiba.

"What debt?" asked Gujie, bewildered, "I've never borrowed a single grain from you!"

"Of course you haven't, but your parents did!"

Gujie knew that Suhaiba was blackmailing him, but he quit arguing for the sake of the red carp. He promised to pay off the alleged debt, and Suhaiba left with his men.

In his sleep, Gujie dreamed of a beautiful young woman dressed in a red costume rising from the jar. She said to him,

"Here at the bottom of the jar, I have a pearl for you. Take it and embed it in your hoe."

Gujie woke up the next morning and rushed to the jar, only to see the carp swimming as usual. But when he took a second look, he was startled. Lying at the bottom of the jar was the pearl that the girl in his dream had given him. He carefully fished it out and stowed it in a safe place. He thought it too precious to be placed on his hoe.

That evening, when Gujie returned from his work, something more astonishing happened. As he entered his poor house, he found the young woman in his dream fixing his dinner. When asked, the girl told him she was the third daughter of Dragon King of the lake where he had been fishing. Adoring his bravery and diligence, she had transformed into a red carp so he could catch her and bring her home. She was so thankful to him for saving her from the cruel landowner that she changed into a human to keep him company. Happily, they became husband and wife.

The dragon princess told Gujie that the pearl she had given him possessed magic power, and it would be tremendously helpful when embedded in his hoe. Sure enough, the first day Gujie tried his hoe, he finished a workload that would have taken him ten days. And in another ten days, the crops tended began to ripen. But no matter how hard he worked and how much he harvested, he was unable to pay off the debt allegedly owed to the treacherous landowner, for the interest grew faster than the payments.

Gujie was demoralized. Dragon Princess, his wife, asked him not to worry. She told him she had handsome savings back at the Dragon Palace in the lake. To get them, however, they had to break through nineteen gates, well-guarded by her father's garrison.

"Nothing can stop me," said Gujie. "Let's go."

When they came to the lakeshore, the baffled Gujie asked, "Where is the Dragon Palace?"

"Don't worry," said his wife. "Here, keep the water I scoop from the lake in your mouth and squirt it as hard as you can over the lake to that peninsula."

No sooner had the water jetted out of Gujie's mouth than a bridge of rainbow appeared over the lake. After they reached the peninsula, Dragon Princess asked Gujie to stop and wait, then she disappeared. In a moment, she returned with a white horse.

"If you have the courage, let's ride on the horse and get to the bottom of the lake, which is twelve layers deep," the princess challenged her husband.

"I can even dive into the twelfth layer of a sea," said the determined husband. Without further ado, they plunged into the water on horseback.

When they reached the seventh layer of the lake, they saw phoenixes flying around a fire-spewing volcano. Gujie shot two of them with his arrows and took them along as a present for his father-in-law, Dragon King.

With their eyes closed, they rode on for thirty-six days, until they arrived at the twelfth layer of the lake and came to the first gate of the Dragon Palace. Gujie asked his wife to wait at a nearby well, where she could use its reflection as a mirror to tidy up her hair. He then set to breaking through the gates.

At the first gate, he found a huge, strange object engraved with patterns of dragons and phoenixes. "It must be a lock," Gujie thought to himself. He thumped it three times with his fist, and to his surprise, it gave out a burst of thunderous bellows. The sound waves soon reached the depth of the Dragon Palace and threw it into great turmoil. At the time, Dragon King and Queen were talking about looking for their lost daughter. Immediately he ordered his marine army to be prepared for an attack.

Hearing weapons clinking in the palace, Gujie mistook Dragon King as belligerent. To preempt a battle, he shot three of his arrows, decorated with phoenix feathers, into the palace, and they dropped in front of the dragon. Before the Dragon King could react to what he deemed an act of war, one of his ministers came forward. He reminded the king of their tradition: Arrows of phoenix feathers meant a proposal of marriage, not hostility. At that, Dragon King ordered all the gates opened wide.

The dragon parents were happy to see their daughter back but resented her unceremonious marriage with a mortal. They blamed Gujie for seducing her and prepared to execute him. Only when Dragon Princess told what had happened to her did her father relent. But he planned to drive Gujie away by assigning him three demanding tasks: cultivating a hillside, growing an orchard, and opening up a pond to farm fish—all had to be done in three days. Gujie was not worried at all; with his magic hoe, he accomplished the tasks in time without much effort. When he finished, Dragon King couldn't find any more exacting undertakings. So he had to grant his consent to their marriage.

When he learned that a day in the Dragon Kingdom was as good as a year on land, Gujie began to miss his fellow villagers. He talked with his wife about returning to them.

"I'll go wherever you go," said Dragon Princess resolutely.

When they shared their thoughts of leaving for Gujie's homeland, the dragon parents gave them not only their approval but also a large dowry, which the couple kindly declined.

"OK," said Dragon King. "Since you asked nothing of me, take this object with you. It can command the forces of nature, send its sound to a distance of a thousand miles, and turn water into silver and earth into gold."

Before the thankful couple had a chance to say anything, Dragon King continued, "Stow it away with great care and don't use it unless there's a war, a death of an elder, or a New Year's celebration. When any of these events takes place, hit the object twelve times. I will hear that and come to help defeat your enemies, release the soul of the dead from purgatory, or rejoice in your New Year's festivity."

After they said good-bye to the dragon parents, Gujie and his Dragon Princess wife left the palace. When they came to the well where she had rested, their precious object immediately turned into a vessel, which carried them up through the twelve layers of the lake.

As soon as they surfaced and hit the shore, the vessel changed into a bronze drum. One of its sides was hollow, and when its was turned upside down, the drum could serve as a container. The couple filled it with the water of the lake. As Dragon King had told them, the water instantly became a silvery fluid. They carried it home and bathed in it. As a result, they remained immune to illnesses for the entire year. When they fed their livestock with the silvery water, the animals grew fatter and stronger. And when they used the water to cook, they both became smarter.

Soon New Year's Day arrived. Gujie and Dragon Princess took the bronze drum out and hit it twelve times, as Dragon King had asked. Upon hearing the magnificent sound of the magic drum, all the villagers, including the vicious landowner Suhaiba, came to see it. Suhaiba elbowed through the crow and maneuvered himself close to it. He wanted to own it, as he did everything he set his eyes or laid his hands on. However, as soon as he touched the drum, he was knocked unconscious by a beam of dazzling light shooting from it.

Since then, the Buyei people have had a tradition of beating their treasured bronze drums during New Year's celebrations. As part of the tradition, girls and newly married women vie with one another in running to the lake to fetch water, as Gujie and his Dragon Princess wife used to do with their magic drum. The villagers believe that whoever gets the first bucket of the water will have her family blessed for the year to come.

Bronze drum.

THE ORIGIN OF THE
EAGLE-BONE FLUTE

This is a legend from the Tajik, one of the ten Chinese Muslim ethnic minorities. Most of the 41,000 (China, 2002) Tajik people live in Xinjiang.

There are at least four different legends about the origin of the eagle-bone flute. One tells of a tragic love story, in which a girl, fatally wounded while escaping from a repressive landlord, turned into an eagle and asked her boyfriend to make a flute with her wing bone after her death. She said that by doing so, he could remember her all the time. The following story has a different ending.

*I*n a village by a river under the foot of the Muztagata Mountain there lived a mean *bayi* ("landlord" in Tajik). His name was Sabir. The villagers were mostly his long- and short-term hired hands. They lived a wretched life because he often made them work overtime and rarely paid them.

Among the long-term hired hands were a boy, Vapa, and a girl, Gulmire. Vapa herded Sabir's sheep and goats and Gulmire looked after his lambs. Although they worked very hard, Sabir still scolded them on the slightest pretext and frequently penalized them by withholding their meals. Therefore, pasturing their herds together was the only time when they could have some fun and relief. Gulmire often danced to the tune of Vapa's cow-bone flute.

As they were growing up, love thrived between them. They were engaged without getting the *bayi*'s consent, as he required his hired hands to do. When he learned of their secret, *bayi* Sabir was very angry. He didn't want them to be married, because if they were, they wouldn't be able to work as much as he expected of them. So he decided to prevent them from seeing each other. He sent Vapa to a remote pasture and made Gulmire work in his manor as a housemaid. The move dealt a heavy blow to the loving couple. The day they parted, Vapa lamented,

The bayi's keeping us apart,
The bayi has a cruel heart,
Your brows you're knitting,
Your heart's evidently aching,
The bayi's making us suffer,
Never can we be together.

Echoing Vapa's melancholy, Gulmire sang tearfully,

Vapa, my loyal lover,
Vapa, my only friend,
Your affection for me is dear,
My love for you is as sincere,
Your love I cherish in my heart,
Never can the bayi keep us apart.

Though separated, Vapa and Gulmire never stopped thinking of each other.

A shepherd likes to play a flute because it can help him fight boredom and rally his herd at the same time. The instrument is often part of a whip handle. At one time, a flute of this nature was made of either yak or cow bones, as was Vapa's. He was not only a good player but also a composer. With his cow-bone flute, he played the tunes he composed for his beloved Gulmire, whom he sorely missed, while roaming with his flock from place to place. He missed her dearly.

One day, Vapa was playing and his herd was grazing when, all of a sudden, a pack of wolves appeared and attacked them. Vapa tried to whip them away but was outnumbered. Just then, a large eagle swooped down to battle the beasts. In the end, the wolves were routed, leaving a number of casualties behind. Unfortunately, the eagle was also fatally wounded. It asked Vapa to pluck a feather out of its wing after its death and use the bone to make a flute. Vapa followed the eagle's instructions with profound grief. When he tried the flute, he found it capable of producing a melody as melancholy as cheerful. It was so enchanting that whenever he played it, larks, partridges, pheasants, and all the other birds would sing and dance to its accompaniment.

The tunes of the eagle-bone flute drifted across grasslands, over mountains, and into Vapa's village. Eventually, everyone came to know Vapa, which irritated the *bayi*. But Gulmire felt very happy and missed Vapa all the more. Whenever she heard the flute, she would be so enthralled that she became absent-minded. The *bayi* would then subject her to all sorts of punishments. He even used his henchman to spy on her whenever she had to work outside his manor—such as going to the river to do his laundry—until he was assured that nothing out of the ordinary would happen.

One day, while laundering at the river, Gulmire saw two eagles circling high above, flapping their wings as if dancing. She couldn't help holding out her arms to mimic their posture. As days went by, Gulmire unwittingly created a set of exceptionally graceful dance movements.

Sabir planned to hold a big party to celebrate his son's birthday. To make it as festive as possible, the stingy *bayi* for the first time invited the entire village, including his hired hands. When word of the party reached Vapa and his fellow herdsmen on the grassland, they encouraged him to go, seeing it as a good opportunity for him to reunite with Gulmire. They offered to look after his herd during his absence.

The party was very dull. When Sabir asked the participants to cheer up, someone in the crowd suggested that Vapa play his popular eagle-bone flute. Both Vapa and the *bayi* were reluctant. Vapa was here for the sake of Gulmire. The *bayi,* on the other hand, was too proud to ask Vapa to help. Eager to give his son a joyous and happy birthday, he finally softened his stance, saying,

"If you can help, I'll let you marry Gulmire."

Vapa's flute playing was soul-stirring. Its electrifying melody immediately changed the atmosphere of the party. Returning from her laundry trip, Gulmire heard the familiar flute, and it sounded very close. She pushed her way into the crowd, only to be thrilled by the sight of her beloved Vapa. She couldn't help dancing to his tune, and the dance that she had learned from the eagles was equally captivating. The couple were delighted to reunite in such a dramatic way. Their joy, however, soon gave way to sadness when, at the end of the party, Sabir dismissed them without mentioning a word about their marriage. Seeing this, the villagers and the hired hands threatened not to leave unless he honored his word. Sabir had no choice but to give in, and the villagers conveniently turned the party into a wedding.

Vapa's eagle-bone flute and Gulmire's dance soon spread among the entire Tajik people in Xinjiang and have since become part of their tradition.

THE FIDDLE WITH A
HORSE HEAD

This is a folktale from the Mongols. The 5,813,900 Mongols (China, 2002) live primarily in the Inner Mongolia Autonomous Region in Northern China.

The horse-headed fiddle, known as "molinhu'er," is very popular among the Mongols. A horse-head sculpture on top of its neck gives this two-stringed fiddle its name. Its drumlike resonator assumes various shapes; originally an upside-down taper, now it can also be a square or an octagon. The sound it produces is deep and melodious, and it can be played solo or as an accompaniment to a vocalist. Its invention is attributed to a young herdsman named Suhe, whose legend is retold below.

*T*here was once an orphan named Suhe, who lived with his grandmother. Every day he went out to herd his two dozen sheep, the only source of the family's income. At the age of sixteen, Suhe had grown to be a handsome young man, popular among his fellow herdsmen for his singing talent.

One day, Suhe failed to come home after sunset. Since this had never happened before, his grandmother was worried. She was talking about looking for him with visiting neighbors when Suhe staggered into the yurt, holding a large, fluffy ball of white hair in his arms. It turned out to be a foal. Suhe told his amazed grandmother and the neighbors that he had found the foal on his way back.

"It was lying still all by itself," Suhe said, catching his breath, "but I couldn't find its mother even though I waited for a long time. That's why I'm late. Sorry, Grandma!"

After he drank a cup of sheep-milk tea, Suhe continued, "I feared that wolves might come and hurt it in the dark, cold night, so I picked it up and brought it home."

"You did the right thing," said his grandmother, who was relieved to see him back and pleased that his grandson was growing to be a kindhearted young man. "What goes around will come around," she added, as the neighbors nodded their agreement.

With great care, Suhe and his grandmother nursed the weak foal back to health, and it soon grew up to be a strong colt. His hair was so white that whoever saw him loved him. The colt was not only handsome but also ran very fast; he could catch up with a deer. As the white colt followed Suhe wherever he went, the two became inseparable friends.

One night Suhe was awakened by quick and urgent neighs.

"It must be the white colt!"

Suhe got up, rushed out of the yurt, and there he saw his friend struggling desperately to keep a big wolf at bay outside the sheep pen. Suhe went up and helped drive the beast away. Only then did he discover the colt sweating all over.

"He must have been fighting the wolf for a long time," Suhe thought aloud. Patting the colt on the back, Suhe said with great sincerity, "I thank you very, very much! You're really my buddy! Without you, we'd have suffered a great loss tonight."

The white colt nodded and sneezed, as if he could understand Suhe's compliment.

As years went by, both Suhe and his white colt grew up. One spring, news circulated throughout the grassland that a prince was sponsoring a horse race in front of a temple and that he had promised to marry one of his daughters to the winner. Prodded by his friends, Suhe rode to the temple on the back of his white horse.

The horse race turned out to be extremely competitive, because the event attracted the best young riders and their steeds from all over the region. Suhe and his white horse, however, beat every one of their competitors with ease. The display of Suhe's horse-riding skills made a deep impression on the prince and his daughter, watching from the rostrum: She had never seen a young man so handsome; he had never seen a horse so speedy. When the race was over, the prince asked that they be brought into his presence.

When he learned that Suhe was from a poor herdsman's family, the snobbish prince retracted his promise to let him marry his daughter, proclaiming that a relationship with him would be beneath the dignity of his noble family. Then he asked Suhe to trade the white horse for three gold coins.

"I'm here to race my horse, not to sell it," Suhe said.

"How dare you speak to me like that, you worthless scoundrel?" roared the enraged prince. With that, he ordered his men to give Suhe a good beating, which rendered him unconscious. Leaving him alone, they went away with his unwilling white horse. His friends, who were outnumbered and could not help, took the black-and-blue Suhe home.

Under the care of his grandmother, Suhe slowly pulled through, but he was never happy again, for he missed his white horse very much and was extremely concerned about his safety.

One night, he was about to get into bed when he heard a few bumps at the door.

"Who is it?"

But his question went unanswered. Curious, he got up and opened the door, only to see his white horse! Soon his joy evaporated as he found the horse's white coat covered with blood, several arrows deeply wedged in his body. With his last breath, the white horse told Suhe what had happened. It turned out that after abducting the white horse, the prince wanted to show him off to his friends. But before the prince could settle himself on the horse's back, he had bucked him off and run away.

"Get it! Get it!" fumed the prince, embarrassed as well as infuriated, "If you can't get it alive, I want it dead!"

Arrows had raced after the white horse, and quite a few had caught up with him, lodging in his back and hips. Knowing he was dying, the white horse had galloped frenziedly toward Suhe's yurt. He would rather die among friends than enemies.

Despite all the efforts to save his life, the white horse passed away. Suhe was so distressed by the loss of his loyal friend that for days he could neither eat nor sleep. One evening, he had finally managed to close his eyes, when he saw his beloved white horse. It trotted over and rubbed its head against him as usual, giving Suhe a great sense of comfort. Suddenly, the horse turned very cold. When the surprised Suhe asked why, he began,

"Suhe, I know you've been thinking of me all this time. I missed you, too, and very much! But there's a way we can be together forever."

"How?" he asked with deep sorrow.

"Don't feel bad, but do as I tell you. Make a fiddle with my bones, tendon, and the hair of my tail. They're parts of me that won't decay for a long time. I know you like to sing, and I enjoyed listening, so when you play the fiddle and sing, you'll feel I'm still with you as your accompanist."

Before Suhe could say anything, the white horse vanished, and he woke up drenched in cold sweat. Keeping the white horse's words in mind, he immediately acted upon them. He made the neck of a fiddle with the bone, twisted two strings out of the tendons, and manufactured a bow using the long hair of the tail. He also crafted a triangular boom box and covered one side with sheepskin. In order to commemorate the white horse, he crafted a wooden horse head after that of the white horse and fixed it on top of the neck.

When he tried playing the fiddle, it produced the best tune he had ever heard in his life. Since that day, the sound of the fiddle with a horse head has become the solace of the herdsmen on the Mongolian prairie, freeing them from the weariness of a day's labor and cheering them up when they are faced with sorrows or difficulties.

The Fiddle with a Horse Head

Legends about Places

  Many of China's landmarks have beautiful stories behind them. A graceful rock standing tall in an ethnic Sani enclave near Kunming is said to be the incarnation of "A Girl Named Ashima." "The River of Hai and Lan," which flows through Yanji in Northeastern China, was named after a brave young Korean couple. The Manchus' ancestor was allegedly born in "A Fairy's Bathing Pond" near the Changbai Mountains. The difference between "The Five-Fingered Mountain and the Seven-Fingered Hill" on Hainan Island at the southern tip of the country was supposedly caused by a pair of contending giants. The Yugur "Young Hero Mola" became the "Red Cliff" in the Qilian Mountains after his conquest of a snow monster. The collective power of the Monba people led to "The Conquest of a She-demon" and thus, as they believe, reshaped some of the geographic features of Tibet.

A GIRL NAMED ASHIMA

This is a folktale from the Sani, one of the twenty major branches of the Yi ethnic group, who have a population of 7,762,300 (China, 2002), living in Sichuan, Yunnan, and Guizhou.

This tale is adapted from a 1,200-line Sani epic. It became nationally known because of a movie produced by the Han Chinese in 1964. The movie, however, turned the relationship of brother and sister into that of two lovers, much to the dismay of the Sani people.

The folktale is said to have taken place in Shilin (Stone Forest), a Sani community near Kunming, which has a stone that resembles the legendary Sani girl (see photo on p. 235).

*T*here were once two families in Azhuodi, one of the Yi people's communities. Though far apart, they welcomed their new babies at the same time. The poor family of Gelu Riming had a twin son and daughter, whom they named Ahei and Ashima. The aristocratic family of Rebu Bala had only a boy, whom they called Azhi.

The baby Ashima was so sweet that her smile resembled a blossom and her cry an agreeable melody. At age five, she began to help her mother look for edible wild herbs to supplement the family's insufficient food supply. As she grew, she learned to weave, cook, and mend clothes. Now a young woman, she looked like a beauty queen in the ethnic costume that the family could afford.

Ashima's twin brother Ahei was as loveable. At an early age, he had learned all the rituals of courtesy required of a grownup. When he was a teen, he had already become an expert herdsman. When this story happened, he had taken his family's herd to a better but faraway pasture three years earlier. During those years, he had learned the skills of archery and the entire set of intricate Yi music.

However, Azhi, the only son of the aristocrat Rebu Bala, was by no means comparable to the twins. He was not only good-for-nothing but, as he came of age, also had a sinister lust for attractive women, despite his apelike appearance. Ever since he got a glimpse of Ashima at a festival celebration, he had been obsessed with her beauty. He was determined to have her. From a priest, Rebu Bala learned of an old, glib-tongued matchmaker known as Gedi Haire and sent for him. At first, Gedi Haire rejected Azhi's request.

"I don't want to be blamed for a bad marriage the rest of my life," he reasoned.

"How about a hundred gold nuggets and a hundred silver ingots?" the desperate Rebu Bala made a generous offer, then continued, "That's not all. I'll also give you horses and cattle. And if that's still not enough, I'll present you a gift every New Year's Day in the future."

Tempted by such a lucrative bribe, the matchmaker gave in. He went to Gelu Riming's house, where he was greeted first by the household's unwelcoming dog.

"What are you here for, Old Pa?" asked Ashima's father.

"I've come to propose to your daughter in the name of Rebu Bala's son Azhi," replied Gedi Haire. "The wealthy Azhi really matches your good-looking Ashima."

"No," Gelu Riming said categorically. "A working family's daughter can never be married to a dandy boy."

"Do you mean you are keeping her at home until she's too old to find a husband?"

"Well, let me tell you this. If I married my daughter into the wrong family, I might get a bottle of wine and be merry for a while. But after that, I'd be sorry for the rest of my life."

"A pot of half-cooked rice spoils only one meal, but a bad marriage would ruin my daughter's entire life," Ashima's mother added. "We'll never marry our daughter into a notorious family like Rebu Bala's."

Gedi Haire then bragged about Rebu Bala's fortune, such as his gilded bed; his gold nuggets, each the size of a horse shoe; and his multitude of cattle and sheep grazing on the hillside. He meant to lure Ashima's parents the same way Rebu Bala had tempted him. Ashima could no longer control her indignation at the shameless matchmaker and began to sing,

> *I'm not livestock for trade;*
> *Nor am I grains for sale.*
> *When you first spoke I listened,*
> *But now you made me mad;*
> *If you dare to ramble further on,*
> *Expect me to call you names bad.*
> *I'm not interested in aristocracies,*
> *Nor will I marry a man of riches.*
> *I'll never marry Azhi, the idler,*
> *No, ninety-nine "no's" I will holler.*

Ashamed and angry, the matchmaker fumed, "Yes or no, Azhi will get you sooner or later." With that, he rushed back to Rebu Bala.

Before long, the matchmaker returned to Gelu Riming again. This time, not only did he bring ninety-nine oxen, ninety-nine yards of silk, and numerous jewelry as dowry, which he would use as carrot, he also brought over a hundred horsemen armed with bows and arrows, which he would employ as a stick.

"Gelu Riming, I hope you are not going to refuse our offer and end up getting nothing while losing your daughter all the same," the matchmaker threatened.

"I only have one thing to tell you: I won't marry my daughter to Azhi under any circumstances," Ashima's father said adamantly.

The humiliated matchmaker ordered the horsemen to take Ashima by force despite her struggles and her parents' objections. The atrocious abduction devastated the parents. Engulfed in tears, her mother wailed, "Ashima, my baby, you've never left me since you were young. You've been my companion and helper all these years. Now that you've been taken from me, when am I going to see you again?"

At the time, Ashima's brother Ahei was herding the family's flock far away. On the night of his sister's kidnapping, Ahei had a nightmare. He dreamt of a green snake coiled in front of his parents' house and ten yellow-faced dogs scrambling for ten bones. When he awoke, he was perturbed and worried. He rounded up the herd and headed for his native land along the river by which he had left it. It took him three days and nights to reach home. Seeing a big mess inside and outside the house, Ahei couldn't help asking his parents what had happened.

"Rebu Bala took your sister," his mother sobbed out.

"Where's my magic horse, Father?"

"It's still in the stable."

Ahei mounted his horse and galloped off, carrying his bow and arrows. On his way, he met an elderly shepherd.

"Uncle Shepherd, have you seen a mob of horsemen passing by with a girl under their control?"

"I would have missed a bee flying by, but I can't miss a hundred horsemen taking a pretty young woman with them. They went by long ago."

"Can I still catch up?"

"Well, you can if your horse is good enough."

Ahei thanked the old shepherd, got on his horse, and galloped away. Climbing over another three mountains, he came across an elderly cowherd. When asked, the cowherd told him that he had seen the armed men and a captive girl. They had gone by hours before.

While Ahei was running after them, the unsuspecting gang, led by the matchmaker Gedi Haire, hurried on. When they approached a dark forest, he flaunted Rebu Bala's riches to Ashima, "This is Rebu Bala's forest, big enough to hide an army."

"So what!" the scornful Ashima chuckled. "He may be wealthy and influential now, but in thirty years when he's less fortunate, we farmers will take the mountain back."

When they came to a lake, the matchmaker bragged again, "This is Rebu Bala's lake, where he cleans his gold and silver bullion."

"So?" Ashima replied contemptuously. "He's rich and powerful now, but in thirty years when he's out of luck, we'll get the lake back."

Along the way, Gedi Haire showed off Rebu Bala's property, such as his cave and flatlands, and each time Ashima responded with disdain.

At the same time, Ahei had doubled his speed and was in hot pursuit. He passed through the black forest, across the lake, and over the flatlands. As he neared Rebu Bala's residence, he shouted out,

"Ashima! Ashima!"

His call reached Ashima, now confined in Rebu Bala's manor, but she was not allowed to answer. Rebu Bala came out to respond instead, "Who's yelling out there?"

Ahei got off his horse and demanded, "Rebu Bala, set my sister free!"

"Well, it's you, twittering like a bird." Rebu Bala recognized Ahei. "Since you like to sing, I challenge you to a singing duel. If you win, I'll let your sister go."

"What creatures open the door of spring?" Ahei began.

"Singing cuckoos in a breeze open the door of spring," Rebu Bala responded.

"What creatures open the door of summer?"

"Crowing frogs in a rain open the door of summer."

"What creatures open the door of fall?"

"Buzzing flies in a wind open the door of fall."

"What creatures open the door of winter?"

Rebu Bala was finally at a loss for words, as if his tongue were glued to the roof of his mouth. Unwilling to admit defeat and give up Ashima, he challenged Ahei to a series of contests with his men, such as cutting down a forest and sowing an acre of his land. Ahei beat his men in each contest, hands down.

Even so, Rebu Bala refused to release Ashima. He demanded that Ahei compete with his men in retrieving grain seeds. When Ahei accomplished the task, Rebu Bala claimed that he had missed three grains. Though angry at Rebu Bala's deliberate attempt to create difficulties, Ahei remained calm. Looking around, he caught sight of three turtledoves perching on a tree. He shot the one in the middle with an arrow and recovered the three seeds from its craw.

Extremely frustrated, Rebu Bala and his men went back to his mansion and shut the door with a bang behind them. He plotted with his henchmen to get rid of Ahei once and for all. As it happened, Ashima overheard their conversation and warned her brother by playing her *kouxian*, a small musical instrument played in the mouth. Its tune carried an encoded message that only her brother could understand. Ahei answered with his flute, telling her not to worry or to fear. They were talking in their encrypted melodies when the door was flung open and three hungry tigers sprang out, charging at Ahei. Without delay, Ahei launched three arrows and killed them.

Rebu Bala was still reluctant to set Ashima free. The furious Ahei let go another five arrows as a warning. They went whooshing over the wall; four lodged in each of the manor's corners and the fifth wedged in the wall of Rebu Bala's bedroom. He asked that the arrows be removed, but none of his men could yank them out, no matter how hard they tried.

However, Ashima plucked them out as if she were picking flowers. Stunned and terrified, Rebu Bala had to release her.

Riding the magic horse, Ahei and her sister Ashima headed home happily. They trotted and galloped alternately, the horse bell jingling beneath its neck as birds circled above them. Soon they arrived at the river. Following it, they should have been able to return home. But a demon wasp changed everything. It appeared from nowhere and invited the fatigued brother and sister to its home for a break.

The demon led the innocent brother and sister to its den in a cave on a hillside. At its opening, Ashima tripped. While trying to regain her balance, she leaned against a rock, which glued her fast to it. Even her powerful brother couldn't pry her off. Then, to their horror, Ashima began to turn into a stone. With the last of her breath, she said good-bye to her mournful brother as well as her parents and fellow villagers at home,

This old, square and yellow stone,
Now, it'll become my permanent home,
The sun may set and the moon may wane,
But I'll be here forever and never move.
My fellow villagers and my playmates,
I'll be always living in your hearts.
Oh, Ahei, my dear, dear brother,
Call me when you miss your sister,
Each call I'll answer with an echo,
But now, I feel I have but to go.

Today, Ashima still stands as a rock looking toward her home. You can find the naturally carved statue in Shilin (Stone Forest), a renowned tourist attraction 78 kilometers (48 miles) from Kunming, the capital city of Yunnan Province in Southern China.

Ashima statue in Shilin

THE RIVER OF HAI AND LAN

This is a folktale from the Koreans. Most of the 1,923,800 (China, 2002) Koreans living in Northeastern China are descendants of immigrants from Korea during the nineteenth century. They share the culture and language of their Korean brethren across the border. Nevertheless, living in China, ethnic Koreans have gradually become attached to the land they call home, as demonstrated in the following story.

A river flows through Yanbian, a Chinese ethnic Korean community, and on each side stands a mountain: the Feiya on the right bank and Zhuya on the left.

Once there was a village at the foot of each of the mountains. Inhabitants of the village beneath Mt. Feiya were fishermen, while residents below Mt. Zhuya were farmers. Both treated the river between them as their lifeblood.

The fishing village boasted a young girl named Lan, who was good at weaving fishnets and had no match for beauty. The farming village prided itself on having a young man called Hai, who was expert at farming and possessed enormous strength. Hai and Lan often crossed the river and helped each other as the other villagers did, and in time they fell in love.

One late autumn day, both the fishermen and farmers along the river had bountiful harvests. Lan and the fishermen were busy drying the fish they had caught, and Hai and his fellow farmers were threshing the crops they had reaped, when all of a sudden, dark clouds engulfed the sky, accompanied by lightning and thunder. Out of the clouds appeared a demon with a pair of horns on his head and long, matted hair over his body. Wielding a thousand-pound *guandao* (Chinese halberd) on horseback, he swooped down as he roared, "The land and the water are mine!" He stormed one village after the other, snatching away the fish and grain, as well as many beautiful girls.

That winter the villagers on both sides of the river went hungry. They had to drill holes in the ice covering the frozen river in the hope of catching some fish so they could survive. Despite their efforts, however, not a single fish turned up. When they looked into the hole in the ice, they were dismayed to find that the water had been turned into mud by the demon.

The next fall, the demon came again, trying to do the same to the villagers. This time, unwilling to put up with the atrocities any more, they revolted, using their oars and hoes as weapons. Leading the uprising was Hai, who was armed with a long sword.

Sneering at Hai, the demon attacked him, brandishing his massive Chinese halberd. The fearless Hai met him head on, wielding his long, heavy sword. The battle was so intense that nothing could be seen but the glint and flash of their blades. They fought until sunset, and yet neither could get the upper hand. The villagers were cheering for Hai, shouting and flourishing their oars and hoes. Before the demon realized it, Hai's long sword had whooshed down and chopped his head off. It rolled onto the riverbank, thumping, thumping, and thumping.

The villagers were bursting with joy as they flocked around their hero. They were about to toss him up in the air to celebrate when something unimaginable happened. The head of the demon started hopping and bouncing on the riverbank, and in no time, it leapt back onto the neck of the demon's body, lying in the sand. The revived demon then sprang up and rushed toward the crowd. Pushing his way out, Hai engaged his enemy again.

Hai was almost exhausted by a an entire day's combat. But encouraged by his fellow villagers, he quickly pulled himself together and made a dash at the oncoming demon. With a single blow of his long sword, he beheaded the demon again. To Hai's amazement, however, the head found its way back to the demon's body a second time. Another combat ensued, resulting in the demon's decapitation a third time. The head was making yet another attempt to get attached to the neck of its body when Lan darted toward it and poured a bagful of quicklime into the gaping wound of the neck, making it impossible for the head to reconnect to it any more. The head bounced about the riverbank aimlessly until the angry villagers kicked it into the river. The water immediately renewed its clarity and vitality.

The joyous and thankful villagers held a wedding for Hai and Lan on the river. They decorated a big dragon boat with fresh flowers and bundles of pine boughs. Surrounding their cherished bride and bridegroom, they sang, danced, and feasted. They later named the waterway between their villages "the River of Hai and Lan" after their hero and heroine.

The River of Hai and Lan

A FAIRY'S BATHING POND

This is a folktale from the Manchu, who have a population of 10,682,300 (China, 2002), the second largest Chinese ethnic minority.

The Manchu believe that Yongšon, their Aisin Gioro (Gold Clan) ancestor, founded the first unified state of Manchu, which eventually dominated China, known as Qing (1644–1911). There is still a monument with the inscription "Fairy's Bath" at a volcanic lake named Bulhūri at the foot of Bulhūri Mountain to the east of the Changbai Mountains in Northeastern China. The following story tells about its relationship to the Manchus' ancestry.

*O*nce three fairies lived in the Palace of Heaven. The eldest was called Enkulen; the second, Zhengkulen; and the youngest, Fekulen. Both of the two elder sisters were faint-hearted and indifferent to things unconcerned with them. Fekulen, on the contrary, was brave and caring. A good archer, she was never seen without her bow and arrows. Besides, she was the most beautiful of the three.

A stellar god named Sky Wolf, who had coveted her beauty for a long time, proposed marriage to her through a matchmaker. Fekulen said no to him because he was a notorious bully. Vexed by her rejection, Sky Wolf would have taken Fekulen as his bride by force but for his fear of her magic power of archery. He had to check his anger and wait for the right time to retaliate.

Spring came, leaving a long, cold winter behind. Everything in the Changbai Mountains came back to life again, revealing a world of fresh green dotted with melting snow. The three fairies, flapping their long, wide sleeves, which they used as wings, snuck out of the Palace of Heaven and landed near the circular Bulhūri Lake on the Bulhūri Mountain. The inviting beauty of the lake, with its clear and tranquil water, was too much of a temptation. Without delay, they took off their clothes, plunged into the water, and began indulging themselves in a bathing party, splashing and giggling. They thought it was such a reclusive place that nobody would know their whereabouts.

The vicious Sky Wolf, however, had trailed after them to the lake. When the fairies were preoccupied with their frolicking in the water, he grabbed Fekulen's costume without their noticing and fled, thinking that the unclad Fekulen would have to look to him for help.

When they finished bathing, the fairies came to shore to retrieve their clothing, only to find that Fekulen's was gone! The two sisters were perplexed and scared. Saying nothing to their younger sister, they took off, leaving her alone on earth. The embarrassed and dumb-founded Fekulen hurried back to the lake to seek cover. She waited and waited, thinking that her sisters would get her clothes from their celestial home. But she was wrong. Fearing that their parents might take them to task, her sisters didn't say a word about their trip to the earth, not to mention their youngest sister's plight. The next day, they simply forgot about her altogether.

Fekulen was still waiting when a white-haired old man came to the lakeshore, a small raft of birch tree logs in one hand and a little ladder in the other.

"You want to return to the Palace of Heaven, right?" he asked the fairy, who stuck only her head out of the water. "That's easy. Prop this ladder up and you'll be able to climb back instantly. But don't forget that Sky Wolf is still waiting to marry you. He's been fanning the flames of war among the various clans on earth and is in dire need of your help."

"I'd rather stay here than be married to that hooligan," declared the angry Fekulen. "He loves war, but I want peace!"

"Great," responded the old man as he handed Fekulen the birch raft. "You'll find it helpful in making peace. Someone will eventually assist you in the cause."

As Fekulen took the raft and looked up, the old man had already vanished. He was in fact the God of the Changbai Mountains.

Soon a magpie fluttered out of the nearby forest and dropped a fruit of hawthorn onto Fekulen's hands. Fascinated by its fragrance and its bright red color, Fekulen put the fruit in her mouth, and strangely, it rolled into her stomach of itself. Before long, she became pregnant. She was so ashamed that she gave up the idea of going back to heaven at all.

Winter set in. To force Fekulen to marry him, Sky Wolf added more piercing winds to the already cold weather. Though in danger of freezing to death, Fekulen wouldn't submit. The God of the Changbai Mountains decided to help her again. He heated a bucket of water and asked a Buddhist, one of his followers, to take it to Bulhūri Lake. He was to pour the water into the lake to turn it into a hot spring. However, too bashful to face the naked fairy, he turned his head away and called to Fekulen to pick up the bucket herself. While he was waiting, he failed to hold the bucket steady. By the time the fairy reached the tipsy bucket, it had already been emptied. Fekulen had to slip back into the lake. There she had almost frozen when she felt a draft of warm steam drifting down and engulfing her. It came from a hot spring formed by the water emptied from the Buddhist's bucket. She clambered out of the icy water and nestled by the spring and thus survived the otherwise lethal winter. Unfortunately, the silly Buddhist, still waiting for the fairy to get the bucket, had already turned into a rock on Bulhūri Mountain, with his hand held out forever.

Spring came. Fekulen went back to the lake. Soon she gave birth to a boy. Placing him on the birch raft that the mountain god had given her, she said to her baby son,

"Let me give you a name. I want it sound as pure as gold. Your last name will be Aisin Gioro (gold clan) and your first name, Bulhūri Yongšon (son of the Bulhūri Lake), since you were born in this lake."

Then, pressing her bow and arrows into her son's little hands, she went on, "Go and settle in a lucky place. Your mother will be here waiting for you to grow into a strong man so you can wipe out evils and bring peace to your people."

With this, Fekulen lifted the raft gently in the air, and it drifted off her hands and onto a five-colored cloud of good luck. The raft glided north for a few days and landed on the Hurha River. Its current then carried it down to the Odoli Castle, where its chieftain adopted the baby. While bringing him up, he taught the boy martial arts along with his only daughter, Duya Boli. When Bulhūri Yongšon was eighteen, the chieftain married his daughter to him.

Not long after their wedding, a war started again among the clans of Nuyalake, Hushihali, and Yikele at the instigation of Sky Wolf. The conflict threatened to spread to the surrounding areas of Odoli. Riding on a steed borrowed from his father-in-law and carrying his mother's magic bow and arrows, Bulhūri Yongšon said good-bye to his bride and set off to the battlefront to make peace.

Arriving at the battleground where the three clans were engaged in close fighting, Bulhûri Yongðon shot three whistle arrows into the air. The sounds of the arrows ripped through the dark clouds and stunned the combatants, who held back their weapons immediately. While the dust was settling, a ferocious wolf dashed out of the troops. It was none other than Sky Wolf, the instigator of the warfare. Bulhūri Yongšon drew his magic bow and sent an arrow deep into the neck of the demon. He fell and then vanished in a streak of firelight.

When peace returned, the three different clans merged into one, and Bulhūri Yongšon was elected leader. Remembering his mother's words, he led his people to a place of good fortune and settled down. He named it Manchu. Bulhūri Yongšon thus became the ancestor of the Manchus.

Bulhūri Yongšon then thought of his mother and hurried to Bulhūri Mountain. Unfortunately, without clothing, her mother Fekulen had to hide deep in the forest. Every day, she stuck her head out to watch her son grow into manhood. As time went by and as she remained in the same position for so long, she transformed into a tall and elegant pine tree. Bulhūri Yongšon paid tribute to his mother by bowing three times to the tree. He then designated the Changbai Mountains as the birthplace of the Manchu and Bulhūri Lake as "Fairy's Bath."

Courtesy of Sarah Martin, WKU

THE FIVE-FINGERED MOUNTAIN AND THE SEVEN-FINGERED HILL

The majority of the 1,247,800 Li people (China, 2002) live on Hainan Island, which is next only to Taiwan in size.

The island is noted for its spectacular mountains, many of which are tourist attractions, incliuding Wuzhishan (Five-fingered Mountain), at 1,867 meters (about 6,124 feet) tall. The Li people have a story to tell about its origin.

*A*long, long time ago, Hainan Island was a plain stretching to the seas in all directions. It was covered with dense vegetation, and all creatures, including humans, enjoyed their idyllic lives as if they were living in heaven.

One day, however, gusts of wind sprang up suddenly and blustered so violently that they shook the sky and the earth. The poor earth creatures were tossed about as if on a boat caught in a furious tempest. An incessant downpour soon followed and threatened to cause a deluge. Seeing this, Jade Emperor of Heaven immediately called in two brothers, named Yangcha and Fayening, both being gods of thunder. Jade Emperor told them that the sky and the earth were at the risk of being overturned unless something was done. He ordered that they descend to the earth and press its foundation hard so that the calamity would be forestalled.

Carrying their tools, Yangcha and Fayening hurried down to rescue the sky and the earth. But for some reason, as they landed, they went their separate ways. They each worked diligently day and night to gather earth and stones with their hands and baskets hanging from their shoulder poles. The stones and earth they transported to their separate locations piled up with each passing day until they formed two mountains. Although both of them had jagged peaks on their ridges, there was a difference between them. The mountain that Yangcha had piled up had five peaks, while the one shaped by Fayening not only had seven crests but was also much higher. They named their mountains respectively Wuzhishan (the Five-fingered Mountain), and Qizhiling (the Seven-fingered Hill).

Like ballast in a ship, the two mountains steadied the shaky sky and the quavering earth, thus heading off the looming catastrophe. The story would have ended here but for the brothers' sudden whim: They wanted to see whose mountain was sturdier. They tried to find out by kicking them hard. As a result, Yangcha knocked off half of Fayening's Seven-fingered Hill. Fayening, on the other hand, found it impossible to do any damage to Yangcha's Five-fingered Mountain. That's why Wuzhishan looks much taller than Qizhiling today. It's also the most popular among the Li people as well as tourists from all over the world.

YOUNG HERO MOLA
AND THE RED CLIFF

This is a folktale from the Yugur. Most of the 13,719 (China, 2002) Yugur people live at the foot of the Qilian Mountians in the Ethnic Yugur Autonomous County in Gansu Province of Northwestern China. Under the setting sun, a peak of the snow-clad Qilianshan Mountains appears crimson in the distance. This natural phenomenon is linked to a beautiful story, retold here.

Some time ago, the Yugur people relocated from Xinjiang to the foot of the Qilian Mountains in Gansu, where they expected to find better pasture. They herded their cattle, sheep, and camels through the Gobi Desert and finally arrived there, only to find that as beautiful as the grassland looked, there was a huge ice cave under the foot of the Qilian Mountains, and in it lived a bad-tempered giant snow monster. When he lost his temper, which he did very often, he would kick up a disastrous blizzard to plague the Yugur herdsmen, depriving them of their fuel and their flocks of their fodder. Most of the calves and lambs, who were the most vulnerable to inclement weathers, died of cold and hunger.

The Yugurs prayed heartily to the monster, burning incense and kowtowing, but he wouldn't heed their prayers because he was bent on creating havoc.

A boy known as Mola couldn't stand these acts of violence any longer.

"Grandpa," he asked, "why don't we get rid of this nasty monster?"

Shaking his head, his grandfather answered, "He's so powerful that nobody dares to confront him."

"Who in this world can beat him, then?"

"The God of Sun," said his grandfather. Pausing a little, he went on, "but he lives in the East Sea, far away from us. Besides, to get there, one has to climb over numerous mountains."

Mola threw out his chest and said with determination, "I'm not afraid of the mountains and the long distance. As long as I can get a magic weapon from the God of Sun to subdue the monster, it'll be worth the trouble."

Having heard that Mola was going to the God of Sun for help, all the herdsmen on the grassland came to see him off. An elderly man from the eastern part gave him a treasure horse that could travel a thousand miles a day, an elderly woman from the west gave him a waterproof garment so he wouldn't get drowned in water, a hunter from the south gave him a magic bow that never missed a target, and a young herdswoman gave him the whip she used to herd her sheep. Mola put on the garment, took the bow and arrows, mounted the magic horse, and spurred it on with the magic whip. At once, he disappeared in the direction of the East Sea, where the sun rises.

On the treasure horse, Mola covered a thousand miles of grassland and climbed ten thousand snow-clad mountains. He galloped and galloped when, all of a sudden, a precipitous cliff stopped him. It was known as the Cliff of a Knife's Edge. Indeed, its top pieced through the clouds like a blade. Mola was at a loss what to do, but a lark hovering above began to sing,

> *Mola, Mola, little brother,*
> *Forget not your treasure horse,*
> *Spur it with your magic whip,*
> *It'll get you over of course.*

At that, Mola lashed his magic whip in the air. With a crack as loud as thunder, the tip of the whip shot out into the clouds and pulled Mola and his horse up and over the cliff.

Mola resumed his journey and traversed another thousand miles before reaching an extensive forest. It was called the Black Tiger Forest because a black tiger devil was lurking in it. When it saw Mola trotting along on horseback, the beast sprang out with a roar and swooped down upon him. Startled, the horse ran toward the west, followed by the beast, in hot pursuit. The tiger was about to catch up when the same lark chanted again,

> *Mola, Mola, little brother,*
> *Forget not your magic bow,*
> *Shoot the tiger with an arrow,*
> *The tiger will surely let you go.*

Mola drew his bow and took aim. Whoosh went the arrow, and the tiger collapsed with a howl of anguish before breathing its last.

Mola got on the horse, steered it toward the east, and set out again. After countless miles, he arrived at the East Sea. Mola saw red radiance shooting up in the distance, where the Solar Palace was dimly visible. As he was wondering how to cross the vast extent of the wavy waters, the same lark sang again,

Mola, Mola, little brother,
Forget not the waterproof garment,
Put it on, you little hero,
And you'll cross the water triumphant!

Sure enough! As soon as Mola put on the waterproof garment and waded into the sea on his horse, the waves made way ahead of him, leaving behind a furrow of tranquil water, as if it were a thoroughfare. He rode toward the brilliant Solar Palace without even getting the horse's hooves wet.

A pretty young goddess dressed in red and green guarded the gates of the palace. When she saw a young boy galloping toward her, she shouted,

"Hey, stop! Don't be so reckless! Or I'll . . . ."

She then let go a magic eagle to capture Mola, who shot it down immediately. Before the goddess could collect herself, Mola had come up under her nose, almost knocking her down. She leapt back through the gate and shut it before Mola could break in. Alighting from his horse, Mola banged on the gilded gates with his fists and hollered,

God of Sun, open the door,
We're suffering on the grassland,
I'm here to ask you for a favor,
Help us subdue the monster.

For three days and nights, Mola kept knocking and shouting until his hands were sore and his voice was gone. Mola's persistence and courage finally moved the God of Sun. He asked the goddess to let Mola in and bring him into his presence. A gold crown on his head and a gold fan in his hand, the God of Sun was glistening in his dazzling red cloak. Stroking his golden beard, he said smilingly,

"I already know your intent, brave boy. I'll loan you a magic gourd and let you know how to unleash and harness the fire from it. When you have vanquished the monster, make sure you return the gourd to me."

Then the God of Sun took the shiny, reddish gourd of fire off his belt and handed it to Mola. He asked the goddess to teach him how to harness the fire from the gourd. Mola thanked the God of Sun and followed the goddess to the gate. He was shocked to find that the hair of his horse had turned gray. When he asked, the goddess told him that he had been there for four days, each amounting to a year on earth. Therefore, his horse had grown old.

Mola was anxious to return to the grassland to fight the wicked monster. He asked the goddess to teach him the tricks of unleashing fire from the gourd and returning it to it. After he had learned the first technique, Mola became impatient. How he wished he could be back on the grassland soon! His rashness took a toll on his ability to learn. He tried forty times before he barely grasped the method of controlling the fire that he could let loose. Despite the goddess's warning, Mola left in a hurry.

Young Hero Mola and the Red Cliff   245

During his absence, Mola's fellow herdsmen had been looking forward to his return. Year after year had passed, and there was no word of him. They became worried, saying, "Poor Mola will probably never be back."

Not until the end of the eighth year did Mola stumble home on foot, his face haggard and his tattered clothes covered with dust. His horse had died of old age on the way back. Undaunted by the numerous mountains, Mola had trudged along on foot.

The day after Mola's return, the snow monster began to spit white mist from his cave and unfettered a ferocious snowstorm. Carrying the gourd of fire, Mola rushed to the Qilian Mountains against the squall, followed at a distance by his spirited herdsmen, who cheered him on with their drums and gongs.

No sooner had Mola arrived at the cave where the snow monster lived than he tossed the magic gourd into the air, its trajectory forming an arc of bright light. The gourd, looking like a fiery ball, flew directly into the monster's cave and turned it into an inferno. The monster was instantly burned to ashes.

After the death of the monster, Mola wanted to recall the fire into the gourd. However, no matter how hard he tried, he couldn't succeed because he didn't remember the correct incantations the goddess at the Solar Palace had taught him. The fire ran amok for three days and nights, showing no sign of going out. To prevent it from spreading to the forests and the grassland, thereby causing a great calamity to his fellow herdsmen, Mola threw himself onto the gourd and covered its fire-squirting opening with his chest. The fire was harnessed, but Mola was tempered into a red rock, standing aloof like a cliff on the edge of the grassland.

The rock was so warm that it melted the ice and thawed the snow dozens of miles around it. Icy water feeding into the White Poplar River nourished the vast grassland and made the herdsmen prosperous from generation to generation.

Courtesy of Sarah Martin, WKU

THE CONQUEST OF A SHE-DEMON

This is a folktale from the Monba. The 8,923 (China, 2002) Monba people live in the southern part of Tibet, having more or less the same culture as the 50,000 Monpas in India. The sixth Dalai Lama and renowned poet Cangyang Gyacuo (1683–1746) was from Monba. His poems were written in Tibetan because the Monba do not have a written language. Nevertheless, oral literary creations have been plentiful.

The Lhebu Valley, once fertile and beautiful, became the crescent-shaped Naga Lake when a catastrophic flood caused the mountains on both sides to collapse into it, forming Wujianxue Hill. Humans, who used to thrive in the valley, had to flee to the mountaintops, where they were deprived of food and shelter.

One day there came a goddess named Chiuji Samo, who was determined to deliver humans from their sufferings. With the sharpened end of a stick, she pushed up the Wujianxue Hill toward the east and cut a canal toward the south, so that the water from the Naga Lake drained first eastward and then southward to form the Niangjiangqu River. With the disappearance of the Naga Lake, the Lhebu Valley reemerged, and humans returned and lived there happily again.

Before long, however, a she-demon named Hanzhu Dunge came to settle in the valley. Lying on her back, she began to release her evil energy, which plunged the humans into misery once again. But this time, the humans decided to take a stand. They talked about how they could get rid of the she-demon. One day, they all gathered at a place known as Bairi Jimuqiong and set to work as planned. They worked nonstop day and night, felling trees on the mountains and carrying stones in the valley. While some pinned her down, others built a temple on the devil's forehead. Then they erected a banner pole thirty feet tall at the front of the temple, where the she-demon's chest was located. The pole, planted deep into her heart, brought her evil life to an end.

The humans resumed their happy lives and eventually changed the name of the place to *Semu Tandan Longba*, which means "the place where everyone worked together to conquer the she-demon."

APPENDIX A:
MOTIFS AND TALE SOURCES

Prepared by Haiwang Yuan

A Golden Deer. The tale is *Type 160. Grateful Animals; Ungrateful man.* A hunter saved a wounded fairy in the form of a doe: *F234.1.4. Fairy in form of deer.* In the form of the fairy, she resuscitated him with a blackened stalk when he fell fatally ill: *F344. Fairies heal mortals. A185.12.1. God resuscitates man.* The motif is also a variant of *E105. Resuscitation by herbs (leaves).* They were married and had a son: *T91.3. Love of mortal and supernatural person. A122. God half mortal, half immortal.* A Shaman priest made the hunter burn the fairy's hidden deer hide to reveal her deer identity: *K2280. Treacherous churchmen. D114.1.1. Transformation: man to deer.* His action caused her to leave him dying of his original illness: This is a variant motif of *C31.1.2. Tabu: looking at supernatural wife on certain occasion.* The doe retrieved their son and raised him so he became a strong hunter: *B631.1. Animal mother of man helps him.*

> *Sources:* Shiyuan Wang, et al, eds. *Zhonghua minzu gushi da xi (Anthology of Chinese Ethnic Stories).* Vol. 16. Shanghai: Shanghai wenyi chuban she, 1995; Changxuan Xu and Huang Renyuan. *Hezhe zu wenxue (The Hezhen Literature).* Beijing: Beifang wenyi chuban she, 1991; Shiyuan Wang. *Heilongjiang minjian wexue, Hezhezu minjian gushi zhuanji (Folktales of Heilongjian, the Hezhen Edition).* Harbin: Zhongguo minjian wenyi yanjiuhui, Heilongjiang fenhui, 1983.

A Muntjac and a Leopard. This is a variant of *Type 85. The Mouse, the Bird, and the Sausage keep house together each with appropriate duties. When they exchange roles, all goes ill.* A leopard and a muntjac (a kind of deer) agreed to do each other's job and feed each other: This motif is a variant of *A2493.17. Friendship between tiger and deer (fawn). A2240. Animal characteristics: obtaining another's qualities.* The leopard forced the deer to look for meat and unknowingly ate its cubs that the deer had killed: *G70. Occasional cannibalism—deliberate. C901.4. Punishment for breaking tabu: assigner of punishment suffers his own penalty.* A boar intervened to save the deer:

B414.1 Helpful boar. In the standoff, it accidentally killed the leopard: *N330. Acciden-tal killing or death.* Its blood smeared and colored the deer: *A2411.1.6.5. Color of deer.*

> *Sources:* Jinhai Tian et al., eds. *Zhonghua minzu gushi da xi (Anthology of Chinese Ethnic Stories).* Vol. 13. Shanghai: Shanghai wenyi chuban she, 1995; Youren Zhang et al., eds. *Cai hui ben Zhongguo min jian gu shi. Achang zu (Illustrated Chinese Folktales: Achang Ethnic Group).* Zhejiang shaonian ertong chuban she, 1992; *Guoxue qimeng jiaoyu zibian shu, minzu fangqing I. (Ethnic Cultures, I. Chinese Studies for Beginners, Self-compiled edition),* 2007. Available at http://zbzx.hcedu.cn/Article/ShowArticle.asp?ArticleID=150. (Accessed June 28, 2007).

Lions Ask a Yellow Ant for Help. This is a variant of *Type 75. The Help of the Weak.* A lion queen accidentally wedged a bone in the lion king's ear while eating and couldn't get it out: *B240.4. Lion as king of animals. N300. Unlucky accidents.* Although big animals they first asked for help didn't succeed, an ant they reluctantly invited did get the bone out, proving that help could come from unexpected sources: *L112.2. Very small hero. L410. Proud ruler (deity) humbled.*

> *Sources:* Kunbo Ou et al., eds. *Zhonghua minzu gushi da xi (Anthology of Chinese Ethnic Stories).* Vol. 10. Shanghai: Shanghai wenyi chuban she, 1995; Zi Bi. *Minjian yuyan (Fables).* Shijiazhuang: Shaonian ertong chuban she, 2004; Fang He and Xin Dechang. *Miren de dongwu gushi (Fascinated Animal Stories).* Jilin: Yanbian daxue chuban she, 2004; Zhenghong Shang. *Jingpo zu wenxue gailun (An Introduction to the Jingpo Literature).* Kunming: Yunnan daxue chuban she, 2003.

A Goat and a Wolf. This tale is *Type 126* The Sheep Chases the Wolf.* A wolf wanted to learn more about a goat before eating it, only to be scared by the goat's witty answers: This motif is a variant of *K1723. Goat pretends to be chewing rock. Frightens wolf. L160. Success of the unpromising hero (heroine). H507. Wit combat.* The wolf got himself killed in flight: *L430. Arrogance repaid. Q341. Curiosity punished.*

> *Sources:* Jinhai Tian et al., eds. *Zhonghua minzu gushi da xi (Anthology of Chinese Ethnic Stories).* Vol. 13. Shanghai: Shanghai wenyi chuban she, 1995; Lu Zhuan. *Xibozu minjian gushi xuan (Selected Xibe Folktales).* Shanghai: Shanghai wenyi chuban she, 1991; Baoxue Guan. *Xibozu minjian gushi ji (Anthology of Xibe Folktales).* Shenyang: Liaoning minzu chuban she, 2002.

A Lion and a Wild Goose. The tale is *Type 76. The Wolf and the Crane.* After a wild goose pulled a fishbone out of a lion's throat, the lion ate the goose after blaming it for causing pain: This is a variant motif of *W154.3. Crane pulls bone from wolf's throat: wolf refuses payment.* The motif is also a variant of *U31.1. Cat unjustly accuses cock and* *eats him. Although all the cock's defenses are good the cat tells him that she can no longer go hungry and eats him.*

> *Sources:* Jiping Wang and Yang Fuxue. "Cong 'huiniao bensheng' dao 'shizi he dayan'—Yindu Fo bensheng gushi yingxiang: Weiwu'erzu minjian wenxue zhi yi li (From 'A Wise Bird's Previous Incarnations' to 'A Lion and a Wild Goose'—An Example of the Indian Sutra Story in the Uygur Folk Literature)." *Minzu wenxue yanjiu* (*Studies of Ethnic Literatures*) 2 (2005): 88–91; *Xingjiang minjin wenxue* (*Xinjiang Folk Literature*) Vol. 3. Urumchi: Xinjiang renmin chuban she, 1982, 142–43; *Xinjiang dongwu gushi xu bian* (*A Sequel to the Xinjiang Animal Stories*). Urumchi: Xinjiang renmin chuban she, 1984, 16–18.

A Bear and a Leopard. This is a variant of *Type 9. The Unjust Partner.* A bear and a leopard painted each other for fun: *A2493. Friendships between the animals. A2411.1.1.1. Color of leopard.* The leopard painted the bear black while he was asleep and caused the bear to hate it: *A2494.2. The leopard's enemies.* The leopard has since had to find and store food for the bear and snarl in repentance: *Q387. Jesting punished. A2211. Animal characteristics: accidental action of ancient animal.*

> *Sources:* Feng Jiang et al., eds. *Zhonghua minzu gushi da xi* (Anthology of Chinese Ethnic Stories). Vol. 8. Shanghai: Shanghai wenyi chuban she, 1995; "Gaoshanzu de wenxue." In *Guojia shuzi wenhua gongcheng* (*The National Digital Cultural Project*), 2007. Available at http://www.ndcnc.gov.cn/datalib/2003/Nation/DL/DL-164847. (Accessed June 29, 2007).

A Clever Man. A king, who wanted to prove he was the cleverest, was cheated of 200 gold coins by a clever man from the street. And the man would distribute it to the poor: *J1705.4. Foolish king. K1200. Deception into humiliating position. Q331.2. Vanity punished.*

> *Sources:* Suo Wenqing, reteller. "A Clever Man." In *Muqiao shutang* (*Muqiao Storytelling Place*), 2006. Available at http://www.mm-bb.cn/story/List/List_284.shtml. (Accessed May 17, 2007); Ye Tao, reteller. "Zi yiwei congming de guowang (A King that Thinks of Himself as Clever)." In *Cai hui ben Zhongguo minjian gushi* (*Illustrated Chinese Folktales*), ed. Zhejiang shao'er chuban she, illus. Wu Song. Hangzhou: Zhejiang shao'er chuban she, 1990.

The Son of a Horse. Part of the tale is *Type 301F. Quest for Precious Objects. The hero goes down a cave or cliff to fetch precious objects but is left down there after the objects are hauled up.* A horse gave birth to a boy: a variant motif of *T566. Human son of animal parents* and *T581.4. Child born in stable.* He went on a quest for brothers: a variant motif of *H1385.8. Quest for lost brother(s).* He found brothers in a man from a tree and another from a rock: *A151.7.1. Deity resides in tree.* Three doves cooked for them in human form. The horse son took away their wings to stop them from flying away. The prettiest of the three fairies smeared her face with soot before they married the brothers: This motif is a variant of *K521.3. Disguise by painting (covering with soot, etc.) so as to escape. T69.1.1. Three brothers married to three sisters*. To get the seed of fire, the three women wandered into the cave of a she-demon: *A1414.7.3. Cave as repository of fire*. The demon had since come to suck their blood, and one day kidnapped the horse man's wife: *G303.3.1.12.1. Devil in form of woman lures and punishes women. G303.9.5. The devil as an abductor*. The brothers traced her to her cave: *H1385. Quest for lost persons*. The horse man was left in the cave while his brothers went away with his wife: and bullied his wife: a variant motif of *K2211. Treacherous brother. Usually elder brother*. An eagle he saved from a snake saved him from the cave: a variant motif of *B521.2.1. Eagle saves man from falling wall. The grateful eagle swoops down and takes the man's hat, and thus gets him away from the wall that is about to fall*. Its parent sent him back home on condition that he feed it with rats: *B542.1.1. Eagle carries man to safety*. He fed his flesh to it: *B322.1. Hero feeds own flesh to helpful animal. The hero is carried on the back of an eagle who demands food. The hero finally feeds parts of his own flesh*. The husband and wife reunited by chance: *N741. Unexpected meeting of husband and wife*. He killed his brothers when they challenged him to a fight: *N731.2.2. Undesired combat between sworn (blood) brothers (foster brothers). K867. Fatal duel: brother kills brother in pretended game*.

Sources: Bohao Jiang, reteller. "Ma de erzi (The Son of a Horse)." In *Zhongguo shenhua gushi daquan (Complete Works of Chinese Fairytales)*, Vol. 3., ed. Ke Yuan. Hangzhou: Zhejiang shaonian ertong chuban she, 1990; Xueyi Ma. "Luotuo quan: Sala zu minjin gushi ji (The Camel Lake and Other Tales from Ethnic Salar)." In *Salazu minjian gushi ji (Works of the Salar Folktales)*, ed. Zhongguo minjian wenxue yishu yanjiu hui, Qinghai fenhui (The Qinghai Chapter of the Chinese Folk Literature Research Society). Xining: Qinghai renmin chuban she, 1982; Yanbian Wen, ed. *Zhonghua minzu gushi daxi (Anthology of Chinese Ethnic Stories)*. Vol. 12. Shanghai: Shanghai wenyi chuban she, 1982.

Three Brothers. The tale is *Type 654 The Three Brothers*. A fairy of fortune visited three brothers: *P251.6.1. Three brothers. Z134. Fortune personified*. Two of them worked hard and became prosperous, but one of them gambled until he was bankrupt: *N102. Fortune comes to deserving and undeserving. Q86. Reward for industry. Q381. Punishment for gambling*.

Sources: The author collected this oral tale from He Jun, a staff member of the Beijing Ethnic Museum, Beijing, China, on July 5, 2006.

Three Neighbors. The tale is *Type 911* The Dying Father's Counsel*. There were three neighboring brothers: *P251.6.1. Three brothers*. One was clairaudient, another clairvoyant, and still another versatile: *F641. Person of remarkable hearing. F642. Person of remarkable sight. F660. Remarkable skill*. Together they fought successfully against a prince of devils: *J1020. Strength in unity*. When the devil asked a river god to flood them, they made a float out of cowhides: *A425. River-god. D1025.5. Magic cowhide*. When the devil made a goddess plague them, they immunized themselves with mugwort and garlic: *F493. Spirit of plague. D1385.2.7. Garlic protects from evil spirits*. The devil prince sent a bird to sow rumors of discord among the brothers: *G303.10.17. Bird as messenger of devil*. They were separated and conquered: a variant motif of *G269.7. Witch estranges brothers*. Before their death, they told their children to live harmoniously: *J10. Wisdom (knowledge) acquired from experience*. Their later generations became three different ethnic groups: *J1021.1. Sons united make living; separated fail*.

> *Sources:* Huihao Liu et al., eds. *Zhonghua minzu gushi da xi (Anthology of Chinese Ethnic Stories)*. Vol. 15. Shanghai: Shanghai wenyi chuban she, 1995; Baoshi Song and Deng Yanli. *Zhongguo shaoshu minzu chuanshuo gushi/ shaonian ertong baike congshu (Legends of Chinese Ethnic Minorities/Juveniles' and Children's Encyclopedic Series)*. Yinchuan: Ningxia shao'er chuban she, 2006; Yang Jie. *Cai hui ben Zhong Guo min jian gu shi: bao an zu*. Zhejiang (China): Zhejiang Juvenile and Children's Books, 1990.

A Feathered Flying Garment. This is *Type 313. The Magic Flight*. An orphan girl was sold by her stepmother: *L111.4.2. Orphan heroine. S31. Cruel stepmother*. She was locked in a room: a variant motif of *T301. Imprisoned virgin to prevent knowledge of men, marriage, impregnation. Usually kept in a tower*. The girl saw the features that she dreamed of doves shedding: a variant of *D812.8. Magic object received from lady in dream. F1068. Realistic dream*. She made a garment out of the feathers and fled in the form of a dove: *D1069.2. Magic feather dress. D671. Transformation flight. D154.1. Transformation: man to dove*. She was adopted by an old man: *N825.1. Childless old couple adopt hero. N825.2. Helpful old man*. He had three magic kettles: *D1171.3. Magic kettle*. He took off her garment and she changed back to her human form: *D1520.35. Magic transformation by feather-dress*. He turned her stepmother and the suitor into two birds: *D665. Transformation of enemy to be rid of him*. Doves have become their natural enemies: a variant motif of *A2494.13.10.6. Enmity between birds of prey and chickens*.

> *Sources:* Dainian Zu et al., eds. *Zhonghua minzu gushi da xi (Anthology of Chinese Ethnic Stories)*. Vol. 9. Shanghai: Shanghai wenyi chuban she, 1995; Yanyi Zhao, reteller. *Bai yu fei yi (The White-feathered Garment)*. Beijing: Zhongguo shaonian ertong chuban she, 1988; Sumin Hao, ed. *Dongxiang zu, Bao'an zu, Yugu zu minjian gushi xuan (Selected Tales from Ethnic Dongxiang, Bonan, and Yugur)*. Shanghai: Shanghai wenyi chuban she, 1987.

A Foolish King. The tale is *Type 1539 Cleverness and Gullibility*. When a thief sued his victim, a foolish king condemned the latter: *J1705.4. Foolish king*. Then, victim after victim tried to exonerate himself and put the blame on others: *J1166. Plea by shifting blame to another*. Before execution, the real thief tricked the king into having himself hanged: *J1169. Clever pleading. K715. Deception into allowing oneself to be hanged*.

Sources: Zhenya Wang et al., eds. *Zhonghua minzu gushi da xi (Anthology of Chinese Ethnic Stories).* Vol. 14. Shanghai: Shanghai wenyi chuban she, 1995; M. Øåâåðãäèí, ed. *Uzbek Folktales,* trans. Zong Qin et al. Shanghai: Shaonian ertong chuban she, 1954; Yang Jie. *Cai hui ben Zhong Guo min jian gu shi: wu zi bie ke zu.* Zhejiang (China): Zhejiang Juvenile and Children's Books, 1990.

A Man with Only a Head. Latter half of the tale is *Type 882C* Chastity Test by Husband.* A widow conceived after drinking from a pool formed by a giant elephant's footprint: This motif is a variant of *T512.7. Conception from drinking dew. D1294. Magic footprint.* She was misunderstood and banned from her community: a variant motif of *Q431.8. Banishment as punishment for adultery.* She gave birth to a living head: *T550.7. Poor woman gives birth to child who has no body (merely head or skull).* The head helped her to farm: a variant motif of *N819.3.1. Helpful speaking skull.* It also helped a heavenly god win his war against a hellish god: *D1400.1.20. Magic (human) head defeats enemy. A106. Opposition of good and evil gods.* The heavenly god promised the head one of his daughters as his wife: a variant motif of *T68.1. Princess offered as prize to rescuer.* The youngest married the head willingly, while her sisters were reluctant: *L54. Compassionate youngest daughter.* The head tested his wife in human form and found her faithful: *H452. Disguise to test bride's chastity. T235. Husband transforms himself to test his wife's faithfulness. T210.1. Faithful wife.* The head turned into a young man: *D437. Transformation: part of animal or person to person.* His sisters-in-law all came to marry him, only to be rejected: *T92.8. Sisters in love with same man. T210.2. Faithful husband.* The couple lived happily and took care of the widow: a variant motif of *Q145.0.1. Reward: happiness during last year of life.*

Sources: Feng Jiang et al., eds. *Zhonghua minzu gushi da xi (Anthology of Chinese Ethnic Stories).* Vol. 8. Shanghai: Shanghai wenyi chuban she, 1995; Dou Dou, reteller. "Du tou wawa (A Boy of Only a Head)." In *Zhongguo shenhua gushi daquan (Complete Works of Chinese Fairytales),* Vol. 2., ed. Ke Yuan. Hangzhou: Zhejiang shaonian ertong chuban she, 1990; Shushen Lin and Weitu Jiang. *Du tou wawa (A Boy of Only a Head).* Taibei: Yuanliu, 2001.

Blessed by Nine Immortals. The first part of the story is *Type 681B Same Dream for Husband and Wife.* A couple's attempt to open up a wilderness was repeatedly frustrated: *N250. Persistent bad luck.* They dreamt of nine immortals revealing that a loach demon was the culprit and two goddesses could subdue it: This motif is a variant of *J157.0.1. Deity appears in dream and gives instructions or advice. J157. Wisdom (knowledge) from dream. G303.3.3.5. Devil in form of fish. F259.1.4. Fairies immortal.* They found the goddesses in a cave: *A151.1.2. Home of gods in cave.* The couple pleased them with rice cakes and musical instruments: *A153.7. God's preference for cooked food. D1359.3.1. Magic music causes joy.* The goddesses came with them riding on cranes: *B463.3. Helpful crane.* The motif is a variant of *A34. Birds as creator's servants.* They helped the couple reclaim the land, one with fire and the other with a magic hoe: *D1271. Magic fire. D1204. Magic hoe. F346. Fairy helps mortal with labor.* The couple thanked the goddesses with offerings, which has become a tradition:

A1405. Culture originated by ancestor of tribes. The nine immortals were so touched by their fortitude that they came to help: *Q81. Reward for perseverance. A185.16. God pities mortal.* They turned into nine mountains to accompany the family: This is a variant motif of *D231. Transformation: man to stone.*

> ***Sources:*** Dainian Zu et al., eds. *Zhonghua minzu gushi da xi (Anthology of Chinese Ethnic Stories).* Vol. 9. Shanghai: Shanghai wenyi chuban she, 1995; Shu Xia, reteller. "Gulong yu Zhahua (Gulong and Zhahua)." Vol. 1. In *Zhongguo shenhua gushi daquan (Complete Works of Chinese Fairytales),* ed. Ke Yuan. Hangzhou: Zhejiang shaonian ertong chuban she, 1990; Nian Dai and Shi Jie, eds. *Shuizu minjian gushi (Folktales of the Sui Ethnicity).* Guiyang: Guizhou renmin chuban she, 1984.

Zhang Guolao and Li Guolao. Two creators created the world: *A2. Multiple creators.* A big flood destroyed it: *A1010. Deluge. Inundation of whole world or section.* They re-created it: a variant motif of *A1036. Earth recreated after world-fire. A1006. Renewal of world after world calamity.* To dry the sodden land, they called in twelve suns to dry it, but they almost scorched it: a variant of the motif *A961.0.1. Several suns, moons in sky simultaneously. Formerly great heat of sun causes distress to mankind. A733.5. Sun dries out earth with its heat.* A frog began to eat the suns with its big mouth: a variant motif of *A737.3. Toad causes eclipses of the sun* and *A1052.1. Sun devoured by monster at end of world.* Creator prevented it from swallowing the last sun, and it has since lost the ability to swallow it: *D1741. Magic powers lost.*

> ***Sources:*** Zhu, Tian reteller. "Zao tian zhi di (Creation of the Heaven and Earth)." In *Zhongguo shenhua gushi daquan (Complete Works of Chinese Fairytales),* Vol. 1., ed. Ke Yuan. Hangzhou: Zhejiang shaonian ertong chuban she, 1990; "Zhonghua minzu yuangu shenhua souji (Collected Chinese Ethnic Tales of the Ancient Times)." In *Baidubaike (Baidu Encyclopedia),* 2007. Available at: http://post.baidu.com/f?kz=140958064. (Accessed June 29, 2007).

Sax—Mother of the Dongs. Part of the tale is a variant of *Type 302B Hero with Life Dependent on his Sword.* A mother drowned herself after her husband's death: *P214.1. Wife commits suicide (dies) on death of husband.* The orphaned son grew up with his adoptive brother: a variant motif of *T678. Adopted child identical with real child reared with him. Z210. Brothers as heroes. L111.4. Orphan hero.* The orphan's daughter was orphaned and fled persecution with the help of an old man: *L111.4.2. Orphan heroine. K640. Escape by help of confederate.* In her flight, she got into a fight with a tiger and her future husband killed it: *B16.2.2.1. Hostile tiger killed.* They withdrew twin swords from a well with ease: *D1654.4.1. Sword can be moved only by right person.* This motif is also a variant of *D813.1.1. Magic sword received from Lady of Lake.* They used them to help villagers farm: *D1081. Magic sword.* This motif is a variant of *D1564.6. Magic sword cuts stone and fells trees.* They defeated their enemies many times with the sword: *D1400.1.4.1. Magic sword conquers enemy.* The enemy stole the swords, rendering the heroes powerless: *D861. Magic object stolen.*

D1741. Magic powers lost. Her men routed, she fought alone: *F614.10. Strong hero fights whole army alone. P555. Defeat in battle.* Cornered, she and her daughters jumped off a cliff: *P232. Mother and daughter. M451.1. Death by suicide.* They were allegedly rescued by an elder: *R122. Miraculous rescue.*

> *Sources:* Long'e Fengqing Wang. *Dongzu nü yingxiong sama hun gui long'e nongtanggai (The Spirit of the Dongs' Heroine Sama Returns to the Nongtanggai of Long'e,* 2006. Available at http://dong.cnwu.net/ shtml/dong1fs/fs2ly/200607/20060712145302.shtml. (Accessed March 17, 2007); Bamo Qubumo. *Dongzu yingxiong shishi: Sasui zhi ge (The Dong Heroic Epic: Ode to Sax).* Zhongguo shehui kexue yuan, minzu wenxue yanjiu suo (Institute of Ethnic Literature, Chinese Academy of Social Sciences), 2002. Available at http://iel.sofoo.com:8181/news_show.asp?newsid=1734. (Accessed June 29, 2007); Caigui Huang. *Nü shen yu fan shen: Dongzu "Sama" wenhua yanjiu (Goddesses and Gods of Pantheism: Studies of the Dong's Sama Tradition).* Guiyang: Guizhou renmin chuban she, 2006.

Liu Sanjie—A Fearless Folk Song Singer. The tale is *Type 875B5 Clever Girl's Other Counter-Tasks.* Includes an episode of *Type 876B* Clever Girl Wins Riming Contest.* An orphan girl singer had great courage: *L111.4.2. Orphan heroine.* Fleeing persecution, she lived with her grandmother: *L111.4.1. Orphan hero lives with grandmother.* She led fellow villagers in defeating a despot and his men in a singing contest held to decide who owned the land: *H503.1. Song duel.* This is also a variant motif of *L151. Peasant girl outwits prince. H217. Decision made by contest. L160. Success of the unpromising hero (heroine). L310. Weak overcomes strong in conflict.* Before the despot caught the girl, fellow villagers helped her flee: *K2247. Treacherous lord. K640. Escape by help of confederate.*

> *Sources:* Dejun Li et al., eds. *Zhonghua minzu gushi da xi (Anthology of Chinese Ethnic Stories).* Vol. 3. Shanghai: Shanghai wenyi chuban she, 1995; *Third Sister Liu: An Opera of Eight Scenes,* trans. Yang Xianyi. Peking: Foreign Languages Press, 1962; *Liu San Jie (Third Sister Liu),* dir. Su Li. 90 min. Changchun dianying zhipianchang, 1960. videodisc.

The Eye of Heaven Reopened. Part of the tale is *Type 300. The Dragon Slayer.* Sky was originally closer to the earth: *A625.2. Raising of the sky. Originally the sky is near the earth.* A dark cloud suddenly appeared to engulf the sky and caused a calamity: *D2147.1. Cloud magically made to cover sun. Z156. Cloud (mist) as symbol of misfortune.* An orphan hero wanted to find out the cause of the cloud: *L111.4. Orphan hero. H1362. Quest for devastating animals.* A fairy phoenix in the form of a white-bearded elder told him it was the smoke vomited by two dragons: *H1233.1.2. Old man helps on quest. F237. Fairies in disguise. B32. Phoenix.* The hero turned a threshold into ashes and then into a sword: This motif is a variant of *D1601.5.1. Stick turns into automatic magic sword. D931.1.2. Magic ashes.* Another fairy in the guise of an old woman turned a hair into a band and tied it to the hero's waist to protect him from being burned to ashes: *H1233.1.1. Old woman helps on quest. D811.1. Magic object received from goddess. D1382. Magic object protects against cold or burning.* He crossed a river of burning blood to reach the lair of the dragons on a mountain: a variant motif of *F142. River of fire as barrier to otherworld* and *A671.2.2. Rivers of blood in hell. F141.1.1. Perilous river as barrier to otherworld.* A raven tricked him into a trap where there was a serpent: *A2493.25. Friendship between snake and crow. F401.3.7.1. Demon in form of crow.* The motif is a variant of *B91.1. Naga. Serpent demon.* The serpent tried to kill the hero but was killed by the light emitted from his waist band and a toad challenging him was killed and bled till it became a bag of skin: *K1626. Would-be killers killed. D1478. Magic object provides light. A2468.2. Why toad dries up when dead.* He encountered the phoenix fairy in the form of a pretty girl: *F234.1.15. Fairy in form of bird.* On the mountaintop perched the dragons spitting smoke that caused the cloud: a variant motif of *B11.2.11. Fire-breathing dragon. D1337.2.3. Dragon's breath renders hideous. J2277.1. Clouds supposed to come from smoke. B11.3.2. Dragon's home at top of mountain.* The girl tossed a pearl to divert the dragons' attention: a variant motif of *D1541.2.2. Magic pearl draws storm away. D1562. Magic object removes obstacles.* They slaughtered the dragons: *B11.11. Fight with dragon. B11.11.7. Woman as dragon-slayer.* Their blood colored the mountains: *B11.2.13. Blood of dragon. F807. Rock of extraordinary color.* To disperse clouds, they turned a pearl into the star and the waistband into a rainbow: *A710. Creation of the sun. A791. Origin of the Rainbow.* They used their dazzling hammer and sword to drive the clouds away: *A1141.2. Lightening from flashing sword. A157.7. Hammer of thunder god.* Their sweat turned into stars: a variant motif of *A702.1. Sky of water. The sky consists of water. A763. Stars from objects thrown into sky.* They are still believed to guard the star that people call the "eye of heaven" against dark clouds: a variant motif of *A661.0.1.1. Gate of heaven guarded by clap of thunder and mysterious sword* and *A714.1. Sun and moon placed for eyes in the sky.*

> ***Sources:*** Feng Jiang et al., eds. *Zhonghua minzu gushi da xi (Anthology of Chinese Ethnic Stories).* Vol. 8. Shanghai: Shanghai wenyi chuban she, 1995; Kong Cheng. *Tian yan chong kai: gei haizi men chuanshuo xilie (Eyes of Heaven Reopened: Legend Series for Children).* Taibei County: Yongquan, 1993; Huimin Chen et al. *Shezu: Tian yan chong kai (She Ethnicity: The Eyes of the Heaven Reopened).* Taibeixian: Yongquan, 1992.

Tan Sanjiu—A God of Perseverance. To help humans fight drought, a deity worked to level a mountain: *A185.16. God pities mortal.* His wife's comment on his bamboo hatchet caused it to break: *C491. Tabu: expressing astonishment at marvel.* The deity then drove the rocks and mountains: *D2152.5. Mountain moved by saints. D1643.2. Rock travels.* The rocks were stopped when someone asked if he saw cattle: *C410: Tabu: asking questions.* Undaunted, the deity invited twelve dragons of rain: *B11.7.*

Dragon as rain-spirit. But roosters crowed early and scared the dragons: a variant motif of *G303.16.19.4. Devil (Satan) flees when cock is made to crow.*

> **Sources:** Wenbian Yan et al., eds. *Zhonghua minzu gushi da xi* (*Anthology of Chinese Ethnic Stories*). Vol. 8. Shanghai: Shanghai wenyi chuban she, 1995; Guorong Meng et al. *Maonan zu wenxue shi* (*Literary History of Maonan*). Nanning: Guangxi renmin chuban she, 1992; Fengchen Yuan. *Maonan zu, Jing zu minjian gushi xuan* (*Selected Stories of Ethnic Maonan and Gin*). Shanghai: Shanghai wenyi chuban she, 1987.

Ginseng Boy. The tale is *Type 1571* The Servants Punish Their Master.* On a land rich in tonic medicinal herbs was a fugitive couple, who named their newborn after ginseng: *R310. Refuges. D1500.1.4.3. Magic healing herb.* The ginseng boy grew to be a good flutist and a deer rider: *H35.1.2. Recognition by unique manner of playing flute. B557.3. Man carried by deer.* His parents made him bring food to a cruel lord's slaves: *Q2. Kind and unkind.* The angered lord had the ginseng boy snared and tortured: *K2247. Treacherous lord.* The boy was rescued by the serfs: *Q40. Kindness rewarded.* When the lord came, the ginseng boy called in millions of deer with his flute: *D1441.1.1. Magic flute calls animals together.* They threw stones into a lake to form a mountain and overran and killed the lord and his men: *B443.1. Helpful deer (stag, doe). D452.1.2. Transformation: stone to mountain. D2153.1.1. Island created by magic. Q285.4. Slave-driving punished.*

> **Sources:** Jun Gu, reteller. "Bang chui hai (The Ginseng Boy)." In *Zhongguo shenhua gushi daquan* (*Complete Works of Chinese Fairytales*), Vol. 4., ed. Ke Yuan. Hangzhou: Zhejiang shaonian ertong chuban she, 1990; Zhidong Meng et al., eds. *Zhonghua minzu gushi da xi* (*Anthology of Chinese Ethnic Stories*). Vol. 11. Shanghai: Shanghai wenyi chuban she, 1995; Zhuping Zhang, reteller. *Shenqi de bangchui hai* (*The Magic Ginseng Boy*), trans. Alatancang. Hohehot: Neimonggu renmin chuban she, 1982.

A Giant and a One-eyed Fairy. Part of the tale is a variant of *Type 851* Tests for Princess' Suitors.* A giant born of a tree found the trees he cut down sprang up from the twigs heaped by a deity in the form of an old man: *A114.4. Deity born from tree. F979.8. Forest springs up from twig (twigs). J151.3. Wisdom from god as old (one-eyed) man.* He promised the giant one of his two niece fairies if he could help him: *T68. Princess offered as prize.* The one-eyed girl loved him and helped to accomplish the tasks: *F512.1. Person with one eye. H335.0.1. Bride helps suitor perform his tasks.* The deity then placed him in a dark forest: *a variant motif of E599.12. Human being transported by a ghost.* A tiger relative sent him home: *B431.3. Helpful tiger.* On his way he met the deity in disguise: *K1811. Gods in disguise visit mortals.* He married the one-eyed fairy: *T111. Marriage of mortal and supernatural being.* The deity gave them bamboo tubes and asked them to do as he bade them: *a variant motif of A1425.1. All the kinds of seed in a bamboo that culture hero cuts down.* Forgetting the deity's warning, they looked into the bamboo tubes and glanced back. Consequently, honey has to be obtained from hives high above, beasts are otherwise domesticated, and women have to bear children instead of men: *C330. Tabu: looking in certain direction. A1351. Origin of childbirth. A1421.1. Man given dominion over beasts. A2813. Origin of honey.* Due to mistrust in a demon, they lost their sick son and gave rise to the tradition of funerals: *A1335. Origin of death. A1547. Origin of funeral customs.*

> *Sources:* Huihao Liu et al., eds. *Zhonghua minzu gushi da xi* (*Anthology of Chinese Ethnic Stories*). Vol. 15. Shanghai: Shanghai wenyi chuban she, 1995; Yang Lian, reteller. "Tan Gapeng." In *Zhongguo shenhua gushi daquan* (*Complete Works of Chinese Fairytales*), Vol. 3., ed. Ke Yuan. Hangzhou: Zhejiang shaonian ertong chuban she, 1990; Jinming Li. *Dulong zu wenxue jian shi* (*A Brief History of Derung Literature*). Kunming: Yunnan minzu chuban she, 2004.

A Mother Who Drives the Sun. Part of the tale is *Type 518 Devils* (*Giants*) *Fight over Magic Objects.* A god created the universe with an axe: *A137.1.1. God with axe.* He created humans and animals with clay: *A1241. Man made from clay* (*earth*). *A1790. Creation of animals—other motifs.* Resenting humans created by that god, another god challenged him to a fight: *A162. Conflicts of the gods.* As he fell dead, his body tipped the heavenly river and caused a devastating flood: *A1015. Flood caused by gods or other superior beings. A778.3. Milky Way as a river.* Only a sister and brother survived, in a leather drum: a variant motif of *A1021.0.2. Escape from deluge in wooden cask* (*drum*). They encountered a devil in the guise of an old woman and escaped: *G302.3.3. Demon in form of old woman.* They ran into a fairy in the same guise and remained: *F311.3. Fairy foster-mother.* They rolled down a mountain and bumped into each other, which they took as a sign that they could marry: *N365.3. Unwitting brother-sister incest.* This motif is also a variant of *H310.2. Brother unwittingly qualifies as bridegroom of sister in test.* The impulsive fairy killed their crying baby and cut it into eight pieces: *A1296. Multiplication of man by fragmentation.* This is also a variant motif of *N325.2. Women, driven mad, devour their infants' flesh.* The pieces turned into young men and women: *D1008. Magic human flesh.* This motif is a variant of *D56. Magic change in person's age.* In her quest for her child, she stumbled on the home of God of Sun: *F17. Visit to land of the sun.* The sun made her wait until her hair grayed: *H1553. Tests of patience.* The god rewarded her with the job of driving the sun: A variant motif of *A725. Man controls rising and setting of sun.*

> *Sources:* Chinese Department of Guangdong Ethnologic Academy et al., eds. *Zhonghua minzu gushi da xi* (*Anthology of Chinese Ethnic Stories*). Vol. 7. Shanghai: Shanghai wenyi chuban she, 1995; Yang Lian. "Tan Gapeng." In *Zhongguo shenhua gushi daquan* (*Complete Works of Chinese Fairytales*), Vol. 3., ed. Ke Yuan. Hangzhou: Zhejiang shaonian ertong chuban she, 1990; Gang Gang. "Juyu taiyang de muqin (The Mother Who Drives the Sun." In *Zhongguo shenhua gushi daquan* (*Complete Works of Chinese Fairytales*), Vol. 2., ed. Ke Yuan. Hangzhou: Zhejiang shaonian ertong chuban she, 1990; Nujiang Lisuzu

Zizhizhou Lisuzu Minjian Gushi Bianji Zu. *Lisu zu minjian gushi (Folktales of the Ethnic Folktales)*. Kunming: Yunnan remin chuban she, 1985.

Ah Dang Seeks the Seed of Fire. A volcano fire provided humans with cooked meat: a variant motif of *G171. Giant roasts camels, elephants for food on crater of volcano. A1518. Why food is cooked.* They sent a hero on a quest for the seed of fire: *H1264. Quest to upper world for fire.* He asked sparrows to help and in return offered them a dwelling place in his home: a variant motif of *A2431.3.7.1. Why sparrow may build nest near people's houses; reward for hospitality.* He asked a wild horse to help and promised to domesticate it: *H1233.6.1. Horse helper on quest. B771. Wild animal miraculously tamed.* He immobilized a dragon by trickery and obtained a magic axe that it guarded: *D830. Magic object acquired by trickery. B11.6.2. Dragon guards treasure. D1206. Magic axe.* With it he turned a river of fire into a path of flags: *F142. River of fire as barrier to otherworld.* This is also a variant motif of *D1524.6. River crossed by means of magic stone.* He brought back the seed of fire along with cooked fish caught in the river of fire: *D1652.1.10. Inexhaustible fish.*

> *Sources:* Li, Shujiang. *Ren zu Adan.* Jin tang mei [1]. Yinchuan shi: Ningxia ren min chu ban she, 2000; *Ren zu Adan.* Yuan-Liou Publishing Co. Ltd., 2007. Available at http://www.ylib.com/search/qus_show.asp?BookNo=P2035. (Accessed June 29, 2007); Jianbing Sun et al., eds. *Zhonghua minzu gushi da xi (Anthology of Chinese Ethnic Stories).* Vol. 1. Shanghai: Shanghai wenyi chuban she, 1995.

The Toad General. First part of the tale is *Type 681B Same Dream for Husband and Wife.* A futile husband and wife dreamed of a boy coming to them: *D1731.2. Marvels seen in dream. V222.0.1. Birth of saint predicted by visions of miracles.* The wife conceived and gave birth to a fragrant and radiant fruit: *T573.1. Woman conceives and bears same day.* This motif is also a variant of *T555.1. Woman gives birth to a fruit. Can transform itself to girl.* Out of it came a toad: *T554.8.1. Woman gives birth to toad.* It helped the emperor to defeat the aggressors: *B493.2. Helpful toad.* It turned out to be the incarnation of a deity worshiped by the villagers: *F234.1.5. Fairy in form of toad.* He punished the officer who looked down upon him: *L460. Pride brought low.* He routed the enemy on a fire-spitting iron horse: a variant motif of *B742.3. Fire-breathing horses.*

> *Sources:* Huihao Liu et al., eds. *Zhonghua minzu gushi da xi (Anthology of Chinese Ethnic Stories).* Vol. 15. Shanghai: Shanghai wenyi chuban she, 1995; Weiguang Su. *Jingzu wenxue shi (The History of Gin Literature).* Nanning: Guangxi jiangyu chuban she, 1993; "Chanchu jiangjun (The Toad General)." *Yiyou wang (Easy Navigation Net)*, 2006. Available at http://www.yiyou.com:1980/gb/guangxi.yiyou.com/html/7/208.html. (Accessed June 29, 2007).

Adventures of Aba Dani. The tale is *Type 836 Pride Is Punished.* A hunter deity had two extra eyes at the back of his head, which were perceptive of demons: *A526.2. Culture hero as mighty hunter. F512.4. Person with eyes in back of head. A123.3. God with many eyes.* This is also a variant motif of *F642.7. Person of remarkable sight can see the soul.* His wife asked him to get back straps from her sun god father: *H934.1. Wife assigns husband tasks. A220. Sun-god. A512.4. Sun as father of culture hero.* He strayed and visited his demon girl friend: *W214. Man will not do a woman's bidding.* She tried to save him from her brother's plot to rid him of his back eyes: *H1233.4.4. Demon as helper on quest.* He showed off his prowess instead and lost his eyes: *C450. Tabu: boasting.* Demons were released but he could only pray, thus giving rise to the tradition of sacrificing and sorcerizing: *A545. Culture hero establishes customs.*

> *Sources:* Ni Dan. "A ba da ni yu nan (Death of Aba Dani)." In *Zhongguo shenhua gushi daquan (Complete Works of Chinese Fairytales)*, Vol. 3, ed. Ke Yuan. Hangzhou: Zhejiang shaonian ertong chuban she, 1990; Liming Chen. "Luoba zu minsu jian zhi (A Brief Account of the Lhoba Folk Traditions)." *Zhongguo Zang xue wang (Chinese Net of Tibetan Studies)*, 2004. Available at http://www.tibetology.ac.cn/article2/ShowArticle.asp?ArticleID=436&Page=8. (Accessed June 30, 2007); Ye Tao, reteller. "*A ba da ni de gushi (The Tale of Aba Dani),*" illus. by Huang Jun illus. In *Cai hui ben Zhongguo minjian gushi (Chinese Folktales Illustrated with Colors)*, ed. Zhejiang shao er chuban she. Hangzhou: Zhejiang shao er chuban she, 1990.

Humans and a Gourd. A deity saved a few humans and creatures in a gourd from a devastating flood: *A1005. Preservation of life during world calamity. A1021.0.3. Deluge: escape in gourd.* In an effort to save them, the deity accidentally beheaded the crab: *A2320.4. Why crab has no head.* The water the crab raised killed all humans but one: *B94.1. Mythical crab.* This is a variant motif of *J1785.2. Crab thought to be the devil.* He caught a fairy with a waist band and made her his wife: a variant motif of *F302.4.4. Man binds fairy and forced her to marry him* and the motif of *A1275.10. First created man catches woman in his snare.* A fire and a subsequent flood decimated humans again: *A1001. Series of world catastrophes.* The family escaped in a gourd: *A1021.0.3. Deluge: escape in gourd.* A giant net of a heavenly spider caught dirt to cover the earth. Heavenly deities ate the dirt and turned into humans: a variant motif of *A1420.6. At beginning people start to eat the earth* and the motif of *A1231. First man descends from sky.* A hellish devil took humans to the heavenly king to ask for seeds of grain: *H1233.4.4. Demon as helper on quest. A1420. Acquisition of food supply for human race.* A king of rats gave them big seeds: *B437.1. Helpful rat.* After the devil left, humans were led back to earth by two rats, a cow, a horse, a python, and an elephant successively: *B411. Helpful cow. B401. Helpful horse. B491.1. Helpful serpent. B443.3. Helpful elephant.* The seeds shrank in size as years went by: a variant motif of *D451. Transformation of vegetable form.*

> *Sources:* The author collected this oral tale from Zao Xiaojie (of De'ang ethnicity), a staff member of the Beijing Ethnic Museum, Beijing, China, on July 5, 2006.

Love Between a Goddess and a Mortal Hunter. The tale is *Type 313A1 The Hero and the Immortal Maiden*. Includes an episode of *Type 851* Tests for Princess' Suitors*. A fairy shepherdess and a mortal hunter fell in love at first sight: *L113.1.4. Shepherd as hero. A526.2. Culture hero as mighty hunter. T15. Love at first sight. T91.3.2. Love of goddess for mortal*. When she had to return to heaven, the mortal followed: *F63.1. Mortal taken to heaven by heavenly maidens. F300.2. Husband pursues fairy wife to heaven*. Her father assigned the hunter tasks meant to kill him: *H931. Tasks assigned in order to get rid of hero*. He accomplished them with the fairy's help: *H335.0.1. Bride helps suitor performs his tasks*. She invited a dragon king to extinguish an otherwise fatal fire with a downpour: *B11.12.5. The dragon-king. B11.7. Dragon as rain-spirit*. She told him to heal his burn in a steam bath: *D2161.2.3. Magic cure of burns*. Eight sympathetic giants made birds and beasts to help him scatter seeds evenly: a variant motif of *Z43.6. Man invites animals to come and work in his field. A185.16. God pities mortal*. The fairy's father made the hunter find missing seeds: *H336. Suitors assigned quests*. The doves that had eaten the seeds gave up seeds in their craws by suicide: *W28. Self-sacrifice. B457.1. Helpful dove*. The fairy and the hunter married: *T111. Marriage of mortal and supernatural being*. When they looked back, the animals following them as a dowry were scared and scattered to become wild beasts: a variant motif of *C331.3. Tabu: looking back during flight. B710. Fanciful origin of animals*.

> *Sources:* Yulan Que. *Qiangzu minjian gushi xuan (Selected Folktales of the Qiang Ethnic Natinality)*. Chengdu: Sichuan minjian wenyijia xiehui (Society of Sichuan Folk Literature), 1999; Shui Yu, reteller. "Douanzhu and Mujiezhu," In *Cai hui ben Zhongguo minjian gushi (Chinese Folktales Illustrated with Colors)*, ed. Zhejiang shao er chuban she, illus. Wang Liduan and Chen Xin. Hangzhou: Zhejiang shao er chuban she, 1990; Zi Ti. *Douanzhu and Mujiezhu*. In *Zhongguo shenhua gushi daquan (Complete Works of Chinese Fairytales)*, Vol. 4., ed. Ke Yuan. Hangzhou: Zhejiang shaonian ertong chuban she, 1990.

A Cloud of Love from a Princess. This is a variant of *Type 575 The Prince's Wings*. A princess fell in love with an orphan hunter she encountered: *N710. Accidental meeting of hero and heroine. A526.2. Culture hero as mighty hunter*. She rejected a marriage arranged by her father: *T131.1.2.1. Girl must marry father's choice*. A talking magpie conveyed her love to the hunter: *B211.3. Speaking bird. B291.1. Bird as messenger. B451.6. Helpful magpie*. A fairy in the form of an old man told him about a magic peach tree that could make him fly: *F237. Fairies in disguise. N825.2. Old man helper. D981.2. Magic peach. D1531. Magic object gives power of flying*. He flew to the palace: a variant motif of *F414.1. transported to girl in fortress by spirit*. He took the princess to his mountain cave: *L130. Abode of unpromising hero (heroine). R111.1.9. Princess rescued from undesired suitor. F531.6.2.1. Giants live in mountains or caves*. An abbot detected their whereabouts with a magic mirror: *K2280. Treacherous churchmen. D1323.1. Magic clairvoyant mirror*. The king hated to marry her daughter to a poor hunter: *T131.1.2.1. Girl must marry father's choice*. The abbot used a crow as his messenger: *B291.1.2. Crow as messenger*. He covered the mountain with snow:

D2143.6.3. Snow produced by magic. The hunter stole the abbot's cassock: *F365. Fairies steal.* He was knocked into a lake, where he turned into a stone: *D231. Transformation: man to stone.* The princess died and her last breath became a cloud hovering over the stone in the lake: *T80. Tragic love. P214.1. Wife commits suicide (dies) on death of husband. D1005. Magic breath. D901. Magic cloud.*

Source: The author collected this oral tale from Duan Yan, an ethnic Bai working in the Kunming Ethnic Village, Yunnan Province, China, on July 18, 2006.

Princess Peacock. The tale is *Type 301A Quest for a Vanished Princess. Her father finally lets her return to the hero.* A pretty princess in the form of a peacock came to bathe with her sisters: *A1996. Peacock. F234.1.15. Fairy in form of bird.* She couldn't return when her winged mantle was stolen by a prince, who married her: a variant motif of *K1335. Seduction (or wooing) by stealing clothes of bathing girl (swan maiden). F302.4.2. Fairy comes into man's power when he steals her wings (clothes). F303. Fairy weds prince.* When the prince went to war, his father's lieutenant made believed that the princess had instigated the war: *F601.3. Extraordinary companions betray hero.* Before her execution by burning, she asked for her winged mantle and fled: a variant motif of *C31.10. Tabu: giving garment back to supernatural (divine) wife. Q414. Punishment: burning alive.* The prince went through hardships to look for the faraway princess. *H1385.3. Quest for vanished wife (mistress). H1301.1.2. Quest for faraway princess.* He used one of three arrows his friend had given him to overcome obstacles: *D1092. Magic arrow. H1236. Perilous path traversed on quest. H1239.3. Quest accomplished by means of objects given by helpers.* His father-in-law asked him to find his wife among the seven sisters by shooting the candle on her head: *H322. Suitor test: finding princess. H326.1.2. Suitor test: skill in archery.* This motif is also a variant of *F661.3. Skillful marksman shoots apple from man's head.* The couple finally reunited: *T96. Lovers reunited after many adventures.* He discovered that the minister was a devilish vulture and killed him with his magic arrows: *F402.1.4. Demons assume human forms in order to deceive. B147.2.2.6. Vulture as bird of ill-omen. Q261. Treachery punished.*

Sources: Lianxiu Qi and Huang Bocang. *Aiqing chuanshuo gushi xuan (Selected Love Stories and Legends).* Kunming: Yunnan renmin chuban she, 1981; Zhu Lanfang, adapter. *Zhaoshutun and Nanmu Nuona,* dir. Dao Guoan. Performed by Daizu Zizhizhou Wengongtuan, 1979; Jin Xi, adapter. *Princess Peacock,* dir. Jin Xi. Produced by Shanghai Meishu Dianying Zhipianchang, 1963.

Two Young Men. Includes an episode of *Type 883A The Innocent Slandered Maiden.* A rich young man and a poor young man loved the same woman: *T92.1. The triangle plot and its solutions. Two men in love with the same woman.* She loved the poor young man despite the rich one's wealth: *T91.5.1. Rich girl in love with poor boy.* She helped the poor young man win a cockfight: *H335.0.1. Bride helps suitor perform his tasks.* The rich man's rooster was handicapped by too much gold embellishment: *Q4. Humble rewarded, haughty punished. L482. Men too prosperous (happy): things are made* *more difficult.* The rich young man then misled the poor young man to a village of witches: *K2221. Treacherous rival lover. F370. Visit to fairyland.* He ran into his sister: *N710. Accidental meeting of hero and heroine.* They were mere refugees from licentious men: *K500. Escape from death or danger by deception.* Meanwhile, the rich man forced the girl to marry him: *T192. Marriage by force.* At their wedding, she heard her love playing his flute and traced it to him: *D1355.1. Love-producing music.* In a dispute, the rich young man died through a misstep: *N330. Accidental killing or death. Q210.1. Criminal intent punished. Q581.0.1. Loss of life as result of one's own treachery.*

> *Sources:* Shiyuan Wang et al., eds. *Zhonghua minzu gushi da xi (Anthology of Chinese Ethnic Stories).* Vol. 16. Shanghai: Shanghai wenyi chuban she, 1995; Lianxiu Qi and Huang Bocang. *Aiqing chuanshuo gushi xuan (Selected Love Stories and Legends).* Kunming: Yunnan renmin chuban she, 1981; Yuting Du. *Jinuo zu wenxue jian shi (A Brief History of Jino Literature).* Kunming: Yunnan minzu chuban she, 1996.

Seventh Sister and Her Snake Husband. The tale is *Type 433D The Snake Husband.* The eldest and the youngest of seven daughters were different in character: *P252.3. Seven sisters. A525. Good and bad culture heroes.* Their father promised a daughter to anyone who could cut a tree: *B620.1. Daughter promised to animal suitor.* This motif is also a variant of *S232. Daughter promised to tiger in marriage for help in carrying load.* When a python, who turned out to be a dragon prince, accomplished the task, only the youngest daughter agreed to marry him, which made the eldest daughter envious and regretful later: *L54.1. Youngest daughter agrees to marry a monster; later the sisters are jealous. D418.1.2. Transformation: snake to dragon. B605. Marriage to dragon.* After talking her sister into changing clothes with her, the eldest daughter pushed her into a well to drown: *K2212. Treacherous sister. Usually elder sister.* Though behaving strangely, she passed successfully as the dragon prince's wife: *K1317. Lover's place in bed usurped by another.* The spirit of the youngest daughter turned into a bird, pestering her sister every day: *F401.3.7. Spirit in form of a bird. F361. Fairy's revenge.* The eldest sister boiled her sister as she sang in defiance and poured her into a vegetable plot in the back yard: *E524.2.1. Cooked cock crows.* The bird turned into a bamboo plant to tease her sister: a variant motif of *D424.1. Transformation: butterfly to bamboo.* The talking bamboo turned into a young woman to cook for them: a variant motif of *D431.10. Transformation: sections of bamboo to persons. F365.7. Fairies steal cooking. F346. Fairy helps mortal with labor.* He snuck back to catch the woman unprepared: a variant motif of *F302.4.4. Man binds fairy and forces her to marry him.* While the husband and wife reunited, the eldest sister drowned herself out of shame: *T96. Lovers reunited after many adventures. F1041.1.13. Death from shame.*

> *Source:* The author collected this oral tale from Wei Xinyu, a tour guide working for the Kunming Ethnic Village, Yunnan Province, China, on July 19, 2006.

Princess Wencheng. Part of the tale is a variant of *Type 851* Tests for Princess' Suitors.* Includes an episode of *Type 851* Tests for Princess' Suitors.* Two kings seek friendship so one marries the other's daughter: *T131.1.2.1. Girl must marry father's choice. T122. Marriage by royal order.* The father put the suitor's envoy through a series of tests: *T51. Wooing by emissary.* This is also a variant motif of *F601.2. Extraordinary companions help hero in suitor tests.* The envoy tied a thread to an ant to go through a zigzagging path of a pearl: *B481.1. Helpful ant.* This motif is a variant of *H506.4. Test of resourcefulness: putting thread through coils of snail shell. Thread tied to ant who pulls it through.* He starved colts so they could find their mothers: *H10. Recognition through common knowledge.* He stood logs in water to tell their tops from their bottoms: a variant motif of *H506.10. Test of resourcefulness: to find relationships among three sticks: they are put in vessel of water; degree of sinking shows what part of tree each comes from.* He spaced out drinking to stay sober enough to accomplish a task: a variant motif of *H941. Cumulative tasks: second assigned so that first can be done.* The envoy pinpointed the princess among many girls: *H324. Suitor test: choosing princess from others identically clad.* The princess and the king were married after her long journey of adventures: *T96. Lovers reunited after many adventures.*

> *Source:* Fajun Liu et al., eds. *Zhonghua minzu gushi da xi (Anthology of Chinese Ethnic Stories).* Vol. 2. Shanghai: Shanghai wenyi chuban she, 1995; Monika Gräfin von Borries. *Wencheng gongzhu ru zang ji (Tale of Princess Wencheng's Entry to Tibet),* trans. Wang Jianbin et al. Hong Kong: Commercial Press, Co. Ltd., 2000; Yao Wang, reteller. *Wencheng gongzhu: Xizang minjian gushi (Princess Wencheng and Other Tales from Tibet).* Beijing: Tongsu duwu chuban she, 1956.

Tale of the Xing'an Mountains. The tale is *Type 403B, The Black and the White Bride.* Includes an episode of type 480, *The Kind and the Unkind Girls.* A hunter was deemed a hero for his strength, appetite, and accuracy in archery: *A526.2. Culture hero as mighty hunter. D1923. Power to hit whatever one aims at.* From a conversation between a deer couple, he learned of a pretty princess of a sun god in the east: *N451. Secrets overheard from animal conversation.* He went on a quest for her: *H1301.1.2. Quest for far-off princess.* The birds he called in with his musical instrument told him what the princess looked like: a variant motif of *D1441.1. Magic musical instrument calls animals together.* The tune he played drove away clouds and caught the attention of the sun god: *D1561. Magic object confers miraculous powers (luck).* The elder sister of the princess intercepted her messenger rabbit and made him lie about the hunter: *K2212. Treacherous sister. Usually elder sister. B291.3.2. Hare (rabbit) as messenger.* The princess fled and was adopted by a spinster: *F394. Mortals help fairies.* This motif is a variant of *N825.1. Childless old couple adopt hero.* The suitor had to marry the elder sister: *K1317. Lover's place in bed usurped by another.* When they met again, the elder sister drowned herself out of shame: *T96. Lovers reunited after many adventures. F1041.1.13. Death from shame.*

> *Sources:* Qing Long, reteller. "Xing'an ling de gushi (Tales from the Xing'an Mountains)." In *Cai hui ben Zhongguo minjian gushi (Chinese Folktales Illustrated with Colors),* ed. Zhejiang shao er chuban she, illus. Wang Dawei.

Hangzhou: Zhejiang shao er chuban she, 1990; Jun Gu. "Xing'anling de gushi (The Tale of the Xing'an Mountains)." In *Zhongguo shenhua gushi daquan* (*Complete Works of Chinese Fairytales*), Vol. 4., ed. Ke Yuan. Hangzhou: Zhejiang shaonian ertong chuban she, 1990; Renyuan Huang et al. *Ewenke zu wenxue* (*The Ewenki Literature*). Harbin: Beifang wenyi chuban she, 2000.

A Mountain Girl and a Giant Hunter. The tale is *Type 304 The Hunter*. A beautiful young woman lived with her father on a mountaintop: *P234. Father and daughter. F721.2. Habitable hill.* She fell in love with a marksman: a variant motif of *F460.4.1. Mountain-girl marries mortal man. F661. Skillful marksman.* A monster took control of the mountain with the help of a boar and an owl: This motif is a variant of *A1111. Impounded water. Water is kept by monster so that mankind cannot use it. B443.5. Helpful wild hog (boar). B147.2.2.4. Owl as bird of ill-omen. B461.2. Helpful owl.* He coveted the beauty of the young woman and abducted her by poisoning her guarding dog and putting her father to sleep: *R22. Abduction by giving soporific.* This motif is a variant of *P19.2.1. King abducts woman to be his paramour.* The woman wouldn't give in: *T325. Chaste woman resists advances of a conqueror.* A tree spoke and gave the hunter a magic leaf: *D1610.2 Speaking tree. D955. Magic leaf.* A flower spoke and gave him a magic tendril: *D1610.4. Speaking flower. D965. Magic plant.* He turned into a caterpillar: *D192.1. Transformation: man to caterpillar.* He alighted on a leaf: *D1532.9. Magic leaf bears person aloft.* The leaf choked the monster: a variant motif of *D1402.1. Magic plant kills.* The tendril changed into a rope and bound him: *D451.2. Transformation: plant to other object. D1411.1. Magic rope binds person.* The marksman killed the monster and rescued the young woman: *R111.1.4. Rescue of princess (maiden) form giant (monster).* A cloud carried them home: *D1520.2. Magic transportation by cloud.* There they found their guarding dog resuscitated and father recuperated: *N730. Accidental reunion of families.*

> *Sources:* Lianxiu Qi and Huang Bocang. *Aiqing chuanshuo gushi xuan* (*Selected Love Stories and Legends*). Kunming: Yunnan renmin chuban she, 1981; Huihao Liu et al., eds. *Zhonghua minzu gushi da xi* (*Anthology of Chinese Ethnic Stories*). Vol. 15. Shanghai: Shanghai wenyi chuban she, 1995; Jun Gu. "Lunjishan and Ayijilun." In *Zhongguo shenhua gushi daquan* (*Complete Works of Chinese Fairytales*), Vol. 4., ed. Ke Yuan. Hangzhou: Zhejiang shaonian ertong chuban she, 1990.

Gumiya—Creator of the Universe. Only black clouds existed at the beginning: *A654. Primary elements of universe. Z156. Cloud (mist) as symbol of misfortune. A605. Primeval chaos.* A creator had twelve children: *D1273.1.5. Twelve as magic number. A2. Multiple creators. A32. Creator's family.* They used a rhinoceros to create the sky, stars, earth, river, plants, humans, and animals: *A1886. Rhinoceros. A610. Creation of universe by creator. The creator is existing before all things.* This motif is also a variant of *A642. Universe from body of slain giant.* The legs of the rhinoceros were used to support the sky: *A665.2.1. Four sky-columns. Four columns support the sky.* A giant turtle was used to carry the earth, and its movement caused an earthquake: *A815. Earth* *from turtle's back. A1145.2. Earthquakes from movements of sea-monster.* The creator asked a rooster to watch over the turtle: a variant motif of *A165.2.2.1. Cock as ambassador of god. B30.2. Mythical cock.* Nine sun sisters and ten moon brothers released heat to destroy the universe: *A736.1.1. Sun sister and moon brother.* This motif is also a variant of *A739.3. Each of sun brothers works for a month and plays for the other eleven; were they to work all together, the world would be burned up by the heat. F961.0.1. Several suns or moons appearing in sky simultaneously.* Crabs lost their heads; fish, their tongues; snake, their limbs; and frogs, their tails: *A2200. Cause of animal characteristics.* The creator shot and killed all but a sun and a moon: A Siberian motif variant is *A716.1. Four suns at first: culture hero shoots three down.* Their blood colored crags and pheasants: *F991. Object bleeds. A2411.2.6.9. Color of pheasant. F807. Rock of extraordinary color.* A sun sister and a moon brother survived and fled to a cave, where they hid and were married: a variant motif of *A713. Sun and moon from cave. A734.1. Sun hides in cave. A736.1.4. Sun and moon married.* The creator sent all animals to invite them out of hiding: *H1371.1.1. Quest for place where sun comes up.* Partridges wouldn't go and have become infamous: *A2234. Animal characteristics: punishment for disobedience.* The creator made a rooster and a boar led the columns of animals: *B256.6. Boar serves saint.* Fireflies lit the way: *B482.1. Helpful firefly.* The rooster pledged to wake up the sun: *B755. Animal calls the dawn. The sun rises as a result of the animal's call.* The timid sun sister came out during the day and would prick the eyes of those who dared to look at her with needles: a variant motif of *A739.9. Sun has weapons of iron to repel enemies. C315.2.2. Tabu: looking at sun.*

> ***Sources:*** Lifan Tao and Li Yaozong. *Zhongguo shaoshu minzu shenhua chuanshuoxuan.* Sichuan: Sichuan minzu chuban she, 1985; Shu Xia, reteller. "Gumiya," In *Cai hui ben Zhongguo minjian gushi* (*Chinese Folktales Illustrated with Colors*), ed. Zhejiang shao er chuban she, illus. Yang Yong. Hangzhou: Zhejiang shao er chuban she, 1990; Shouchun Wang, ed. *Yunnan mingjian gushi wushi pian* (*Fifty Yunnan Folktales*). Kunming: Yunnan renmin chuban she, 1979.

The White-swan Fairy. The tale is *Type 400D Other Animal Wives.* A white swan led a soldier dying of thirst to a body of river and saved his life: *B469.2. Helpful swan.* The swan turned into a beautiful fairy: *D361.1. Swan maiden. F234.1.15.1. Fairy as swan.* They married and had a son: *B652.1. Marriage to swan maiden. A122. God half mortal, half immortal.* The son begot three sons who became different branches of an ethnic group: *A592. Cultural heroes and descendants. A1610. Origin of various tribes.*

> ***Sources:*** The author collected this oral tale from Wang Yanan, born of a Han and a Kazak family and a staff member at the Beijing Ethnic Museum, Beijing, China, on July 5, 2006.

Forty Girls. A brother and sister wandered into a cave where immortals lived: *P253. Sister and brother. A151.1.2. Home of gods in cave.* The king had them hanged for mingling with the immortals: *C920. Death for breaking tabu. Q221. Personal offenses against* *gods punished*. Their ashes were scattered over a river: *E431.9. Ashes of dead thrown on water to prevent return*. They impregnated forty of the king's concubines who were swimming in it: *D931.1.2. Magic ashes. T510. Miraculous conception*. The king banned them from the court: *Q431. Punishment: banishment (exile)*. Their descendants became different branches of an ethnic group: *A1610. Origin of various tribes*.

Sources: Jihong He, ed. *Ke'erkezi minjian wenxue jingpin xuan (The Selected Best of the Kirgiz's Folk Literature)*. Vol. 1. Beijing: Zhongguo wenlian chuban she, 2003; Kunbo Ou et al., eds. *Zhonghua minzu gushi da xi (Anthology of Chinese Ethnic Stories)*, Vol. 10. Shanghai: Shanghai wenyi chuban she, 1995; Zhenhua Hu. "Guanyu Ke'erkezi de 'sishi ge guniang' (About the Kirgiz's Tale of 'Forty Girls')." *Heilongjiang minzu congkan (Heilongjiang Ethnic Journal)* (4) (2005).

The Origin of the Naxi People. At the beginning, trees talked, rocks walked, and heavenly objects were not solid: *A605. Primeval chaos. D1610.2. Speaking tree. F809.5. Traveling stones*. A deity in the form of a white chicken gave birth to gods, and a deity in the form of a black chicken gave birth to devils: *A114.2. God born from egg. B30.2. Mythical cock. A106. Opposition of good and evil gods*. Nine gods and seven goddesses propped up the sky with columns of different qualities: *A2. Multiple creators. A665.2.1.3. Sky extended by means of pillars*. Air and sound gave birth to dews that turned into oceans, where the ancestors of humans emerged: *A1132. Origin of dew. A1261. Man made from water*. Men incurred wrath from heaven by committing incest: *A1018.2. Flood as punishment for incest*. A repentant human survived the crowning flood: *Q36. Reward for repentance*. He was told to make a vessel out of a yak's hide, filling it with grain seeds and selected animals: This motif is a variant of *A1021.1. Pairs of animals in ark* and of *K1861.1. Hero sewed up in animal hide so as to be carried to height by bird*. He was told to tie the vessel with twelve ropes to trees, to the sky, and to the earth: *D1203. Magic rope. D1273.1.5. Twelve as magic number*. A white-bearded old man told him of two fairies, one with vertical eyes and the other with horizontal eyes, and asked him to marry the latter: *N825.2. Old man helper. A123.3. God unusual as to eyes. J260. Choice between worth and appearance*. The man married the vertical-eyed fairy, so she gave birth to animals; he looked at the puppets the deity gave him and they failed to turn into humans: *Q325. Disobedience punished. F230. Appearance of fairies*. The deity cut the puppets into pieces and they became echoes, waves, and wild animals: *D450. Transformation: object to another object. D440. Transformation: object to animal*. He wandered into a twilight garden: This is a variant motif of *H1057. Task: coming neither by day nor by night*. There he encountered a pretty goddess escaping an arranged marriage: *T320. Escape from undesired lover. F234.2.5. Fairy in form of beautiful young woman*. They fell in love: *T91.3.2. Love of goddess for mortal*. In the form of a crane, the goddess carried the man to her heavenly home: a variant motif of *F63.1. Mortal taken to heaven by heavenly maidens. F234.1.15. Fairy in form of bird. D162. Transformation: man (woman) to crane*. Her father put him through a series of tests in an attempt to deter or even kill him: *H931. Tasks assigned in order to get rid of hero*. Each time, the goddess helped him: *H335.0.1. Bride helps suitor perform his tasks.* She called in butterflies and ants to cut trees for him: *Z43.6. Man invites animals to come and work in his field. B481.1. Helpful ant.* He shot a turtledove and left indelible marks on its neck: a variant motif of *A2521.1. Why turtle-dove is sad. A2410. Animal characteristics: color and smell.* He then tied an ant's waist and made it thin: *A2355.1.2. Why ant has small waist.* The god asked him to get a tigress's milk: *H506. Test of resourcefulness.* When the newlywed stole a cat, it was condemned to purring: *A2236.8. Origin of cat's purring.* The turnips they stole were cursed as side dishes: *A2720. Plant characteristics as punishment.* Their children spoke different languages and became ancestors of three different peoples: *A1616. Origin of particular languages. A1610. Origin of various tribes.*

> *Sources:* Dainian Zu et al., eds. *Zhonghua minzu gushi da xi (Anthology of Chinese Ethnic Stories).* Vol. 9. Shanghai: Shanghai wenyi chuban she, 1995; Mei Xiao, reteller. "Renlei qianxi ji (The Migration of Humankind)." In *Zhongguo shenhua gushi daquan (Complete Works of Chinese Fairytales),* Vol. 3., ed. Ke Yuan. Hangzhou: Zhejiang shaonian ertong chuban she, 1990; Dongba wenhua yanjiu suo, ed. and trans. *Naxi Dongba guji yi zhu quanji (A Complete Annotated Collection of Naxi Dongba Manuscripts),* annot. He Kaixiang. Kunming: Yunnan renmin chuban she, 1999.

Seven Brothers. The tale is *Type 465A The Quest for the Unknown.* A father sent his seven sons of different capabilities away and asked them to be back with a gift in ten years: *H1210.1. Quest assigned by father. H500.1. Sons tested for skill. H1557. Tests of obedience.* On their quest, each helped a girl in need and married her: *Z71.5.8. Seven brothers marry seven sisters.* Their children became ancestors of seven different ethnic groups: *A1610. Origin of various tribes. A1620. Distribution of tribes.*

> *Sources:* Chinese Department of Guangdong Ethnologic Academy, Faqing Zhu, et al., eds. *Zhonghua minzu gushi da xi (Anthology of Chinese Ethnic Stories).* Vol. 7. Shanghai: Shanghai wenyi chuban she, 1995; Haizhen Hu. *Qi Xiongdi (Seven Brothers).* Vol. 2 of *Zhongguo shenhua gushi daquan (Complete Works of Chinese Fairytales),* ed. Ke Yuan. Hangzhou: Zhejiang shaonian ertong chuban she, 1995.

Miluotuo—A Goddess Who Creates the World. A creator used his master's rain hat to create the sky and his limbs and trunk to prop it up: *A15.1. Female creator. A40. Creator's advisers. D1067.1. Magic hat. A614.1. Universe from parts of man's body.* She then created the features and creatures of the earth: *A630. Series of creations.* Another deity was asked to create mountains but accidentally burned everything: *A37. Joint creators. A1031.6. Miscellaneous reasons for world-fire.* She covered the scorched earth with cloth: *D1051. Magic cloth.* She asked a third deity to purchase and plant tree seeds: *A1036. Earth recreated after world-fire. A30. Creator's companions.* The shape of plants and insects gave them the idea to invent saws, with which they built houses for humans: *A1402. The gods build houses, and fashion tools. A1446.1. Origin of the saw.* The creator tried making humans out of various materials and turned them into different things and animals: *A630. Series of creations*. She tried pumpkins and sweet potatoes but produced monkeys: *D441.4. Transformation: plant to animal*. The creator punished the birds and animals that failed to carry out her instructions by changing their characteristics: *A2230. Animal characteristics as punishment*. The eagle succeeded: *A165.1.2. Eagle as god's bird*. The creator made humans with bees and breast fed them until they grew up and worked as diligently as bees: a variant motif of *A1224.7. Creation of man by creator from ants. A1226. Man created after series of unsuccessful experiments. D382.1. Transformation: bee to person*.

> *Sources:* Shengzhen Zhang, ed. *Miluotuo gu ge* (*The Ancient Song of Miluotuo*), collec. trans., and annot. Lan Yonghong and Lan Zhenglu. Nanning: Guangxi minzu chuban she, 2002; Shengxing Su et al., eds. *Zhonghua minzu gushi da xi* (*Anthology of Chinese Ethnic Stories*). Vol. 5. Shanghai: Shanghai wenyi chuban she, 1995; Ye Hong, reteller. "Miluotuo." In *Zhongguo shenhua gushi daquan* (*Complete Works of Chinese Fairytales*), Vol. 1., ed. Ke Yuan. Hangzhou: Zhejiang shaonian ertong chuban she, 1990.

The Origin of the Gelao Ethnicity. Heavenly god dispatched the weaving fairy in the form of an eagle to take the suffering Gelao family to heaven: *A211. God of heaven. A185.16. God pities mortal. A451.3.1. Goddess of weaving and spinning. F234.1.15. Fairy in form of bird. A165.1.2. Eagle as god's bird. B542.1.1. Eagle carries man to safety. Q172. Reward: admission to heaven*. He gave a sister and brother pills of immortality: *D1851. Immortality bestowed. D1346.7. Pill of immortality*. He had them sent to earth to multiply: a variant motif of *A1231. First man descends from sky*. God of heaven sent the weaving fairy to get the sister and brother married: *A1273.1. Incestuous first parents*. Millstones and needle and thread were used as signs to convince the hesitant siblings: *D1262.1. Magic millstone. H509.1. Test: threading needle. N365.3. Unwitting brother-sister incest*. With a palm fan, the fairy called in a dragon princess as their witness: *D1077. Magic fan. B498.1. Helpful dragon*. The couple's child became the ancestor of the Gelao people: a variant motif of *T131.5.1. Marriage within clans sanctioned because of incest-origin of tribe*.

> *Source:* The author collected this oral tale from Cha Sailuo and Li Niga, staff members at the Beijing Ethnic Museum, Beijing, China, on July 5, 2006.

The Surviving Nu Ancestry. A flood destroyed the earth: *A1010. Deluge. Inundation of whole world or section*. Heavenly god sent a brother and sister to populate the earth: *A1271.3. First parents children of god. A1273.1. Incestuous first parents*. Sister asked brother to shoot at a loom to see if they were destined to marry: *N365.3. Unwitting borther-sister incest. H326.1.2. Suitor test: skill in archery*. Their seven children either married each other or bees, fish, snakes, and tigers: *A1552.3. Brother-sister marriage of children of first parents. B653.1. Marriage to bee in human form. B603. Marriage to fish (whale). B604.1. Marriage to snake. B601.9. Marriage to tiger*. A fire showed them that cooked meat was delicious: *X1208. Animals already cooked for eating. A1518. Why food is cooked*. They rubbed bamboo to get fire: *A1414.1. Origin of* *fire—rubbing sticks.* After their death, their descendants relocated and spoke a language of the locals: *A1405. Culture originated by ancestor of tribes.*

Sources: Ye Hong, reteller. "Lapu and Yaniu." In *Zhongguo shenhua gushi daquan* (*Complete Works of Chinese Fairytales*), Vol. 3., ed. Ke Yuan. Hangzhou: Zhejiang shaonian ertong chuban she, 1990; Yanchun You. *Nu zu wenxue jian shi* (*A Brief History of Ethnic Nu*). Kunming: Yunnan minzu chuban she, 2003; Daji Lü. *Zhongguo yuanshi zongjiao ziliao cong bian* (*A Compilation of Materials about Chinese Primitive Religions*). Shanghai: Shanghai renmin chuban she, 1993.

The Deluge. Last part of the tale is *Type 400A The Disappearance of the Immortal Spouse.* A frog told one of three brothers of an imminent flood because he treated it well: *F234.1.6. Fairy in form of frog. B521. Animal warns of fatal danger. Q40. Kindness rewarded. L10. Victorious youngest son.* The brother escaped the flood by tying himself to a tree top: *A1023. Escape from deluge on tree.* The cat, dog, and pestle he cast into the water repelled the flood: a variant motif of *D1541.2.1. Magic pestle draws storm away. B184. Magic cat. B182.1. Magic dog.* He fed flesh from his leg to an eagle that took him to a highland: *B322.1. Hero feeds own flesh to helpful animal. The hero is carried on the back of an eagle who demands food. B542.1.1. Eagle carries man to safety.* He encountered a devil couple with heavy eyelids: a variant motif of *G631. Ogre so old that his eyelids must be propped up. F402.7. Family of demons.* The she-devil swallowed him, but the frog made her spit him out: a variant motif of *A535. Culture hero swallowed and recovered from animal. B493.1. Helpful frog.* His fingers were no longer flushed and his ears became smaller: *A1310. Arrangement of man's bodily attributes. A1316.4. Origin of ears.* He went on a quest for a mountain god with three beautiful daughters: *H1289.4. Quest to see deity. F234.2.5. Fairy in form of beautiful young woman.* He shot and killed a monster in the form of a log: *H326.1.2. Suitor test: skill in archery. G303.3.4. Devil in form of inanimate objects.* He married the god's third daughter: *L50. Victorious youngest daugher. F460.4.1. Mountain-girl marries mortal man.* He was given a task of fighting a tiger, a leopard, and a python, which in fact was the third daughter: *H332.1. Suitor in contest with bride. F234.1. Fairy in form of an animal.* They settled on Earth: a variant of *A316. Goddess divides time between upper and lower worlds.* The fairy meant to get grains from heaven, but her plan was foiled because her husband didn't follow her instructions: Part of the motif is a variant of *D2105.2. Provisions provided by messenger from heaven. W214. Man will not do a woman's bidding.* She made a woman out of ashes to keep her husband company: *A1268. Man created from ashes (cinders).* Her husband married the ash girl: *K1317. Lover's place in bed usurped by another.* She returned to heaven: *C31.12. Unfaithful husband loses magic wife.* The man shot grains and domestic animals down from the fairy as she ascended to heaven: a variant motif of *J2196. Grain shot down with guns.*

Sources: Xi Yi, reteller. "Hongshui tao tian (The Flood That Soared to the Sky)." In *Zhongguo shenhua gushi daquan* (*Complete Works of Chinese*

Fairytales), Vol. 3., ed. Ke Yuan. Hangzhou: Zhejiang shaonian ertong chuban she, 1990; "Hongshui tao tian (The Flood that Soared to the Sky)." *Qian tu wang* (*The Net of the Road to Guizhou*), 2007. Available at http://www.chiyou.name/page/whyz/mjgs/7.htm. (Accessed June 30, 2007); Zhenya Wang. *Pu mi zu min jian gu shi. Yunnan min zu min jian gu shi cong shu.* Kunming Shi: Yunnan ren min chu ban she, 1990.

A Monkey Boy Stealing Rice from Heaven. Part of the tale is a variant of *Type 519 The Strong Woman as Bride* (*Brunhilde*). Includes an episode of *Type 532 The Helpful Horse*. A childless widow adopted a monkey: *T676. Childless couple adopt animal as substitute for child*. It turned into a boy as she received him: *D646.2. Transformation to child or pet to be adopted*. He rode a flying horse to heaven to ask the heavenly god for more productive grain: *B41.2. Flying horse. H1254. Journey to otherworld for magic objects*. The twelve grain seeds were the god's daughters: a variant motif of *A433.2. The seven grain sisters*. The boy had to draw a heavy bow to see them: *H1562. Test of strength*. Rice turned into a pretty young woman and wooed the boy: *D431.6. Transformation: plant to person. T55. Girl as wooer*. He asked for the rice plant and learned how to grow it from her: a variant motif of *D1810.1. Magic knowledge from queen of other world. A1423.2. Acquisition of rice*. He got her drunk and fled to Earth with the help of the horse: *K332. Theft by making owner drunk. B401. Helpful horse*. The fairy hit the horse with her magic sword: *D1081. Magic sword*. Both the horse and the boy plunged to their death: *C51.2. Tabu: stealing from god or saint*. The rice shoots the horse had swallowed burst out of its belly and began to grow in the fields: a variant motif of *A1441.3. Origin of water wheel and rice growing*.

> *Sources:* Meng Wu, reteller. "Yingxiong Mamai (The Hero Mamai)." In *Zhongguo shenhua gushi daquan* (*Complete Works of Chinese Fairytales*), Vol. 2., ed. Ke Yuan. Hangzhou: Zhejiang shaonian ertong chuban she, 1990; Huihao Liu et al., eds. *Zhonghua minzu gushi da xi* (*Anthology of Chinese Ethnic Stories*). Vol. 6. Shanghai: Shanghai wenyi chuban she, 1995; Zu'e Bai et al., eds. and trans. *Hani zu minjian gushi* (*Folktales from Ethnic Hani*). Kunming: Yunnan minzu chuban she, 1993.

Sky Mended with a Dragon's Teeth. A childless couple parented a child that was born of cotton: *N825.1. Childless old couple adopt hero. T543. Birth from plant*. Two dragons, one from the sea and the other on the mountain, fought and broke the sky: *B11.3.1. Dragon's home in bottom of sea. B11.3.2. Dragon's home at top of mountain. A1015.1. Flood from conflict of gods. A1050. Heavens break up at end of world*. The cotton boy went to seek objects that could mend the sky: *H1286.2. Quest to fairyland for magic object*. A long-bearded old man living in a bird's nest on a cliff referred him to a bear king on a column-like tall mountain: *H1233.1.2. Old man helps on quest. D1292. Magic bird nest. A151.1. Home of gods on high mountain. A132.5. Bear-god* (*goddess*). In his magic sandals, gloves, and hat he kicked, pushed, and bumped the mountain to shake it: *D1065.5. Magic sandals. D1066. Magic glove. D1067.1. Magic hat. F1006.3. Mountain trembles*. Each time he did so, a fairy girl came down in a basket from a vine, but only the third one, in white, agreed to help: *L111.2.1. Future hero found in boat (basket, bushes). F234.2.5. Fairy in form of beautiful young woman. P252.2. Three sisters. D1293.3. White as magic color.* As the girl suggested, the cotton man made nails out of one of the dragon's teeth and a hammer of the other dragon's horn: *D1009.2. Magic tooth. D812.7. Magic object received from dragon king. D1252.1.2. Magic nails. D1209.4. Magic hammer.* The girl made two mantles from the sheep wool; they flew to the sky: *D1532.6. Magic robe bears person aloft. D1053. Magic mantle (cloak).* They mended the sky with the dragon's teeth: a variant motif of *V229.10. Broken objects restored to their original forms by saint.*

> *Sources:* Jian Shun, reteller. "Long ya bu tian (Mending the Sky with Dragon's Teeth)." In *Zhongguo shenhua gushi daquan (Complete Works of Chinese Fairytales)*, Vol. 1., ed. by Ke Yuan. Hangzhou: Zhejiang shaonian ertong chuban she, 1990; Peikun Wang. *Long ya ke ke ding man tian (Every Dragon Tooth Is Nailed On the Sky)*. Shanghai: Shaonian ertong chuban she, 1956; Yue Chen, reteller. *Long ya bu tian (Mending the Sky with Dragon's Teeth)*. Taibei: Zhixing wenhua, 1999.

Why Are Oxen Preferred to Till Our Land? After the heavenly emperor created humans, he wanted to know about their lives: *A1210. Creation of man by creator. A185.16. God pities mortal.* He sent an ox to tell them how to eat and do their toilet: *B291.2. Domestic beast as messenger.* But his arrogance caused him to give the wrong decree and the emperor to kick his front teeth out: *A2345.7.1. Why cow has no upper teeth.* The ox developed an oxbow as he stretched his neck to allay his fear: *A2213.4. Animal characteristics changed by stretching.* The ox descended to earth to help humans produce more food: *A2515.1. Why ox is draft animal. A2513.5. Why ox serves man.*

> *Sources:* Kunbo Ou et al., eds. *Zhonghua minzu gushi da xi (Anthology of Chinese Ethnic Stories)*. Vol. 10. Shanghai: Shanghai wenyi chuban she, 1995; Liubao Jin, reteller. "Wei shenme yong huangniu gengdi (Why Ox Is Used to Till the Land)." In *Zhongguo shenhua gushi daquan (Complete Works of Chinese Fairytales)*, Vol. 4., ed. Ke Yuan. Hangzhou: Zhejiang shaonian ertong chuban she, 1990; Sangji Renqian. "Huang niu shen: Tu zu yuanshi nongye wenhua yixiang (The God of Yellow Cow: The Imagination of the Primeval Agriculture of Tu Nationality)." *Zhongguo tuzu (China's Tu Nationality)* (3) (2006): 45–47.

The Origin of the Bronze Drum. The tale is *Type 555* The Grateful Prince (Princess)*. Part of the tale is *Type 471 The Bridge to the Other World.* An orphan caught a carp and kept it in a jar: *L111.4. Orphan hero.* A dragon princess, the fish gave him a pearl in his dream: a variant motif of *B375.1. Fish returned to water: grateful. B11.2.1.3. Dragon as modified fish. D813.2. Magic object received from grateful fairy.* It gave his hoe magic power: *D1561. Magic object confers miraculous powers (luck).* The princess cooked for him stealthily: *F365.7. Fairies steal cooking. F346. Fairy helps mortal with labor.* The orphan married her: *F300. Marriage or liaison with fairy.* They went to the dragon palace in a lake for help: a variant motif of *H1286.0.1. Quest to fairyland at bottom of lake. B11.3.1.1. Dragon lives in lake*. The man squirted water so that it became a rainbow bridge: *A791.3. Rainbow made as bridge by the gods. F152.1.1. Rainbow bridge to otherworld*. The hero rode on a horse into the twelve layers of lake water: *F141. Water barrier to otherworld*. He gave the dragon king phoenixes: *B32. Phoenix*. The king assigned him three tasks, which he accomplished easily with his magic hoe: *H941. Cumulative tasks*. The dragon king gave the couple a magic object: *D812.7. Magic object received from dragon king*. It could manipulate the weather and turn water into silver: a variant motif of *D475.2.2. Transformation: water to money*. The magic object turned into a vessel to ferry them over a river before changing into a bronze drum: *D1171. Magic vessel. A2824. Origin of drum*. The couple used it only on important occasions as the dragon king asked, so it has become a tradition: *A1405. Culture originated by ancestor of tribes*.

> *Sources:* Dejun Li et al., eds. *Zhonghua minzu gushi da xi (Anthology of Chinese Ethnic Stories)*. Vol. 3. Shanghai: Shanghai wenyi chuban she, 1995; "Buyi zu tonggu de laili (The Origin of the Buyei's Bronze Drum)." In *Qian tu wang (The Net of the Road to Guizhou)*, 2007. Available at http://www.chiyou.name/page/whyz/mjgs/55.htm. (Accessed June 30, 2007); Luta Yang. "Tong gu de chuan shuo." In *Gui zhou shao shu min zu gu shi xuan*, ed. Guizhou sheng minzu shiwu weiyuanhui and Guizhou sheng jiaoyu kexue yanjiusuo. Guiyang: Gui zhou ren min chu ban she, 1985.

The Origin of the Eagle-bone Flute. The tale is a variant of *Type 780, The Singing Bone*. A shepherd and a shepherdess fell in love: *P412.1. Shepherd as hero*. When they were separated by force they pledged their love for each other: *M149.1. Lovers vow to marry only each other*. The shepherd was a good flutist: *L113.10. Flute player as hero*. An eagle fought wolves to save his flock but was mortally wounded: *B455.3. Helpful eagle*. This motif is also a variant of *J715.1. Eagle warns shepherd that wolf is eating sheep*. He asked that the shepherd use his feather bone to make a flute: *B560. Animals advise men. E632. Reincarnation as musical instrument*. With it, he gained access to the rich man's home and was reunited with the shepherdess: *Q95.1. Reward for flute-playing. T96. Lovers reunited after many adventures*.

> *Sources:* Zhenya Wang et al., eds. *Zhonghua minzu gushi da xi (Anthology of Chinese Ethnic Stories)*. Vol. 14. Shanghai: Shanghai wenyi chuban she, 1995; Xia Fang, reteller. "Ying Di (The Eagle Flute)." In *Cai hui ben Zhongguo minjian gushi (Chinese Folktales Illustrated with Colors)*, ed. Zhejiang shao er chuban she, illus. Feng Yuan and Qian Jiwei. Hangzhou: Zhejiang shao er chuban she, 1990; "Ying di chuanshuo (The Legend of Eagle Flute)." In *Tianshan.net*, 2006. Available at http://www.tianshannet.com.cn/travel/content/2006-09/19/content_1183901.htm. (Accessed June 30, 2007).

The Fiddle with a Horse Head. The tale is a variant of *Type 780 The Singing Bone.* A shepherd saved an abandoned colt and it won in a race to win a princess: *P412.1. Shepherd as hero. B360. Animals grateful for rescue from peril of death. T68.1. Princess offered as prize to rescuer.* It won a horse race to win a princess, but the father rescinded his promise: *K231.2. Reward for accomplishment of task deceptively withheld.* He even forfeited the horse: *K2247. Treacherous lord.* The defiant horse returned to the shepherd fatally wounded: *B301.4.4. Faithful horse allows only its master to catch and ride it.* At its request, the shepherd made a fiddle using its bone and hair: *B560. Animals advise men. E632. Reincarnation as musical instrument.*

> *Sources:* The author collected this oral tale from Yue Songmin (a Mongolian, whose original name is Naren Chaogetu), a staff member at the Beijing Ethnic Museum, Beijing, China, on July 5, 2006.

A Girl Named Ashima. An episode is *Type 875D2 Clever Woman Interprets Important Message.* A twin brother and sister were born to a poor family concurrently with a boy to a rich one: *A515.1.1. Twin culture heroes. U60. Wealth and poverty.* When grown up, the rich boy coveted the girl's beauty, but she resented him: *F575.1. Remarkably beautiful woman. T70. The scorned lover.* Parents objected to matchmaker's proposal that bad husband would ruin daughter's life: *L143.2. Poor suitor makes good husband; rich suitor cruel.* While her brother was away herding, the rich family kidnapped the girl: *P412.1. Shepherd as hero.* This motif is a variant of *P19.2.1. King abducts woman to be his paramour.* She wouldn't yield to the temptation of their wealth and fled with her brother, who came to her rescue: This motif is a variant of *T320.5. Girl gives up wealth and flees to escape lecherous emperor.* Brother had to undergo tests of survival to get sister free: *H1510. Tests of power to survive. Vain attempts to kill hero. P253.2.1. Brother faithful to persecuted sister.* On their way to freedom, they were misled by a wasp to a trap laid by the rich family, which turned the girl into a stone: *F401.3.4.1. Demon in form of wasp. D231. Transformation: man to stone. M458. Curse of petrifaction.*

> *Sources:* Deguang Zhao, ed. *Ashima yuanshi ziliao huibian* (*Compilation of the Source Materials about Ashima*). Kunming: Yunnan minzu chuban she, 2002; Dejun Li et al., eds. *Zhonghua minzu gushi da xi* (*Anthology of Chinese Ethnic Stories*). Vol. 3. Shanghai: Shanghai wenyi chuban she, 1995; *Ashima*, dir. Liu Qiong. 90 min. Haiyan zhipian chang, 1964. videodisc.

The River of Hai and Lan. A village of farmers on one side of a river had a hero, and a village of fishers on the other side had a heroine: *L113. Hero (heroine) of unpromising occupation.* A hairy devil with a sword robbed the villagers of the fruits of their labor and abducted women: *G303.3.1.21. The devil as a great hairy man. G346.2. Devastating demon. Kills and eats people.* He even turned the river muddy, making fishing in it impossible: This motif is a variant of *D478.12. Transformation: water to rocks. D2085.1. Curse makes river barren of fish.* Villagers revolted against the hairy devil, but each time the hero cut its head, it grew back to its body: *D1602.12. Self-returning* head. *F531.1.2.3. Giant's self-returning head. E783. Vital head. Retains life after being cut off.* The heroine prevented its last effort by applying quicklime to the wound: *D931.1.4. Magic lime.* The river was named after the hero and heroine: *Q53. Reward for rescue.*

> *Sources:* The author collected this oral tale from Xu Jizi, an ethnic Korean and a staff member at the Beijing Ethnic Museum, Beijing, China, on July 5, 2006.

A Fairy's Bathing Pond. The youngest of three fairies was a skillful archer: *P252.2. Three sisters. L50. Victorious youngest daughter. F273.1. Fairy shows remarkable skill as marksman.* A god of a star coveted her beauty but was rejected: This motif is a variant of *T91.6.2.0.1. King covets subject's wife. A250. Star-god.* When the fairies bathed in a lake on a mountaintop, he took away her clothes: a variant motif of *F441.2.1.4. Tree maidens bathe at midnight in lake. F265. Fairy bathes. K1335. Seduction (or wooing) by stealing clothes of bathing girl (swan maiden).* She had to stay behind as her sisters left and forgot about her: a variant motif of *S142. Person thrown into the water and abandoned. U150. Indifference of the miserable.* When a mountain god gave her a ladder accessible to heaven and a raft, she chose the latter: *A418. Deity of particular mountain. A657.1. Ladder from earth to heaven.* The motif is a variant of *D1121. Magic boat.* A magpie impregnated her by dropping fruit into her mouth: a variant of *T511.1.1. Conception from eating apple. B.451.6. Helpful magpie.* She placed her baby on the raft, which drifted away on a cloud: *D1520.2. Magic transportation by cloud.* A shy arhat who tried to keep the nude fairy warm with hot water became a stone by accident: *F238. Fairies are naked. D231. Transformation: man to stone.* A chieftain adopted the baby: This motif is a variant of *N836.1. King adopts hero (heroine).* He grew up and, with her mother's magic bow and arrows, stopped a protracted tribal war by killing the god of the star who had instigated it: *D1091. Magic bow. A172. Gods intervene in battle.* He became the ancestor of the Manchu people: *A1405. Culture originated by ancestor of tribes.* His mother became an arching tree on the mountain, still watching him: *D215. Transformation: man to tree.*

> *Sources:* "Jianzhou Nüzhen de Nu'erhachi (The Jurchens' Nurhaci in Jianzhou)." In *Tanmi dongfang* (*Exploring the Mysterious Orient*), dir. Zhi Qun et al. 30 min. Haixia Weishi (Fujian Satellite TV); Jun Gu, reteller. "*Tiannü yu gong chi (The Fairy Girl's Bathing Pond*." In *Zhongguo shenhua gushi daquan* (*Complete Works of Chinese Fairytales*), Vol. 4., ed. Ke Yuan. Hangzhou: Zhejiang shaonian ertong chuban she, 1990; Wenliang Sun and Li Zhiting. *Qing taizong quan zhuan* (*The Complete Biography of the Second Emperor of Qing*). Nanjing: Jiangsu jiaoyu chuban she, 2005.

The Five-fingered Mountain and the Seven-fingered Hill. Wind and incessant rain brought a deluge to an idyllic earth: *A1067. Extraordinary wind at end of the world. F962. Extraordinary precipitation (rain, snow, etc.)* and made it shake: *A1145. Cause of earthquakes.* Jade Emperor sent two giant brothers to steady the earth: *A211. God of heaven. N817.0.1. God as helper. A523. Giant as culture hero.* They each built a mountain with dirt and stones, one with five peaks and the other seven: *A969. Creation of mountains and hills. A962. Mountains (hills) from ancient activities of god (hero).* They tested the fruits of each other's labor by kicking them and halved one of the mountains: *F626.2. Strong man kicks mountain down.*

> *Source:* Chinese Department of Guangdong Ethnologic Academy et al., eds. *Zhonghua minzu gushi da xi (Anthology of Chinese Ethnic Stories).* Vol. 7. Shanghai: Shanghai wenyi chuban she, 1995; Yue Wu. *Hainandao lizu minjian gushi xuan (Selected Tales from the Ethnic Li on the Hainan Island).* Guangzhou: Guangdong renmin chuban she, 1980; Zhen Fu. *Li zu minjian gushi ji (A Collection of the Ethnic Li's Folktales).* Guangzhou: Huacheng chuban she, 1982.

Young Hero Mola and the Red Cliff. The Yugurs migrated to a new location only to run into a devastating snowstorm monster: *A1630. Wandering of tribes. F433. Storm-spirit. F433.1. Spirit of snow. F436. Spirit of cold.* A boy volunteered to seek help: *Z251. Boy hero. H1320. Quest for marvelous objects or animals.* Carrying a magic bow and wearing a magic garment, he set out on a magic horse with a magic whip: *D1091. Magic bow. D1388.0.4. Magic garment protects from drowning. B184.1.4. Magic horse travels on sea or land. D1208. Magic whip.* Repeatedly reminded by a lark, he used them to surmount a formidable mountain, kill a tiger, and cross a sea: *B451.1. Helpful lark. B16.2.2.1. Hostile tiger killed. H1199.14. Task: climbing extraordinary (high, thin) cliff. F1057. Hero (giant) wades across sea.* A pretty goddess unleashed an eagle to attack him, and he killed it: *A125.4. Beautiful goddess. A165.1.2. Eagle as god's bird.* He banged on the heavenly gate for three days until his persistence moved the God of the Sun: *A220. Sun-god. A661.0.1 Gate of heaven. Q81. Reward for perseverance.* He lent him a gourd of fire and the goddess taught him how to release fire: *N817.0.1. God as helper. D965.2. Magic calabash (gourd). D1548. Magic object controls weather.* He left for home before learning the trick of recalling the fire, and consequently he couldn't put out the fire that had burned the monster to ashes: *W196. Lack of patience. D806. Magic object effective only when exact instructions for its use are followed. G512.3. Ogre burned to death.* This motif is a variant of *A871.0.2. Unextinguishable fire at end of earth.* He covered the gourd with his body and turned into a red crag: This motif is a variant of *A969.3. Mountains and valleys formed from great fire. D231. Transformation: man to stone. W28. Self-sacrifice.*

> *Sources:* Huihao Liu et al., eds. *Zhonghua minzu gushi da xi (Anthology of Chinese Ethnic Stories).* Vol. 15. Shanghai: Shanghai wenyi chuban she, 1995; Shan Bai, reteller. "Mola." In *Zhongguo shenhua gushi daquan (Complete Works of Chinese Fairytales),* Vol. 3., ed. Ke Yuan. Hangzhou: Zhejiang shaonian ertong chuban she, 1990; Bianji weiyuan hui. *Zhongguo shaoshu minzu wenxue zuopin xuan (Selected Works of Folk Literature from China's Ethnic Minorities).* Shanghai: Shanghai wenyi chuban she, 1981.

The Conquest of a She-Demon. A fertile land turned into a lake as a flood demolished mountains: *A910.4. Bodies of water remnant of flood. A920.1. Origin of lakes.* Humans fled to the mountaintops: *A1022. Escape from deluge on mountain.* A goddess cut a canal and led water out to form a river so humans coud go back: *N817.0.2. Goddess as helper. A934. Various origins of rivers.* A she-demon came and lay on her back in the valley, causing humans to suffer: *D486.1. Demon becomes larger. F531.2.11. Demon looks like a mountain.* Humans built a temple on the demon's forehead and killed her as they erected a pole where her heart was: *F773. Remarkable church (chapel, temple).* Part of this motif is a variant of *A992.1. Origin of sacred post (placed there by ancestral culture hero).*

Sources: Shiyuan Wang et al., eds. *Zhonghua minzu gushi da xi (Anthology of Chinese Ethnic Stories).* Vol. 16. Shanghai: Shanghai wenyi chuban she, 1995; Shengqi Zhao and Zhang Lifeng. *Zou guo Zang dong nan (Traverse the Southeast of Tibet).* Kunming: Yunnan daxue chuban she, 2005; Jianshang Li. *Luoba zu Menba zu minjian gushi xuan (Selected Tales from the Ethnic Lhoba and Monba).* Shanghai: Shanghai wenyi chuban she, 1993.

APPENDIX B: LIST OF CHINESE NATIONAL MINORITIES

(Listed alphabetically)

Romanized Name	Chinese Name	Pinyin (Pronunciation)
Achang	阿昌族	Āchāng Zú
Bai	白族	Bái Zú
Blang	布朗族	Bùlǎng Zú
Bonan	保安族	Bǎoān Zú
Buyei	布依族	Bùyī Zú
Dai	傣族	Dǎi Zú
Daur	达斡尔族	Dáwòěr Zú
De'ang	德昂族	Dé'áng Zú
Derung	独龙族	Dúlóng Zú
Dong	侗族	Dòng Zú
Dongxiang	东乡族	Dōngxiāng Zú
Ewenki	鄂温克族	Èwēnkè Zú
Gaoshan	高山族	Gāoshān Zú
Gelao	仡佬族	Gēlǎo Zú
Gin	京族	Jīng Zú
Han	汉族	Hàn Zú
Hani	哈尼族	Hāní Zú
Hezhen	赫哲族	Hèzhé Zú
Hui	回族	Huí Zú
Jingpo	景颇族	Jǐngpō Zú
Jino	基诺族	Jīnuò Zú
Kazak	哈萨克族	Hāsàkè Zú
Kirgiz	柯尔克孜族	Kēěrkèzī Zú
Korean	朝鲜族	Cháoxiǎn Zú
Lahu	拉祜族	Lāhù Zú
Lhoba	珞巴族	Luòbā Zú
Li	黎族	Lí Zú

Lisu	傈僳族	Lìsù Zú
Manchu	满族	Mǎn Zú
Maonan	毛南族	Màonán Zú
Miao	苗族	Miáo Zú
Monba	门巴族	Ménbā Zú
Mongolian	蒙古族	Měnggǔ Zú
Mulao	仫佬族	Mùlǎo Zú
Naxi	纳西族	Nàxī Zú
Nu	怒族	Nù Zú
Oroqen	鄂伦春族	Èlúnchūn Zú
Pumi	普米族	Pǔmǐ Zú
Qiang	羌族	Qiāng Zú
Russ	俄罗斯族	Éluōsī Zú
Salar	撒拉族	Sǎlá Zú
She	畲族	Shē Zú
Sui	水族	Shuǐ Zú
Tajik	塔吉克族	Tǎjíkè Zú
Tatar	塔塔尔族	Tǎtǎěr Zú
Tibetan	藏族	Zàng Zú
Tu	土族	Tǔ Zú
Tujia	土家族	Tǔjiā Zú
Uygur	维吾尔族	Wéiwúěr Zú
Uzbek	乌孜别克族	Wūzībiékè Zú
Va	佤族	Wǎ Zú
Xibe	锡伯族	Xíbó Zú
Yao	瑶族	Yáo Zú
Yi	彝族	Yí Zú
Yugur	裕固族	Yùgù Zú
Zhuang	壮族	Zhuàng Zú

GLOSSARY

Antiphonal:	Of responsive singing, a style known as *duige* in Chinese
Appliqué:	Fasten a cutout decoration to a larger piece of material
Bazaar:	Market
Bharal:	Sheep on high mountains
Bodhisattva:	A Buddhist god
Cattail:	A plant having long, strap-like leaves
Centipede:	A wormlike bug with multiple segments, each with a pair of legs
Contrapuntal:	Marked by one or more independent melodies added above or below a given melody
Craw:	Stomach of fowls and insects
Crochet:	To make by looping thread with a hooked needle
Crotch:	The angle or region where two branches join
Epic:	A long narrative poem telling the deeds of a legendary or historical hero
Eurasian:	Of mixed European and Asian descent
Glossy ganoderma:	A medicinal herb said to have tonic effect, known as *lingzhi* in Chinese
Hieroglyphic:	A writing that uses pictures to represent meaning
Imam:	The Muslim male prayer leader in a mosque
Jaundice:	A disease caused by the disorder of one's bile, characteristic of yellow skin
Khanate:	The realm of a khan, a medieval ruler of a Mongol, Tartar, or Turkish tribe
Li:	Measure of distance: half kilometer (about ? of a mile)
Märchen:	Folktales or fairy stories

Mugwort:	A medicinal herb used in Chinese acupuncture
Mythology:	Body of myths associated with a culture
Papaya:	Large oblong yellow fruit of a tropical tree
Parterre:	An ornamental flower garden having the beds and paths arranged to form a pattern
Pigment:	A substance used as coloring
Polytheistic:	Of multi-god
Ruminant:	Of animals with four stomachs that chew regurgitated and partially digested food
Serration:	Formation of a row of small, sharp, projections resembling the teeth of a saw
Shaman:	A priest believed able to heal or foretell the future through communication with spirits
Shoton:	A Tibetan festival featuring the Tibetan Opera
Stilt:	One of two poles with footrests used for walking high above the ground
Tendril:	A twisting, threadlike structure by which a twining plant grasps an object for support
Ventriloquism:	The art of speaking in such a manner that the voice appears to come from another source

REFERENCES

"Afanti de gushi (Tales of Efendi)." 1980–1991. In *Zhongguo da baike quanshu* (*The Great Chinese Encyclopedia*). Beijing : Zhongguo da baikequanshu chubanshe.

Ahmed, Syed Jamil. 2006. "Tibetan Folk Opera: Lhamo in Contemporary Cultural Politics." *Asian Theater Journal* 23 (1) (Spring): 155.

Aikebaier Wulamu. 1994. *Shijie Afanti xiaohua daquan* (*Complete Collection of Efendi's Funny Stories from the World*). Beijing: Zhishi chubanshe.

Archer, Kirstie. 2002. "A Celebration of Chinese and Jewish History." *Lancet* 359 (9307): 715.

Ashima, dir. 1964. *Liu Qiong*. 90 min. Haiyan zhipianchang (videodisc).

"Baisha xiyue (The Xiyue Music of Baisha)." 2006. In *Wikipedia*. Available at http://en.wikipedia.org/wiki/Baisha_xiyue. (Accessed June 18, 2006).

Bender, Mark. 2003. "Oral Narrative Studies in China." *Oral Tradition* 18 (2): 236–238.

Bender, Mark. 2006. "Ethnic Diversity in China and Japan." *East Asian Humanities*. Available at http://people.cohums.ohio-state.edu/bender4/eall131/EAHReadings/module01/module01ethnicdiversity.html. (Accessed June 6, 2006).

Chen, Jing, and Tang Cao. 2006. "Hulu yu renlei qiyuan shenhua—Yunnan shaoshu minzu hulu congbai de wenhua jiedu (Gourd and the Mythology of Human Origin—A Cultural Explanation of Gourd Worshiping among the Ethnic Minorities in the Yunnan Province)." *Hubei shehui kexue* (*Hubei Social Sciences*) 9: 82–86.

China. 2002. *Zhongguo 2000 nian ren kou pu cha zi liao*. Beijing Shi: Zhongguo tong ji chu ban she.

"China—Paradise of Foreign Immigrants." 2006. *Deutsche Welle* (*Voice of Germany*). Available at http://www.deutsche-welle.de/dw/article/02144199308900.html. (Accessed June 18, 2006).

Deng, Qiyao. 1991. *Minzu fushi: yi zhong wenhua fuhao : Zhongguo xi nan shaoshu minzu fushi wenhua yanjiu* (*Ethnic Costumes and Ornaments—A Cultural Symbol: Study of the Costume and Ornament Cultures of the Ethnic Minorities in Southwestern China*). Kunming: Yunnan renmin chubanshe.

Di jiu jie quanguo renmin daibiao dahui changwu weiyuan hui di ershi wu ci huiyi (The 25th Session of the Standing Committee of the Ninth People's Congress of PRC). 2001. "Zhonghua renmin gonghe guo renkou yu jihua shengyu fa (PRC Law on Population and Family Planning)." *People.com.* Available at http://www.people.com. cn/GB/shizheng/20011229/638471.html. (Accessed May 30, 2006).

Eber, Irene. 1986. *Passage through China: The Jewish Communities of Harbin, Tientsin and Shanghai.* Tel-Aviv: Beth Hatefutsoth, v–xxii.

Eber, Irene. 1999. "Kaifeng Jews: The Sinification of Identity." In *The Jews of China,* ed. Jonathan Goldstein, 23–24. New York: M.E. Sharpe.

"Exhibition on Costumes of China's Ethnic Minorities Tells of Folklore, History." 2002. *People's Daily.* Available at http://english.people.com.cn/200203/04/eng20020304_ 91373.shtml. (Accessed June 6, 2006).

Fan, Yunxing, et al., eds. 1997. *Zhongguo shaoshu minzu tese cai (Characteristic Dishes from China's Ethnic Minorities).* Nanning: Guangxi kexue jishu chubanshe.

Gao, Limei. 2005. "Shaoshu minzu xiaoshuo, sanwen, dianying wenxue yicaifencheng (Great Achievements Made in Minority Ethnic Novels, Prose, and Screenplays)." *Zhenshi Yunnan (The True Yunnan).* Available at http://www.oayn.net/Topic. aspx?id=1857. (Accessed November 27, 2006).

"Gesa'er wang zhuan (Biography of King Gesa'er)." 2006. In *Baidubaike (Baidu Encyclopedia).* Available at http://baike.baidu.com/view/26414.htm. (Accessed November 27, 2006).

Gladney, Dru C. 1996. *Muslim Chinese: Ethnic Nationalism in the People's Republic.* Cambridge, Mass.: Harvard University Press.

Gladney, Dru C. 2004. *Dislocating China: Reflections on Muslims, Minorities and Other Subaltern Subjects.* Chicago: University of Chicago Press, 9.

Guan, Ming, ed. 2001. *Minzu caipu (Ethnic Recipes).* Kunming: Yunnan keji chubanshe.

Guan, Yanpo. 2005. *Wenhua yu yishu: Zhongguo shaoshu minzu toushi wenhua yanjiu (Culture and Art: Study of the Head Ornament Culture of China's Ethnic Minorities).* Beijing: Zhongguo jingji chubanshe.

"Guangbo dianshi (Radio and Television Broadcasts)." 2006. In *Dongfang minzu wang (Orental Ethnic Minorities Net).* Available at http://www.e56.com.cn/minzu/west/ yunnan4-7.htm. (Accessed June 11, 2006).

Guojia minzu shiwu weiyuan hui jingji fazhan si he guojia tongji ju guomin jingji zonghe tongji si (Department of Economic Development of the State Ethnic Affairs Commission of China and Department of Comprehensive Statistics of the National Bureau of Statistics of China). 2000. *Zhongguo minzu tongji nianjian (China's Ethnic Statistical Year Book).* Beijing: Minzu Chubanshe.

Guowuyuan (State Council). 2001. "Quanguo nian jie ji jinian ri fangjia banfa (Methods for Having Days Off for Annual Festivals and Commemoration Days throughout the Country)." *People.com*. Available at http://www.people.com.cn/GB/shenghuo/200/ 3475/3478/20001228/364694.html. (Accessed September 15, 2006).

"Gushi daquan (Complete Collection of Stories)." 2002. In *Minjian gushi* (*Chinese Folktales*). Available at http://www.yuda-edu.com/yang/1.htm. (Accessed November 6, 2005).

"Guya chunpu de Naxi zu fushi (Primitively Graceful and Simple Costumes of Naxi)." 2006. *Shiji zaixian zhongguo yishu wang* (*Art & Design*). Available at http:// cn.cl2000.com/artdesign/fashion/culture/wen08.shtml. (Accessed June 6, 2006).

He, Yihong. 2006. *Zhijian shang de lücheng: tanfang Zhongguo shaoshu minzu shougong yi de lüxing* (*A Tour on the Fingers: A Journey to the Exploration of China's Ethnic Minorities' Handicrafts*). Urumchi: Xinjiang renmin chubanshe.

Heberer, Thomas. 1989. *China and Its National Minorities: Autonomy or Assimilation?* New York: M.E. Sharpe.

Ho, Wan-Li. 2003. "Jews in China: A Dialogue in Slow-Motion." *Journal of Ecumenical Studies* 40 (1/2) (Winter/Spring): 171–200.

Hou, Hui, ed. 2003. *Zhongguo shenhua gushi jing xuan—yuwen xin keben bidu congshu* (*Selected Chinese Tales: Compulsory Readings for the New Edition of Chinese Textbooks*). Beijing: Zhongguo da baike quanshu chubanshe.

Hu, Qiaomu, et al, eds. 2000. *Zhongguo da baike quanshu* (*The Great Chinese Encyclopedia*). Beijing: Zhongguo da baike quanshu chubanshe.

Hu, Qiwang, and Meizhen Xiang. 1996. *Zhongguo shaoshu minzu jieri* (*Festivals of China's Ethnic Minorities*). Beijing: Shanwu yinshuguan.

Ji, Xiaobin, ed. 2003. *Facts about China*. New York: Wilson, 53.

Jiang, Rong. 2006. "Zhongguo shaoshu minzu renkou buju de bianqian jiqi youyin fenxi (The Changes in the Population Distribution of Chinese Minorities and Analysis on Its Inducement)." *Heilongjiang minzu congkan* (*Heilongjiang Ethnic Series*) 1: 46–50.

Lai, H. H. 2006. "Religious Policies in Post-Totalitarian China: Maintaining Political Monopoly over a Reviving Society." *Journal of Chinese Political Science* 11 (1) (Spring): 55–77.

Langxingtianxia. 2005. "Fushi shi wenhua de biaozheng (Costumes Indicate Cultures)." *C'est La Vie*. Available at http://yaowang.yculblog.com/post.1019714.html. (Accessed June 6, 2006).

"Laran (Batik)." 2006. In *Baidu baike* (*Baidu Encyclopedia*). Available at http://baike. baidu.com/view/15332.html. (Accessed December 7, 2006).

Lee, MaryJo Benton. 1997. "Ethnic Minorities in the People's Republic of China." *The Great Plains Sociologist* 10:68–83.

Li, Kunsheng, and Zhou Wenlin, eds. 2005. *Yunnan shaoshu minzu fushi* (*Minority Nationalities' Costumes and Ornaments in Yunnan*). Kunming: Yunnan meishu chubanshe.

Liu, Xiang. 2002. *Shan hai jing* (*Classics of Seas and Mountains*): *77 B.C.–6 B.C.* Collated by Liu Xin (?–A.D. 23). Beijing: Hualing chubanshe.

Liu, Zhiqun, 2000. "Zangju ('Tibetan Drama)." In *Zhongguo da baike quanshu* (*The Great Chinese Encyclopedia*), ed. Hu Qiaomu et al. Beijing: Zhongguo da baike quanshu chubanshe.

Lu Yilu. 2001. "Yanjing de shenhua—cong yizu de yi mu shenhua, zhi mu shenhua tan qi (Mythologies of Eyes—A Discussion of Tales with One-eyed and Vertical-eyed Protagonists)." *Dongwu zhongwen xuebao* (*Soochow Journal of Chinese Studies*) 8: 1–22.

Ma, Rongrong. 2004. " 'Yunnan yingxiang': minzu wenhua baohu de 'Yang Liping moshi' ('Yunnan Images': The 'Yang Liping Model' for Ethnic Cultural Preservation)." *Sanlian shenghuo zhoukan* (*Sanlian Life Weekly*) 282: 14.

Ma, Xueliang, and Tao Lifan. 1980. "Shaoshu minzu wenxue (Literature of Chinese Ethnic Minorities)." In *Zhongguo da baike quanshu* (*The Great Chinese Encyclopedia*), ed. *Zhongguo da baike bianweihui* (*Encyclopedia of China Editorial Board*). Beijing: Zhongguo da baike quanshu chubanshe.

Mackerras, Colin. 1995. *China's Minority Cultures: Identities and Integration since 1912.* New York: St. Martin's Press.

Mamet, Rizvan, et al. 2005. "Ethnic Intermarriage in Beijing and Xinjiang, China, 1990s." *Journal of Comparative Family Studies* 36 (2) (Spring): 187–204.

"Music of China." 2006. In *Reference.com.* Available at http://www.reference.com/browse/wiki/Music_of_China. (Accessed June 18, 2006).

"Music of China." 2006. In *Wikipedia.* Available at http://en.wikipedia.org/wiki/Chinese_Music. (Accessed June 18, 2006).

"Nüshu (Women's Scripts)." 2006. In *Wikipedia.* Available at http://en.wikipedia.org/wiki/Nushu. (Accessed January 3, 2006).

The Peacock Maiden: Folk Tales from China. 1981. Beijing: Foreign Language Press.

Peng, Xiaoyuan, ed. 2006. "Zhonghua minzu' gainian shi zenyang tichu de (How Did the Concept of 'Chinese Nation' Come to Be)." JBNews. Available at http://www.ben.com.cn/bjxw/mtdd/rbjx/200604/t20060421_18434.htm. (Accessed June 4, 2006).

Qi, Qingfu. 1999. *Zhongguo shaoshu minzu jixiang wu* (*Cultural Symbols of Luck of China's Ethnic Minorities*). Kunming: Sichuan minzu chubanshe.

Schwartz, Benjamin I. 1999. "Jews and China: Past and Present Encounters." In *The Jews of China.* ed. Jonathan Goldstein, 299–304. York: M.E. Sharpe.

"Shaoshu minzu cixiu (Embroidery of Ethnic Minorities)." 2006. In *Zhongguo yishu ba* (*China Art*) Available at http://www.chinaart8.com/show_art.asp?art_id=4780. (Accessed December 7, 2006).

"Shaoshu minzu shougongyi (Arts & Crafts of Ethnic Minorities)." 2006. In *Weike* (*Wiki*). Available at http://wiki.cn/. (Accessed December 7, 2006).

"Shaoshu minzu zongjiao xinyang (Religious Beliefs of Chinese Ethnic Minorities)." 2006. *Qiantuwang* (*Road to Guizhou Net*). Available at http://www.chiyou.name/page/whyz/zjxy/tjzxy.htm. (Accessed June 3, 2006).

"Shaoshu minzu wenxue (Literature of Ethnic Minorities)." 1980–1991. In *Zhongguo da baike quanshu* (*The Great Chinese Encyclopedia*). Beijing : Zhongguo da baikequanshu chubanshe.

"Shou tai shaoshu minzu yuwen dianshi jijiang toufang shichang (The First TV Set with Ethnic Minority Languages Is for Sale)." 2006. *Dongfang caijing* (*Finance East*). Available at http://finance.eastday.com/epublish/gb/paper94/20020625/class009400004/hwz738404.htm. (Accessed June 30, 2006).

Stone, Caroline. 1996. "The Dye That Binds." *Aramco World* 47 (5) (September/October): 38–43.

Sun, Jianjiang, ed. 1994. *Zhongguo shenhua gushi da quan jing bian lianhuan hua* (*Picture Books of Selected Classic Chinese Mythologies*). Hangzhou: Zhejiang shaonian ertong chubanshe.

"Tibetans Enjoy More Holidays than Other Ethnic Groups." 2003. *People's Daily*. Available at http://english.people.com.cn/200303/29/eng20030329_114177.shtml. (Accessed September 14, 2006).

"Tujia Ethnic Minority, The." 2006. In *China.org*. Available at http://www.china.org.cn/e-groups/shaoshu/shao-2-tujia.htm. (Accessed December 7, 2006).

"Tuwaren: yi-ge bu jie de mi (The Tuwa People: an Unsolved Mystery)." 2000. *Zhongguo guojia dili* (*Chinese National Geography*). Available at http://www.zh5000.com/GJDL/zghp/2006/01/gns-0003.htm. (Accessed September 16, 2006).

Wang, Haitao. 2005. "Qian tan hami Weiwuerzuren minjian jianzhi (A Brief Introduction to the Folk Paper-cut of the Uygurs in Hami)." In *Wang haitao wenji* (*Collection of Wang Haitao*). Available at http://www.hami.cn/1$001/1$001$042/1$001$042$011/911.jsp. (Accessed December 7, 2006).

Wang, Jiping, and Yang Fuxue, 2005. "Cong 'huiniao bensheng' dao 'shizi he dayan'—Yindu fo bensheng gushi yingxiang Weiwu'er zu minjian wenxue zhi yi li (An Example of the Influence of Indian Sutra Story in Uighur Flok Literature)." *Minjian wenxue yanjiu* (*Studies of Ethnic Literature*) 2: 88–91.

Wang, Yonghong. 2001. "Shen gu sheng sheng zhen Beijing (Sacred Drums Rumbling in Beijing)." *Zhongguo wenwu bao* (*China Cultural Relic Press*). Available at http://www.ccrnews.com.cn/tbscms/module_wb/readnews.asp?articleid=12581&serarchText=%C9%F1%B9%C4%C9%F9%C9%F9%D5%F0%BE%A9%B3%C7. (Accessed December 9, 2006).

Wei, Ronghui. 2004. *Ershiyi shiji Zhongguo shaoshu minzu fushi* (*Costumes of the Chinese Ethnic Minorities in the 21st Century*). Beijing: Zhongguo huabao chubanshe.

Wendu, Zongzhelajie. 2002. *Zang hua yishu gailun* (*Overview of Tibetan Paintings*). Beijing: Minzu chubanshe.

References

"Wenhua yishu (Culture and Art)." 2006. *Minzu wang* (*Ethnic Network*). Available at http://www.e56.com.cn/minzu/west/yunnan4-5.htm. (Accessed June 12, 2006).

Wu, David Y. H. 1995. "Ethnicity, Identity and Culture." *The Humanities Bulletin* 4 (December): 5.

"Xizang yishu (Tibetan Art)." 2006. In *Guojia shuzi wenhua wang* (*National Digital Cultural Network*). Available at http://www.ndcnc.gov.cn/datalib/2004/Nation/DL/DL-163267. (Accessed October 10, 2006).

Xu, Xin. 2005. "TV Programs in Ethnic Languages Have Increased," *People's Daily*. Available at http://culture.people.com.cn/GB/22219/3908661.html. (Accessed June 11, 2006).

Yang, Fuxue. 2006. *Shaoshu minzu dui gudai Dunhuang wenhua de gongxian (The Contribution of Ethnic Minorities to the Ancient Culture of Dunhuang)*. Available at http://gansu.yiyou.com/html/21/459.html. (Accessed November 25, 2006).

Yang, Ming. 2000. "Baiju ('Bai Drama)." In *Zhongguo da baike quanshu* (*The Great Chinese Encyclopedia*), ed. Hu Qiaomu et al. Beijing: Zhongguo da baike quanshu chubanshe.

Yang, Shengneng. 2001. *Xishuangbanna Daizu meishi qutan* (*Interesting Observations on the Dainty Food of the Dai Ethnic Minority in Xishuangbanna*). Kunming: Yunnan daxue chubanshe.

Yang, Yueping. 2004. "Chumo shaoshu minzu guji (Touching the Ancient Classics of the Chinese Ethnic Minorities)." In *Government of the Guangxi Zhuang Autonomous Region*. Available at http://www.gxi.gov.cn/200409/200492792802.htm. (Accessed November 8, 2006).

Yu, Naichang. 2004. "Zhongguo shaoshu minzu wenyi lilun gailan (An Overview of Chinese Ethnic Minorities' Literary Theories)." In *Zhongguo minzu wenxue wang* (*Chinese Ethnic Literature Network*). Available at http://www.iel.org.cn. (Accessed November 8, 2006).

Yu, Rong. 2004. "Tibetan Finery Brightens an Austere Land." *China Daily*. Available at http://www.chinadaily.com.cn/english/doc/2004-05/22/content_332809.htm. (Accessed June 6, 2006).

Zhang, Yue. 2006. "Minzu yuyan zhujian xiaowang, tu liu sheng sheng tan (Gradual Extinction of Ethnic Languages Leaves Only Helpless Sighs Behind)." *Wenweipo*. Available at http://slave.wwpnews.net/news.phtml?news_id=NS0603250001&loc=any&cat=037NS&no_combo=1. (Accessed May 26, 2006).

Zhao, Jingdong. 2003. *Yunnan sheng teyou minzu chuantong tiyu wenhua* (*Sports Culture of the Ethnic Minorities Unique to the Yunnan Province*). Kunming: Yunnan minzu chubanshe.

Zhao, Shilin. 2002. *Yunnan shaoshu minzu wenhua chuancheng lun gang* (*An Outline of the Cultural Inheritance of Yunnan Minority Nationalities*). Kunming: Yunnan minzu chubanshe. pp. 49-50.

Zheng, Xianlan. 2002. "Canlan de wenhua, xuanli de guibao: guotu cang shaoshu minzu wenxian jianjie (A Brief Introduction to the Collection of Ethnic Minority Documents in the National Library of China)." In *Wenjin liushang* (*Visible Traces*). Available at www.nlc.gov.cn/service/wjls/pdf/03/03_01_a4b16c1.pdf. (Accessed November 25, 2006).

"Zhongguo fengqing—quanguo wenhua xinxi ziyuan gongxiang gongcheng (Chinese Folk Culture—National Cultural Information Resources Sharing Project)." 2002. In *Guojia shuzi wenhua wang* (*National Digital Cultural Network*). Available at http://www.ndcnc.gov.cn//libpage/mzfq/index.htm. (Accessed November 6, 2005).

"Zhongguo minjian wenhua qiangjiu gongcheng (The Project to Salvage Chinese Folk Cultural Heritage)." 2005. In *Zhongguo minjian* (*Chinese Folk Culture*). Available at http://www.folkcn.com/news/Class/pczn/pcsc/21011609.htm. (Accessed November 6, 2005).

Zhongguo minwei (The State Ethnic Affairs Commission of PRC). 2006. "Zhongguo minzu (Chinese Ethnicities)." In *The Central People's Government* (*CPG*) *of the People's Republic of China*. Available at http://www.gov.cn/test/2005-07/26/content_17366.htm. (Accessed May 30, 2006).

"Zhongguo shaoshu minzu fuzhuang liushi yanzhong (There's a Heavy Drain of Chinese Ethnic Minority Costumes.)" 1999. *Sina.com*. Available at http://news.sina.com.cn/culture/1999-12-28/46619.html. (Accessed June 6, 2006).

Zhonghua renmin gonghe guo guojia tongji ju (National Bureau of Statistics of PRC). 2006. "2005 nian quanguo 1% renkou chouyang diaocha zhuyao shuju gongbao (Communiqué of Major Results of the 2005 National 1% Sample Survey of China's Population)." In *Zhongguo renkou xinxi wang* (*China POPIN*). Available at http://www.cpirc.org.cn/tjsj/tjsj_cy_detail.asp?id=6628. (Accessed May 29, 2006).

Zhou, Wen. 2003. "Jiedu 'wupu' de shaoshu minzu renkou (Decoding the Demographic Numbers of Ethnic Minorities)." *Zhongguo minzu* (*China's Ethnicities*) 9 (5): 10.

Zhou, Yang, and Liu Zaifu. ed. 1995. *Zhongguo da baike quanshu* (*The Great Chinese Encyclopedia*). Beijing: Zhongguo da baike quanshu chubanshe.

Zong, He. 2000. *Dongfang nishang jing yan chuncheng* (*Oriental Costumes Vie to Display Their Beauty in the City of Spring*). Available at http://www.yndaily.com/zl/daguan/0715/dg07151.htm (Accessed November 26, 2006).

Zou, Yilin. 2004. "Zhongguo duo minzu tongyi guojia xingcheng de lishi beijing he diyu tezheng (The Historical Background and Geographic Characteristics of the Formation of China as a Unified, Multi-ethnic Nation)." In *China Economic History Forum*. Available at http://economy.guoxue.com/article.php/587. (Accessed June 4, 2006).

INDEX

Leaf, 118
  magic. *See* "Mountain Girl and a Giant
      Hunter, A"
  palm, 161, 195–96
Legend, 23, 31, 59, 105, 110, 144, 161,
      168, 195, 202, 208, 220, 224, 227,
      230–31
Leopard, 56–58, 70, 74–75, 77, 82–83,
      207. *See also* "Bear and a Leopard,
      A"; "Muntjac and a Leopard, A"
Lhasa, 168, 170
Lhoba, 6, 11–12, 39, 60, 131, 146, 209,
      247
Li, 8, 22–23, 25, 59, 111, 148
Lion. *See* "Lion and a Wild Goose, A";
      "Lions Ask a Yellow Ant for Help"
"Lion and a Wild Goose, A," 80–81. *See
      also* Uygur
Lioness. *See* "Lions Ask a Yellow Ant for
      Help"
"Lions Ask a Yellow Ant for Help,"
      76–78. *See also* Jingpo
Lisu, 8, 27, 32, 39, 51, 54–55, 131, 135,
      202–3, 205
Literature, 31–33
"Liu Sanjie—A Fearless Folk Song
      Singer," 115–21. *See also* Zhuang
"Love Between a Goddess and a Mortal
      Hunter," 151–53. *See also* Qiang
Lu Tongtsan, 169–70. *See also* Songtsan
      Gambo
Lunar brother. *See* Brother(s): lunar

Magistrate, 110, 120
Magpie, 154–55, 206, 239
"Man with Only a Head, A," 102–4. *See
      also* Lahu
Manasi, 31. *See also* Kirgiz
Manchu, 4, 8, 17, 20, 25, 30, 32, 34, 41,
      60, 79, 238, 240
Mandala, 30
Mandarin, 8, 27, 106, 117, 122. *See also*
      Language
Mantle, 159, 217
Maonan, 52, 60, 105, 127, 198

Marriage, 103, 111, 126, 137–38, 146,
      149, 193, 207, 240
  brother-sister. *See* "Mother Who Drives
      the Sun, A"; "Origin of the
      Gelao Ethnicity, The";
      "Surviving Nu Ancestry, The"
  in defiance of social conventions, 177
  forced, 163. *See also* "Fairy's Bathing
      Pond, The"; "Girl Named
      Ashima, A"
  interethnic, 4, 168
  proposing, 118, 154, 173, 222
  refusing to consent, 152, 188, 224
  with a snake. *See* "Seventh Sister and
      Her Snake Husband"
Martial arts, 56, 89, 110–12, 240
Matchmaker, 118, 232–33, 238
Miao, 6, 8, 11, 20, 25, 32–33, 39, 52,
      59–61, 112, 115, 148, 212, 220
Millstone, 200
"Miluotuo—A Goddess Who Creates the
      World," 195–97. *See also* Yao
Monastery, 30, 155–56, 170
Monba, 20, 30, 247
Mongol, 8, 13, 19, 20, 23, 25–26, 31, 39,
      60–61, 140, 182, 204, 227
Mongolian, 8, 10, 13, 21, 30, 32, 41, 55,
      60, 91
  dancer, 26
  house. *See* Yurt
  matouqin. *See* Fiddle, horse-headed
  painters, 30
  xiaokeyare, 34. *See also* Storytelling
Monkey, 118, 187, 196, 204, 208
"Monkey Boy Stealing Rice from Heaven,
      A," 208–11. *See also* Hani
Monster, 23, 82, 124, 150, 174–76, 207
  of drought, 14
  mud fish, 107–8
  snow. *See* "Young Hero Mola and the
      Red Cliff"
Moon, 14, 64, 107, 179–81, 186, 205–6,
      235
  brother. *See* Brother(s): lunar
Mosuo, 20, 40, 191

plantation, 116–17
suyoucha 39. *See also* Ghee
Television, 25, 28
Thangkas, 29
"Three Brothers," 90. *See also* Tatar
"Three Neighbors" 91–94. *See also*
    Bonan
Third brother, 90–93, 193, 205–7
Thunder, 94, 141–42, 207, 236, 241, 244
Tianjin, 3, 5, 7
Tibet, 4, 17, 20, 25, 27, 29, 146, 168, 230,
    247. *See also* Autonomous: region
Tibetan
    dance, 26
    diet, 40
    drama. *See Zangju*
    New Year, 23
    shengu, 26. *See also* Drum
    xiangsheng, 34. *See also* Storytelling
Tiger, 45, 77, 111, 133, 141, 172, 193,
    203, 207
    devil, 244
    milk, 189–90
    skin, 189
    totem, 23. *See also* Yi
Tigress, 189
Toad, 124. *See* "Toad General, The"
"Toad General, The," 144–5. *See also* Gin
Tu, 8, 11, 17, 23, 30–31, 52, 56, 60, 204,
    218
Tubo, 168, 170. *See also* Songtsan
    Gambo; Tibet
Tujia, 6, 25, 30–31, 52, 59, 94, 105, 109,
    148
Turtle, 178
Turtledove, 188–89
"Two Young Men," 161–63. *See also* Jino

Universe, 135–36, 177–78, 185–86
Uygur, 7, 8, 10, 17, 19, 25–6, 28, 31–32,
    34–35, 39, 42–43, 55, 60–61, 70,
    80, 85, 90
Uzbek, 17, 25–26, 42, 84, 99

Va, 8, 22, 26, 39, 54, 56, 58, 148, 192,
    194, 220
Venison, 51, 206

Wax, 179
    dye . *See* Batik
    printing, 15
Weaving Girl. *See* "Origin of the Gelao
    Ethnicity, The"
Wedding, 15, 153, 162–63, 168, 173,
    175–76, 200, 202, 210, 226, 237,
    240
    ceremony, 55, 137
    of ethnic Bai, 20
    performed by God of Heaven, 211
    of Tujia, 31
    of Yao, 20
Wheat, 39, 43
Whip, 225
    magic, 244
"White-swan Fairy, The," 182–3. *See also*
    Kazak
"Why Are Oxen Preferred to Till Our
    Land?," 218–19. *See also* Tu
Widow, 102, 209
Wing, 95–96, 124, 200, 209
    bone, 224–5
    of a horse, 211
    mantle with, 158–59
    of a sheep, 217
    sleaves used as, 238
    stealing, 87
Witch, 162
Wolf, 79, 174, 193, 228
    blood, 113
    and a goat, 70
    Sky, 238–40
Woman, 5, 35, 106, 138
    bamboo turned into 167
    beautiful/gorgeous, 71–72, 115, 125,
        187, 200, 221, 233
    Dai, 4
    Jino, 17
    loved by two men, 161

Index   **301**

ABOUT THE THE AUTHOR
AND FOREWORD AUTHOR

HAIWANG YUAN is the author of *The Magic Lotus Lantern and Other Tales from the Han Chinese*, to which this book is a companion. He is a professor and the Web Site & Virtual Library Coordinator in the Department of Library Public Services at Western Kentucky University. He is also an adjunct instructor of Chinese in the Department of Modern Languages. A native of China and an American citizen, Mr. Yuan maintains a Web site, a large portion of which is devoted to Chinese traditions and folktales. Having published widely in professional journals, he is also a contributor to *The Encyclopedia of Contemporary Chinese Culture* (2004) and editor of *Chinese Peoples: Encyclopedia of Chinese Ethnic Groups,* to be published by Greenwood Press. He is the recipient of the 1999 Kentucky Libraries Award.

ZHANG CHUNDE, a Yi native originally named Dele Anan, was born in a *bimo*, or religious scholarly, family in the Luquan region of Kunming, China. He is a professor at the Yunnan Nationalities University and director of its Institute of Western Chinese Ethnic Groups. He is also on the Advisory Committee of the Ethnic Society of Yunnan Province. His dedication to the study of Yi history, culture, and languages and his devotion to collecting, salvaging, and preserving the Yi classics have won him the name *"Bimo* of the New Era."* He is the author and coauthor of several books and helped with the production of five newsreels on the Yi culture. He runs a family ethnic museum.

Recent Titles in the
World Folklore Series

A Fire in My Heart: Kurdish Tales
Retold by Diane Edgecomb; with Contributions by Mohammed M.A. Ahmed and Çeto Ozel

The Flying Dutchman and Other Folktales from the Netherlands
Theo Meder

Folktales from the Japanese Countryside
As told by Hiroko Fujita; Edited by Fran Stallings with Harold Wright and Miki Sakurai

Mayan Folktales; Cuentos Folkloricos Mayas
Retold and Edited by Susan Conklin Thompson, Keith Thompson, and Lidia López de López

The Flower of Paradise and Other Armenian Tales
Translated and Retold by Bonnie C. Marshall; Edited and with a Foreword by Virginia Tashjian

The Magic Lotus Lantern and Other Tales from the Han Chinese
Haiwang Yuan

Brazilian Folktales
Livia de Almeida and Ana Portella; Edited by Margaret Read MacDonald

The Seven Swabians, and Other German Folktales
Anna Altmann

English Folktales
Edited by Dan Keding and Amy Douglas

The Snow Maiden and Other Russian Tales
Translated and Retold by Bonnie C. Marshall, Edited by Alla V. Kulagina

From the Winds of Manguito: Cuban Folktales in English and Spanish (Desde los vientos de Manguito: Cuentos folklóricos de Cuba, en inglés y español)
Retold by Elvia Perez, Edited by Margaret Read MacDonald

Tales from the Taiwanese
Retold by Gary Marvin Davison

Additional titles in this series can be found at www.lu.com